Girls on Film

Clare Bundy, Lise Carrigg, Sibyl Goldman, Andrea Pyros

This is not your father's film site

"We think you'll love . . . Clare, Lise, Sibyl, and Andrea. Forget the thumbs-up or -down reviews—there aren't any. But there are plenty of insightful—and caustic—critiques on everything from a film's poor plot to a character's bad coif."
—*Newsweek*

"As they romp across the pop culture landscape, the *Girls'* personalities shine through in their reviews, which are thoughtful but never stuffy. Finally, an urban female answer to Joe Bob Briggs."
—*Entertainment Weekly*

Praise for Girls on Film Web site

The creators of the Web site Girls on Film bring you the ultimate de facto video guide, featuring:

- All original material
- ories from the Girls
- and fun film chat
- ovie recommenda-
- ery film genre, for
- .e-watchin' mood
- Side-splittin' sidebars

Clare Bundy, **Lise Carrigg**, **Sibyl Goldman**, and **Andrea Pyros** have been friends since their college days at Vassar. They are founders and writers/reviewers for the "Girls on Film" Web site, part of the "Girls on" Network—which gets 7 million viewers each month!

More Praise for "Girls on Film" Web site:

"Chatty, cheeky film talk."
—Cynthia 0Wang, *People* magazine

"GOF is full of personality, doesn't take itself
too seriously, and even looks fun. *I was hooked.*"
—Krissy Harris, *Los Angeles Times*

"Politics in the GOF world are more in-your-makeup-case
than in-your-face. No blanket ideologies, other than their
pursuit to get beer served in cinemas. They [are] more
into Drew Barrymore and Ralph Fiennes than pre- or
poststructuralist anythings. Which as far as I'm
concerned. . . is good strategy. As long as we're being
entertained, we'll forget we're being challenged."
—Susan Gerhard, *San Francisco Bay Guardian*

"Feminists with funny bones."
—*Time* magazine

"I'm not sure who they are or why they are,
but they are good writers and funny."
—Roger Ebert, Siskel and Ebert Online, Yahoo! Internet Life

"A tart departure from the male-dominated
World Wide Web."
—Anthony Ramirez, *New York Times*

Girls

on

film

Clare Bundy
Lise Carrigg
Sibyl Goldman
Andrea Pyros

HarperPerennial

HarperCollins books may be purchased for educational, business, or sales promotional use. For information please write: Special Markets Department, HarperCollins Publishers, Inc., 10 East 53rd Street, New York, NY 10022.
FIRST EDITION

Illustrations ©1999 Shannon McGarity
Designed by Joel Avirom and Jason Snyder

Library of Congress Cataloging-in-Publication Data

ISBN 0-06-095310-1
99 00 01 02 03 / 10 9 8 7 6 5 4 3 2 1

*To every member
of each of our
families, thank you*

&Contents

Contents

ACKNOWLEDGMENTS

Special thanks to:

All the Girls of the "Girls on" Network: Mary Augus... Diane Goodman, Lorna McDou... Ardy ... Vi...ia Watkins (Deanna Avery, ...d, Liza Powel, Jennie Sharf, ... Tucker Shaw; Gregor Eh... Robert Kessel; Jim Haygoo... Bar... Schwartz, and Paul Wolff; ... Burns and Stacy Horn; Jane Mount and HK Dunston; Dan Pelson and everyone at Concrete Media.

Our total gratitude to Shannon McGarity for all her great illustrations.

A big thanks to all our partners in movie-watching, who kept us company during all those hours of "research"—you made this book even more fun to write.

Lastly, a special thank-you to Trena Keating and Bronson Elliott for your suggestions, your patience, and your humor!

ACTOR I WANT TO PLAY ME IN THE MOVIE OF MY LIFE

LISE: love to have Samantha Mathis play me. It can be her big comeback.

SIBYL: Miranda Richardson—she's perfect, talented, beautiful, classy!!

ANDREA: The totally funny and smart Janeane Garofalo, who I think would be able to pull off "L'Essence du Dre."

CLARE: Clare: I'd want that perky Sandra Bullock to play me so she could prove to everyone that she had the range to portray such a highly intelligent, sensitive, and nuanced character as myself.

INTRODUCTION

We're Girls on Film! Stuff About Us

ather 'round, film buffs and film novices alike! We are proud to present a few obscure but vital moments in the student film history of Clare, Lise, Sibyl, and Andrea—college friends, once-budding actors and directors, and founders of Girls on Film:

Budding starlet Clare suffers the ultimate indignity of low-budget student filmmaking: a cheap, dime-store special-effect scar. The scar, which looks like old, chewed-up gum but is actually made of silly putty, is stuck to her neck every day for a week. Still, Clare, the consummate professional, delivers a heart-wrenching performance in the highly acclaimed coming-of-age film, **Bloodlines**.

Brilliant auteur Andrea struggles with a most difficult task: how to properly capture the angst and misery that is college a capella singing. Dedicated to her craft, this talented film studies major endures more than twenty-five takes of the happy warblers harmonizing through an endless medley of Doobie Brothers tunes.

Affable gal-about-town Sibyl agrees to be a party-going extra for an indie film with a heart. Arriving on the set in her pajamas (the set is her living room, the director her roommate), she is advised to sit on a couch and drink a beer. Sibyl hears "action!" and grabs the beer, guzzling with passion and zest. Little does she know that one of the guys from the crew (another roommate) used that very bottle for an ashtray.

Visionary student filmmaker Lise writes, produces, and directs an epic of love and loss aptly titled **Doin' the Do**. From the rustic sidewalk-chalk title sequence to the cross-dressing keg party with Technicolor vomiting, the film is pure artistry. Hundreds of gallons of coffee are consumed during the production, friendships are ruined, and a lovely mannequin painted with clouds is stolen.

Not familiar with any of these films? Phew, that's a relief. See, we Girls dabbled in filmmaking during our college years at Vassar, and we still have the videotapes (stashed away under lock and key) to prove it. That's part of why it's fun for us to write about movies now. We know filmmaking isn't all glamorous; we know how hard it is to tell a story well; we know that sometimes things on the set randomly catch fire. *We know the pain*. Though none of our films made the festival circuit, we did learn a lot about the art of filmmaking. The glory days may be gone, but the passion remains.

Since then, we've decided to stick to something we're good at: watching movies and talking about them endlessly. It was in this capacity that, four years ago, we started *Girls on Film* (www.girlsonfilm.com), a Web site devoted to movie reviews, pop culture commentary, and whatever else we felt like talking about at any given moment.

Our inkling that lots of other people were as consumed with movies as we were was confirmed in a big way. The feedback we got from the site in terms of E-mail and publicity was the fuel that allowed us to continue the project for two years while working full-time at unrelated (paying!) jobs. We worked nights and weekends, and we sometimes sneaked in an hour here or there at our respective day jobs. *Girls on Film* brought us closer together as friends and gave us an outlet to say whatever we wanted, whenever we wanted. In the end, it was acquired by a company here in New York City, and our two-year labor of love became a real profession.

We still get a lot of feedback on the site, and a lot of challenging E-mail; Lise recently got a message that said simply, "Who made you Film Reviewer of the Universe?" Lise replied by saying that she'd been given the title by Clare, who then jockeyed for the title of Supreme Critic of the Solar System. Then, of course, Sibyl and Andrea wanted promotions, too. We had to get new business cards made and everything. Quite a production.

That E-mail did pose an interesting question: Who told us we could be critics in the first place? Well, we did. And who told Roger Ebert or Leonard Maltin or Pauline Kael that they could be critics? Well, they probably did. So, what exactly are our qualifications for being movie critics? Well, the biggest one is simple: We love movies. Among the four of us, we have a decent shared knowledge of film history (the Muybridge horses and the whole nine yards) and no shortage of opinions, but we don't have a million advanced degrees or anything. As dedicated, full-time professional amateurs, we firmly believe that movie-going is a very subjective experience—there is no "right" opinion, even if it's the one that we give.

We're excited for this opportunity to recommend some great films to you. Three things to remember: First, there is more to your local video store than the "new releases" section; we're not here to advertise the latest, biggest movies to hit the shelves. Nor are we here to spend entire chapters discussing the amazing through-the-skylight crane shot in **Citizen Kane**; we've heard all that before, and you've heard all that before. Lastly, we were kids in the seventies, and teens in the eighties, so our movie tastes will definitely reflect a certain *je ne sais quoi* of the last thirty years, if you'll excuse our French.

We're talking about movies that you might want to rent with your friends and family this weekend, and we're talking about them as if we were all sitting in a coffee shop together. We'll recommend

1 DRAMAS:
Not for the Faint of Heart

When you're staring into a character's eyes and you've forgotten the actor's name completely; when you can't press "pause" even though you're pretty certain that you hear Ed McMahon and Dick Clark on your doorstep, yelling something about a check; when you go back to see a movie a second time because someone sneezed five minutes before it ended, and you absolutely must hear every bit of dialogue . . . chances are, you are watching a drama.

Drama is at the core of the movie-watching experience. You will find it in most comedy, romance, and horror movies, because if you don't care at least a little about the talking pig or the scorned lover or the axe murderer, you're not going to find things funny, sad, or scary. (And this, dear friends, is why makers of megabudget Hollywood flicks should pay more attention to the characters they create, and not just to the special effects, but that's another book entirely . . .)

Think about all those interviews you see with major directors and actors talking about why they wanted "to be in pictures": It's always because they saw John Ford's **The Searchers**, or maybe

Orson Welles's **The Magnificent Ambersons**, not because they saw, say, **The Jerk**, which we happen to love, but that's not the point. Dramas touch us because they are, on their most basic level, an exhibition of a life. And what could we possibly want to watch more than someone else's life unfolding in Technicolor? In the best of the genre, some brilliant person has created characters and situations that are so compelling that they make you look inward to examine your own life and beliefs. Take a film like Tim Robbins's **Dead Man Walking** (1995), which shows a man named Matthew Poncelet (Sean Penn) who is about to die by lethal injection. The final scenes are presented in close to real time, which is almost unheard-of in movies. This is so we are forced to feel, even a teeny-weeny bit, what it would be like to look at the clock and see that you have an hour to live, then a half hour, and then . . . no more. What would we do? And think and feel? What would we say, knowing that our lives would shortly end?

Then there's Woody Allen's **Crimes and Misdemeanors** (1989), which we Girls have all watched several times. Its complex tale of morality and murder boils down to some basic questions

 FAMILY HEIRLOOMS

LISE: My mother made me watch *The Sound of Music* every holiday season when I was growing up. I know every word to every song, and most of the dialogue too. You'd think I'd hate it by now, but it still gets me! Edelweiss!

SIBYL: Esther Williams's films, all that swimming and fancy costumes.

ANDREA: *On the Waterfront.* My mom adored Marlon Brando, and she definitely thought this film was him at his best.

CLARE: *All About Eve* is one of my mom's favorites; *Europa Europa* is one of my dad's.

that relate to each and every one of our lives: If you don't get caught doing something awful, did you really get away with it? Or is there a higher power watching over us? If nothing else, movies like this make for some good debates as soon as you hit "rewind."

Another important aspect of the drama—and really, of all films—is voyeurism. It's good old-fashioned curiosity that makes us welcome an opportunity to watch someone doing even the most mundane chores, like washing the dishes, without that person's seeing us. This is the theme of Hitchcock's masterpiece **Rear Window** (1954), which features Jimmy Stewart as L. B. Jeffries, a professional photographer with a broken leg, who is confined to a wheelchair in his New York City apartment. Hand that guy a set of binoculars and we've got ourselves a movie here—several movies, actually, since he has a clear view into almost an entire building of apartments. Eventually, he focuses in on what he finds to be the most compelling story, that of a man who appears to have murdered his wife. **Rear Window** works not only as a movie but also as an exploration of what movies actually are—a window into another person's life, which, ultimately, is a mirror back into our own. In **Rear Window**, Stewart's character is watching his neighbors in precisely the same way that we are watching him; his camera is pointed at his neighbors, and our camera is pointed at him.

Then there's the guilty and somewhat uncomfortable pleasure of watching a movie like **Who's Afraid Of Virginia Woolf?** (dir. Mike Nichols, 1966). Here, the movie camera is more like a video camera. In front of this forgotten camera unfolds the life of George and Martha (Richard Burton and Elizabeth Taylor), a completely dysfunctional alcoholic couple who invite guests (Sandy Dennis and George Segal) over and then torture them with their twisted, drunken arguments. We are tormented along with this couple because not only do we feel like we're there with them (almost all the action takes places in one room, giving it an incredibly claustrophobic feel), but it also makes us think, have I ever behaved like that? Do I know someone who has? What would I do and think and feel if I were there?

On a lighter note, dramatic films also can provide what we think of as the perfect movie moment. During the perfect movie moment, you may get a little misty and grab the hand of the person next to you, because you can't believe that some director you don't even know got it so, so, so right. These perfect moments surpass verbal communication; they're the sum of an almost fortuitous combination of writing, acting, direction, music, lighting, cinematography, and whatever else is thrown into the mix to create the magic. Here's an example: the scene in **Quiz Show** (dir. Robert Redford, 1994) where Charles Van Doren (Ralph Fiennes) drives from New York City back to his parent's house in the country, late at the night. He is sitting at the old kitchen table, eating a piece of chocolate cake that his mother baked, clearly trying to escape the reality of his life. See, we already know that Charles has been given the answers in advance to questions on "Twenty-One," the game show on which he has been a champion contestant. We also know that this scandal is about to blow up and become national news. So when his father (Paul Scofield) comes downstairs for a midnight chat and cake-sharing session with his son, we feel Charles's guilt and pain, and we wonder whether he will reveal the truth to his father, who is so proud of him. Charles's father speaks to him about the joy and pride of having a son, oblivious to the huge disappointment that is coming his way. It's such a bittersweet and truly touching moment—the cake, the dad, and Charles's worry that nothing will ever be that good and that simple again. Sigh. Don't worry, though, perfect moments come in the happy variety, too! (As for whether Charles tells his father the truth, you will have to rent the movie to find out!)

Drama is obviously a huge category in film history, and we are each drawn to different categories within it. What all four of us seem to look for and find in the genre, though, is something a little darker, something not for the faint of heart. Clare loves war movies; Sibyl is a champion of epics; Andrea loves film noir. If we ever wanted to get rid of Andrea for a week (we wouldn't—it's just an example), we'd need only to show up at her apartment with some food and a bag of videos like **The Big Sleep, The Third Man,** and **Double Indemnity**. She'd probably crawl out eventually, calling us all "dollface" and smoking from a foot-long cigarette holder. For Lise, it'd be a slightly more embarrassing situation, since her weakness is the psychological thriller, a type of film by which she is repulsed and to which she is strangely drawn. We'd probably have to orchestrate some kind of intervention in which we pried **The Manchurian Candidate** (best-case scenario) or **Whispers in the Dark** (worst-case scenario) from her hands while she screamed, "They're trying to get me!" over and over.

So whether the word "drama" makes you think of **The Ten Commandments** or **Twelve Angry Men, Bambi,** or **Blue Velvet,** we think you'll probably find a common kernel if you put your drama of choice under the microscope: a story that really makes you think about love, loyalty, life. This is the power of the mother lode that is drama, and it's not for the timid.

EMBRACING THE EPIC

By Sibyl

When I was twelve years old, I went to see **Gone With the Wind** at the Fox, an old restored movie palace in St. Louis. Chuck (my personal version of Charles in Charge, only much smarter and less cheesy than Scott Baio) took me; he felt it was important for me to see this Southern sentimental classic on the big screen. A movie on a school night, cool! When we returned home, after midnight, my mom was sitting up in the kitchen, about to call the police. Oops, maybe a four-hour movie on a school night wasn't the greatest idea. That night began my lifelong passion for the big, grand, so-long-that-someone-might-report-you-to-Missing-Persons epic movie.

What is an epic? Well, it's not just a really long movie (average movies are between 90 and 120 minutes), because Kevin Costner's **The Postman** (1997) is really long—170 minutes—but an epic? I don't think so. I decree, here and now, that bad, over-long movies don't deserve inclusion in the highly esteemed epic genre! For me, "epic" implies quality! An epic must be as vast in scope as it is in length; look for romance, war, tragedy, several decades covered. The great epics are bursting with information, but also visually dazzling and heart-breaking, too.

There are some people who will never, ever have the capacity to savor an epic. You know those people, the ones who tap their feet nervously, the ones who can't wait in a line, the ones who have ants in their pants, the ones who enjoy "Short Attention Span Theater"—those people should probably forget it. But for the rest of us, particularly

I LOVE THE SOUND OF YOUR VOICE

LISE: Bogey. He can call me "sweetheart" anytime.

SIBYL: Rupert Everett. What a lovely accent. Totally charming.

ANDREA: Katharine Hepburn. She's so distinctive and sassy-sounding.

CLARE: Morgan Freeman. He can say any line with that great voice of his and make it sound credible.

those who like to get a lot of bang for their buck, a massive, mega-movie is just the thing.

Epic novices might want to start with a classic like **Gandhi**, directed by Richard Attenborough (1982, 188 minutes). A big Oscar-winner, **Gandhi** is like a history lesson. It's slow in parts (all epics are), but Ben Kingsley gives a mind-blowing performance as the unassuming young lawyer who becomes the spiritual leader of India and a symbol for passive resistance worldwide. There's so much to learn from this film about Indian politics and culture; this is three hours well spent.

If you're feeling cocky, then David Lean's **Lawrence Of Arabia** (1962) is the right choice. Clocking in at a whopping 221 minutes (that's almost four hours), the movie consists largely of sandy, panoramic desert shots. You might want to turn this film into a miniseries (watching it over two nights), or wake up early and watch it on a Sunday with breakfast in bed.

Biography is perfectly suited to the epic form; the length allows for a thorough examination of a whole lifetime. **Malcolm X** (1992, 201 minutes) and **Nixon** (1995, 190 minutes) generated a lot of controversy when they were released, but didn't receive much criti-cal acclaim. Both Spike Lee and Oliver Stone are known for creating films that inspire heated debate. Lee is cantankerous and uncom-promising in his vision; Stone is paranoid and what I like to call a "creative historian." These traits alienate many viewers and tend to overwhelm any real understanding or appreciation of the films.

Put aside any preconceived notions you might have about Spike and Oliver (sounds like a kids' puppet show) and settle in for two supersatisfying epics. **Malcolm X** is a loving portrait of the title character (played by Denzel Washington, in an Oscar-worthy performance)on his journey from low-level con artist to convict to Muslim convert to charismatic Nation of Islam spokesman. The film doesn't really hit its stride until Malcolm's religious conversion in prison, but once it does, we get a very intimate view of a man's spiritual evolution. Malcolm's assassination is heart-wrenching, particularly since it is unclear who wants him dead more, the government spooks trailing him or the radicals in his own movement.

Nixon is, in many ways, the reverse of **Malcolm X**. While **Malcolm X** gives us the story in chronological order, **Nixon** begins at the end—the end for Nixon (Anthony Hopkins), at least—on the eve of his ouster from the White House. Then, through Stone's bizarre, disorienting, signature style, we're shown Nixon's whole life. His childhood is shot in stark, Walker Evans black-and-white. His political career is documented like a series of news reels. We see his successes in China, his disasters in Vietnam, his long-suffering wife, Pat (Joan Allen), and his power-hungry, paranoia-driven decisions to approve the Watergate break-in and set up a taping system in his offices. Stone's portrait of Nixon is surprisingly sympathetic; Nixon seems more pathetic than evil.

While most epics bore a bit, thrill a bit, and teach a bit, a truly great epic manages to sustain a feeling of suspense over an extremely long period of time. **Malcolm X** and **Nixon** both succeed. Though I know that Malcolm will be brutally gunned down in front of his wife and children, I cry each time I see it. Though I know that Tricky Dick slithers out of the White House, weirdly waving the victory symbol in the air, I watch, engrossed, waiting to see what will happen. And, though I know that Rhett tells Scarlett he doesn't give a damn, I wait almost four hours to see it happen, time and time again.

BRAINWASHING, MIND CONTROL, AND OTHER FUN WAYS TO PASS TIME

By Lise

At some point during your teen years (possibly around the time you started writing poetry and/or smoking clove cigarettes), you and your cohorts undoubtedly pondered some age-old and ultimately ridiculous questions along the lines of "What if you and I have totally different perceptions of the color green?!? What if—whoa—we're seeing two completely different colors?!?!" Very heavy stuff. If you were in a particularly thoughtful mood, you may have reached the ultimate in teen existentialism: What if our entire world existed on the head of a pin, or on the back of a flea on a dog, in some larger universe? (Incidentally, I think this may have been the topic of an early **Twilight Zone** episode.)

Okay, confession time: I still kinda like that one. In fact, it influences my movie choices quite often, as I find myself drawn to the psychological dramas at the video store. I'm obviously not the only one, because there are lots of top-notch directors out there—from Hitchcock to Frankenheimer to Weir—who have delved into the theme that I like to think of as, "Uh-oh. Things are not as they appear." To different extents, films in this broad category deal not only with the themes of paranoia and deception, but with even more sinister topics like mind control and brainwashing. It's worth noting at this stage that I'm not a conspiracy-theory fanatic. But, whereas some of my friends get their thrills from horror or sci-fi movies, with gory and implausible plots, I've always been more interested in the idea that your actual present-day, normal-seeming life could be, well, not as it appears. I'm not entirely certain when I got so beguiled with the idea of deception (insert evil cackle here), but what do you say we just talk about some fun and creepy movies and leave the psychoanalysis to a professional, capische?

In **The Truman Show** (dir. Peter Weir, 1998), a seemingly normal insurance salesman named Truman Burbank (Jim Carrey) discovers that his entire life has quite literally been a television show called, appropriately, "The Truman Show." Truman was born on camera, as the first baby ever legally adopted by a corporation. His friends and family are really just actors, his job is fake, and the entire island on which he lives is an elaborately designed set. As Truman begins to realize that things are amiss in his life (in one darkly comic scene, he is trying to tell his wife that something is wrong, but she just smiles broadly and recommends a product called "mococoa," which she holds up for the camera), a debate heats up in the real world between people who love "The Truman Show" and people who think that it is highly unethical.

The Truman Show deals more overtly with the theme of deception than some of director John Frankenheimer's films, such as **The Manchurian Candidate** (1962) and **Seconds** (1966). In *Seconds*, an average, 1960s, Connecticut commuter named Arthur Hamilton (John Randolph) is led, by an old friend whom he thought had passed away, to a company that promises to

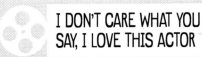

I DON'T CARE WHAT YOU SAY, I LOVE THIS ACTOR

LISE: Woody Harrelson. His hemptastic outfits are getting a little out of control, but his acting is improving with age.

SIBYL: Jeff Goldblum—Some may say he's a buffoon, but check out his sexy alien in *Earth Girls Are Easy.*

ANDREA: Keanu Reeves. Leave the poor man alone! *He can act!*

CLARE: Michael Keaton! Love him! Brilliant, sexy, funny … *Mr. Freakin' Mom!* (So there, Andrea.)

exchange his excruciatingly ordinary life for an entirely new identity. At the initial meeting, the company's executives explain how they will orchestrate Hamilton's "death," planning every detail so that even his wife will be fooled. He agrees to their plan.

At first, Hamilton's new life seems pretty great. Plastic surgery has completely changed his appearance to make him younger (for the rest of the movie, he is played by Rock Hudson!), and he is living under an assumed identity, as a swinging artiste-type in an ocean-front cottage. I was about to start thumbing through the Yellow Pages myself! Unfortunately, Hamilton gets a little more than he bargained for and when he tries to reclaim his real identity, he finds out what "seconds" really are. (Hint: If you remember Charlton Heston's unfortunate discovery in **Soylent Green**? It's along those lines.)

Seconds has the surreal look and feel of another 1960s film, **The Trial** (dir. Orson Welles, 1962). Although obviously lesser-known than **Citizen Kane** (1941) and **Touch of Evil** (1958), **The Trial** is, visually speaking, pure Welles. The sparse story line is an adaptation of a Kafka novel of the same name, and it concerns a man (Anthony Perkins) who is woken up in the middle of the night, arrested, and told only that he is on trial. Held as a prisoner in an official building, he is unable to mount any defense because no one will tell him what crime he is accused of committing! Movies like this can be intensely frustrating to watch; this one in particular is most interesting as a visual experiment. Made about twenty years after **Citizen Kane**, **The Trial** has the same Expressionist look and power-related themes as the film that Welles will always be remembered for.

In recent years, there has been a whole slew of films about deception and, despite their range of quality, I have seen most of them. From **The Usual Suspects** (1995) to **Deceived** (1991), there's something fun about watching your favorite actor be the Bad Guy for a change. Alan Alda has since proven his range of acting ability in movies like **Crimes and Misdemeanors** and **The**

Object of My Affection (where he provided some much-needed comic relief; watching that movie was like watching toenails grow). But I'll always remember my shocked laugh when I saw him in **Whispers in the Dark** (dir. Christopher Crowe, 1992), as Dr. Leo Green. Throughout the movie he plays friend and mentor to fellow psychiatrist Dr. Ann Hecker (Annabella Sciorra). It's only in the final scene of the film that Leo reveals himself as not only a creep, but a murderer! The confession is hilarious and shocking and completely schlocky; there's something so satisfying about watching an actor like Alan Alda, whom we've always known as the ultimate sensitive guy, go off the deep end like that. I made Clare watch this one too and she liked it, but may not admit that.

In **Jacob's Ladder** (dir. Adrian Lyne, 1990), a postal worker named Jacob Singer (Tim Robbins) begins to realize that many men in his Vietnam platoon may have killed one another while under the influence of a brainwashing drug. In **Malice** (dir. Harold Becker, 1993), a seemingly caring and devoted wife (Nicole Kidman) undergoes surgery as part of an elaborate plan to frame her husband (Bill Pullman). And let us not forget the dated and jocular **The Stepford Wives** (dir. Bryan Forbes, 1975), in which an entire town of housewives have been replaced by robot look-alikes who love housework and sex. Now, how could cheap costumes and fake blood ever compare to the intrigue of gripping psychological dramas like these? What's scarier: little green men, or the idea that something is terribly amiss in your everyday life? Good, I'm glad you have joined me on the dark side!

WAR IS BAD!

By Clare

Okay, so I'm into war movies—Vietnam movies in particular—and I'm not quite sure where that came from. I think it's usually guys who dig war movies, but hey, I was a bit of a tomboy growing up. I used to wear my hair short, beg my mom to let me keep off my bikini top at the pool, play "Big Boys" with my older brother and call myself "Steve"—you know, the usual stuff. But my biggest influence had to have been my dad, who not only adores overwhelmingly depressing movies (as do I), but is obsessed with World War II—Hitler and the Holocaust in particular. Me? I can't get enough of those Viet Cong!

Actually, my favorite war movies are more about the war at home, because, for one thing, that's the only time you get to see any women. By "war at home," I mean that you don't see a lot of battle scenes; in fact, none of my three top picks shows much of Vietnam at all, although one takes place in Cambodia. I like this more indirect representation of the war (excuse me, "conflict") not only because it shows the ladies' side, but because it leaves more to my rather fertile imagination.

A good example of a "war at home" movie is **Coming Home** (dir. Hal Ashby, 1978). This flick could be in our Moving Pictures chapter, but it's also just a fantastic Vietnam movie. (Don't let the fuzzy pastel smoochy-couple picture on the video box fool you.) Jane Fonda plays Sally, dutiful wife of Army man Bob (Bruce Dern). On the eve of Bob's tour in Vietnam, we're treated to what is probably one of the most accurate depictions of good old-fashioned American sex, circa 1967, ever filmed: She lies on her back patiently while he grunts and plugs away. Not a word passes between them. It's sad and funny and a little chilling.

Once he's off, she finds herself with nothing to do, so she volunteers at the local veteran's hospital, where she meets up with angry, wheelchair-bound rabble-rouser Luke Martin (Jon Voight, who, as always, is intensely magnetic). Gradually, she learns how to be her own person. She takes down her fussy bouffant, smokes a little pot, falls in love. I may sound glib, but this movie is anything but. With scenes in the veteran's hospital that make Oliver Stone's **Born on the Fourth of July** look like a Sunday walk in the park (one disturbed patient locks himself in an office and kills himself while the others look on helplessly and "Sympathy for the Devil" pounds in the background), **Coming Home** gets under your skin. Sally changes. And, just as important, Bob has changed when he gets back. Vietnam has changed them both.

I suppose that's what intrigues me the most about war movies: They give you a clear definition of a turning point, of a time when a person has finally seen so much death and violence that they can't ignore it anymore. The scene in **The Deer Hunter**

A MOVIE THAT DROVE ME TO DRINK—DURING THE MOVIE

LISE: *Working Girl.* In fact, I have some not-so-great feelings for most of the Melanie Griffith oeuvre.

SIBYL: *M*, that German classic with creepy Peter Lorre whistling and killing children. Cheap no-name vodka from the bottle.

ANDREA: *Bad Lieutenant.* I drank, I napped, I cleaned my apartment. Yet this Harvey Keitel vehicle still wouldn't end.

CLARE: I've gotten loaded during so many action movies that I can't even count the times. But Lise and I swilling beer during *Forrest Gump* will always stick in my mind as a low point.

(dir. Michael Cimino, 1978), in which a glassy-eyed Christopher Walken plays Russian roulette, will always haunt me. I think that, in life, we often feel a vague sense of dread lying just at the edge of our circumscribed existence. We read about it in the papers—massacres in Rwanda, Bosnia, Beijing—but war movies put a face to it, crystallize it, bring it home. They make us see that war is as much a part of human nature as anything else. Scary.

Which brings me to **Apocalyspe Now** (dir. Francis Ford Coppola, 1979). More so than any other Vietnam movie, **Apocalypse Now** gives the insanity of war a name, and that name is Colonel Walter Kurtz (Marlon Brando—bald, fat, and mumbling, lingering in the shadowy recesses of a spooky villa). Loosely based on Joseph Conrad's book **Heart of Darkness**, the movie follows Captain Ben Willard (Martin Sheen, in his best role ever), sent on assignment to find Kurtz, who went missing after an illustrious career as a highly decorated Green Beret. Well, it seems he's "gone native," as they say, appointing himself as the ruler of a remote group of Cambodians.

As Willard travels upriver, he encounters all sorts of soldiers run amok—Lieutenant Colonel Kilgore (Robert Duvall), who loves the smell of napalm in the morning; an unnamed photographer (Dennis Hopper), who's an ardent follower of Kurtz, and various other disenchanted soldiers (played by, among many others, a fifteen-year-old Laurence Fishburne!). All of these people have found a sort of alternate universe in the jungle: They have discovered power, the power to control and fight and even kill with impunity, and for some it has proved deathly intoxicating.

Full of sweat, gore, LSD, and ritual beheading, **Apocalypse Now** can be a bit tough to take. It's beautifully shot in lush greens and browns and uses that amazing Doors song, "The End," to great effect, in a scene juxtaposing two very different slaughters. Yikes!

Dogfight, another "war at home" movie, features Lili Taylor as Rose, a sweet, idealistic young woman who wants to be the next Joan Baez, and the late River Phoenix (sigh—he was so beautiful and talented) as Birdlace, a soldier about to go off to war who picks her up in an attempt to win a "dogfight." The careless bravado and indifference of Birdlace and his friends is perfectly characterized by this competition: They each try to pick up the ugliest girl they can find and bring her to a dance. Sadly, the gentle Rose figures out why she's having such good luck with Birdlace, and she's humiliated.

Dogfight is a quiet, tame movie—you only see the actual war for about five minutes. But once again, you see the effect that it has on Birdlace when he comes back, and on Rose. It's almost a coming-of-age film, in the way that both characters learn the truth about life.

From the violence and loud music of **Full Metal Jacket** (Eek! Who's that relentless sniper?!) to the Christ motif in **Platoon** (oh, Mr. Stone, you are so deep), even to the recent **Courage Under Fire** (about the Gulf War, and P.S., featuring a prehype Matt Damon), war movies never cease to enthrall me. (Plus, those Vietnam films have such great sixties music!) I am no gun fetishist (certainly not!), I am no rubbernecker (well, maybe), but I am fascinated by the primal urges and brutal devastation that these movies depict. It's like a beast that, once unleashed, cannot be stuffed back into its cage.

Unless, of course, you numb yourself with repeated viewings of **Sleepless in Seattle**, which I plan to do presently. Even Steve needs a break sometimes.

P.I.'S, MOLLS, AND DIMLY LIT STREETS: MY LOVE OF FILM NOIR

By Andrea

Growing up, while all of my friends dreamt of being scientists, doctors, or even media moguls (hey, they gotta start somewhere), I longed only to make my living as a private detective.

I dreamt of sporting a long trench coat, a fedora tilted rakishly over one eye. Tough as nails, I'd be able to crack cases that baffled the police. When my friends would come over after school and ask what I wanted to do, I'd break out my spiffy black notebook (which I had covered with purple glittery nail polish, like any good P.I.) and say, "Let's be private detectives." I spent many an afternoon pretending to chase after clues, or tracking down the bad guys. My dad bought me the Hardy Boys detective manual, which explained in some detail how to shadow a criminal without being spotted—a skill I attempted to hone while walking to school every day. I also spent hours reading mysteries like the Trixie Belden series and watching "Nancy Drew & the Hardy Boys" on television, along with good old Peter Falk as Columbo.

As I got older, I realized I didn't actually want to be a detective; however, I never grew out of my love of the detective story. While in school studying the films of the forties and fifties, I discovered a passion for one type in particular, the film noir. (Noir, by the way, is French for "black," and it's pronounced *nooooowaaaaaah-hhrrrr*. Kind of. Say it with confidence and you should be golden.)

Even if I bungle the pronunciation, I can still say that I love these films noir. They tell the gripping crime/P.I. story I so enjoy; these movies look great; and most of all, they have the kind of brooding, cynical mind-set that meshes perfectly with an urban kid like myself, someone who's never been able to get into other film classics like **The Sound of Music** or **Mary Poppins**.

You may ask, "what is noir?" Feel free, although agreeing on a formal definition of film noir is darn near impossible. I always considered it a genre (like the western, or the musical, for instance), but in reality, it's closer to a mood or style than anything else. Even which films fall into the noir category is up for debate, though most film historians seem to agree that the noir period began with 1941's **The Maltese Falcon** (dir. John Huston) and pretty much had its heyday during the next fifteen years or so.

Sidebar TK?

I have always been drawn to certain qualities of the film noir, namely the palpable sense of disillusionment that emanates from them; their highly stylized lighting and camerawork; their focus on the criminal world (there's my P.I. fixation again!); their lack of reverence toward authority figures. Perhaps best of all, I was drawn to their hard-boiled characters, men and women who dance around each other, spitting out biting, caustic dialogue, with a total lack of trust or faith in one another.

Film noirs were the "B" movies of their time, in other words, low-budget and considered pulp rather than quality. For years they flew under the radar of most American critics, and it took the French film theorists (who also hailed the genius of Alfred Hitchcock and, um, er, Jerry Lewis, and, um, er, Mickey Rourke) to recognize that something rather amazing was going on in postwar Hollywood. These days, noir flicks get the respect they certainly deserve, but would never have bothered asking us for.

To say the average film noir is cynical is an understatement along the lines of saying it's been known to drizzle a teensy bit in England. There's no other film out there that manages to have such an antipathetic attitude towards humanity than the average noir. One of the best examples of this cynicism: **Out of the Past** (dir. Jacques Tourneur, 1947), starring Robert Mitchum as a former criminal trying to go straight with a new life, a new job, and a new girl. Of course, he's pulled back into his past by bad guy Kirk Douglas and femme fatale Jane Greer. Mitchum, as always, turns in a stunning performance as a man caught uneasily between two worlds, resigned to his fate and his true nature.

Another consummate noir is **Kiss Me Deadly** (dir. Robert Aldrich, 1955) about detective Mike Hammer (one of pulp author Mickey Spillane's inventions), a mean, violent, selfish S.O.B. who's still the nicest guy in this story about a murder, a wicked girl with a pixie haircut, and a briefcase that glows with something that could signal the end of the world.

The fact that both **Out of the Past** and **Kiss Me Deadly** feature femme fatales is no surprise, since another recurring trope of the noir is the bad woman, who's always beautiful and usually deadly. Much has been made of the tension between the sexes in postwar America, with GIs returning home to find their wives and girlfriends working in droves, the traditional balance of power turned on its head. Films noir are filled with anxiety about this state of affairs, showcasing dysfunctional families (if any are even visible at all) and greedy, duplicitous babes who seem to be able to take care of themselves just fine, thank you. It's hard to say whether this was a step forward for actresses, who got to shine in powerful, sexy roles, or a step backward in society's suspicions about the evil that women do. What isn't up for debate is that some of the most enduring villainesses of all time showed up during this period, and they are something to behold.

Take, for instance, a blond, sinewy, seductive Barbara Stanwyck in **Double Indemnity** (dir. Billy Wilder, 1944). One look at her as she descends the staircase of her husband's house, wrapped in a formfitting dress and a sparkling ankle bracelet, we know both her husband and the insurance salesman (Fred MacMurray) hawking him a policy are in for a bumpy ride. I'm also partial to the gun-slinging Peggy Cummins from **Gun Crazy** (dir. Joseph Lewis, 1950) who manages to seduce some poor schnook, not with her beauty (though she is quite lovely), but with her deadly aim with a pistol. Before you can say "prison sentence," the two are on a road trip/crime-spree from hell, à la **Bonnie and Clyde**.

There are good people in film noir, they're just few and far between. You've got to look closely, too, since the heroes usually have their own code of morality and a definition of right and wrong that's not quite in sync with society at large.

All in all, films noir—like Lise's psychological thrillers, Sibyl's political dramas, and Clare's war movies—are not for the faint of heart. Cold and cynical, they're filled with murky plots and shady characters. Watch them on a cold, rainy night, with a cool cocktail and the lights on low, and know that your world isn't just sweetness and light.

Drama: 25 to Rent!

1 **ALL ABOUT EVE** (dir. Joseph L. Mankiewicz, 1950) Classic tale of a famous Broadway actress (the incomparable Bette Davis) whose seemingly devoted assistant (Anne Baxter) does everything but don hiking boots in her attempt to climb over her mentor. *All About Eve* boasts top-notch acting and writing, with lines like "Fasten your seatbelts—it's going to be a bumpy night!" Also, check out the hilarious performance by Marilyn Monroe.

2 *APOCALYPSE NOW* (dir. Francis Ford Coppola, 1979) Based on Joseph Conrad's *Heart of Darkness*, this superintense movie took years to make. Starring Martin Sheen, Marlon Brando, and Robert Duvall, this film could cause panic attacks. It's ultimately a story of power and shrunken, severed heads—the horror indeed! You'll feel the heat and hear the insects, like you're actually on a riverboat in the Vietnamese jungle.

3 **APOLLO 13** (dir. Ron Howard, 1995) Our old friend Opie directs the true story of 1970s *Apollo 13* space mission, which was considered "a successful failure" when astronauts who were supposed to land on the Moon were instead faced with serious technical problems in the spacecraft. One of Tom Hanks's understated and great performances; Kevin Bacon, Gary Sinise, Kathleen Quinlan, and Ed Harris are also remarkable. Really puts you in the middle of the drama . . .

4 **CHINATOWN** (dir. Roman Polanski, 1974) "She's my daughter! She's my sister!" If you don't know what that means, rent this movie. Right now. Jack Nicholson plays Los Angeles P.I. Jake Gittes, and Faye Dunaway is the femme fatale in this noirish story of power, paranoia, and corruption.

5 **CITIZEN KANE** (dir. Orson Welles, 1941) Tops almost every critic's list of the greatest films of all time. We're not telling you to see this flick because it's good for you, but because it's really good.

At age twenty-five, Welles starred in, directed, and cowrote this masterpiece about a powerful businessman's life story. Broke all sorts of ground, and even now, more than fifty years after its release, it's an original and powerful movie.

6 **CRIMES AND MISDEMEANORS** (dir. Woody Allen, 1989) Despite a wickedly funny performance by Alan Alda as a cheesy TV producer, this really is a drama, in which Allen poses provocative questions, like if you don't get caught doing something immoral (never mind illegal!), did you really get away with it? Or is there a Higher Power tallying all of our scores? Conversation-inspiring, so watch it with a friend or date.

7 **THE DEER HUNTER** (dir. Michael Cimino, 1978) A truly epic Vietnam film, this flick finds some friends in a small Pennsylvania steel town on the eve of three of them going off to war. Brilliantly capturing the subtle dynamic among these friends (played by Robert De Niro, Christopher Walken, and John Savage) and one of their girlfriends (played with heartbreaking simplicity by Meryl Streep), this movie shows how each of them reacts to the experience of Vietnam.

8 **DOGFIGHT** (dir. Nancy Savoca, 1991) Takes place in San Francisco in 1963. Lili Taylor is Rose, an idealistic young woman who wants to be the next Joan Baez, and the late River Phoenix is Birdlace, a Marine who is shipping off to Vietnam the very next day. Birdlace woos Rose; only later does Rose figure out that she is his entry in a "dogfight," where he and his buddies are competing to find the ugliest girl.

9 **DO THE RIGHT THING** (dir. Spike Lee, 1989) This fresh flick from Spike Lee takes place in the Brooklyn neighborhood of Bedford-Stuyvesant on a very, very hot summer day, as racial tensions rise along with the barium in the thermometer. The action centers around Sal's Pizzeria; Lee has mastered the art of telling one small story that is a metaphor for a much larger situation. Amazing performances by Danny Aiello, John Turturro, and Lee himself.

Closing quotes from Malcolm X and Martin Luther King Jr. leave you with something to think about.

10 **THE GODFATHER, PARTS I & II** (dir. Francis Ford Coppola, 1972, 1974) So you want to hear an epic tale of crime, family, corruption, and redemption—*and* you have about six hours to spare? We couldn't decide which one to recommend, so we went with both. Amazingly enough, studio execs were incredibly nervous about releasing the original *Godfather*, and Coppola was admonished for making a film so dark. Hmm, guess they didn't notice some of the best performances of all time, by Al Pacino, Robert De Niro, and Marlon Brando, among others. Based on the novel by Mario Puzo.

11 **GOODFELLAS** (dir. Martin Scorsese, 1990) This violent and sometimes sad gangster flick also has its share of funny moments. Ray Liotta plays a regular guy who always wanted to be a gangster. Be careful what you ask for, 'cause you just might get it. This is beautifully edited with great music; too bad it was robbed of an Oscar the year that *Dances with Wolves* won!

12 **THE ICE STORM** (dir. Ang Lee, 1997) Every detail from the cowl-neck sweaters to the rubber Nixon mask is in place in this tragic story of suburban Connecticut in the 1970s. Sigourney Weaver, Kevin Kline, Joan Allen, Christina Ricci, Tobey Maguire— wait, *everyone* is amazing in this film. Notice how the adults behave like children and the children behave like little adults. So gorgeous and so, so sad.

13 **L.A. CONFIDENTIAL** (dir. Curtis Hanson, 1997) Kevin Spacey, Russell Crowe, and Guy Pearce star in this superb and gorgeous ensemble flick. What starts with some corrupt police officers and some murders at the Night Owl Café turns into, well, a story that requires some serious attention to understand (how refreshing!). Kim Basinger won a well-deserved Oscar for her portrayal of an upscale Veronica Lake look-alike hooker who captures the heart of one of the officers. A tense thriller that's even better the second time around.

14 **LAURA** (dir. Otto Preminger, 1944) In this romantic noir, Dana Andrews plays a detective who becomes heavily involved in a murder investigation. The victim, Laura (Gene Tierney) left behind a trail of broken hearts and suspects. Her beauty even entices the detective from the fetching painting of her in her home. Clifton Webb plays a snooty newspaper columnist who adored Laura a little too much, and Vincent Price plays a gigolo! Yikes!

15 **MALCOLM X** (dir. Spike Lee, 1992) Denzel Washington pretty much becomes Malcolm X in this flick based on *The Autobiography of Malcolm X* (a great book, by the way). The story of one man who affected millions, this movie is stirring, thoughtful, and epic. Angela Bassett stars as the heroic Betty Shabazz, Malcolm's wife. It's a personal, political, religious, and important story that sheds some light on race relations today.

16 **THE MALTESE FALCON** (dir. John Huston, 1941) Densely plotted mystery of a stolen statue (above-mentioned falcon) and the detective, Sam Spade, who's searching for it. Huston directs with enough bite to leave marks, and as Spade, Humphrey Bogart delivers enough cynicism and toughness to make us wish he'd show these new 1990s whippersnappers a thing or two.

17 **THE MANCHURIAN CANDIDATE** (dir. John Frankenheimer, 1962) Oliver Stone's got nothing on Frankenheimer, who directed this conspiracy flick war hero Raymond Shaw (Laurence Harvey), who has been brainwashed to be a political assassin. An amazing scene where a ladies' gardening party "becomes" a brainwashing demonstration by Chinese Communists is sick, hilarious, and brilliantly edited. Vintage Frank Sinatra and Angela Lansbury, and a completely bizarre-o performance by Janet Leigh!

18 **THE PIANO** (dir. Jane Campion, 1993) This lush, breathtaking film stars Holly Hunter as a mute Scottish woman, betrothed to a vacant New Zealander (Sam Neill). Harvey Keitel, of all people, captures her heart. Little Anna Paquin plays the brilliant, defiant daughter who has learned to speak for her mother. There's some-

thing so heartbreaking about seeing the piano in the middle of a deserted beach, with waves lapping close by. . . sigh.

19 **QUIZ SHOW** (dir. Robert Redford, 1994) Redford goes behind the camera for this alternately funny and sad story of the 1950s quiz-show scam. A handsome Columbia University teacher (Ralph Fiennes) was given the answers to questions in an attempt by the show's producers to oust Herb Stimple (John Turturro), who was disliked by the sponsors because he, uh, had a face made for radio. Turned out this wasn't the first time the show had been rigged. Even Rob Morrow can't ruin this film!

20 **RAN** (dir. Akira Kurosawa, 1985) King Lear only better. *Ran* is so vast and gorgeous, woweee!! Three sons duke it out for their aging father's turf in feudal Japan. The battle scenes (with vibrant flashes of color—the flags showing who's who) are intense yet beautiful like a complicated ballet. Even after many viewings, you'll still be caught up in the intrigue.

21 **THE SWEET HEREAFTER** (dir. Atom Egoyan, 1997) If there's a way to make pain and suffering beautiful, then Egoyan does it in this grim but not maudlin movie. Traveling freely through time, we see a town devastated by the loss of fourteen children in a bus accident. Then we see the accident. Ian Holm is a lawyer looking to make some dough off of the citizens' tragedy, but he's got problems of his own. Exquisitely directed and acted, this is the ultimate portrait of family, mourning, and life in the aftermath of tragedy.

22 **THE USUAL SUSPECTS** (dir. Bryan Singer, 1995) Who is Keyser Soze?! That was the question in this film that took us completely by surprise in 1995. Kevin Spacey, Chazz Palminteri, and Benicio Del Toro became three of our favorite actors after their performances in this totally enjoyable and engrossing story. The scene where the usual suspects are dragged in for their mug shots is hilarious, and the ending took every one of us by surprise!

23 **VERTIGO** (dir. Alfred Hitchcock, 1958) It's Hitchcock's version of the Pygmalion myth; gorgeous Kim Novak and handsome Jimmy Stewart star in this dramatic tale of an ex-cop who is hired by a supposed old college acquaintance, Gavin Elster, to trail Gavin's wife, who is apparently suffering from some kind of "spells." Poor "Scottie" (Stewart) doesn't know that he's been targeted because of his severe vertigo. Great titles by Saul Bass. P.S. We love Midge!

24 **WHO'S AFRAID OF VIRGINIA WOOLF?** (dir. Mike Nichols, 1966) Known among certain circles (um, ours at least) as The Dinner Party from Hell, this film, based on an Edward Albee play, features a haggard Richard Burton and a braying Elizabeth Taylor as two insane alcoholics who drag an innocent young couple into their twisted world for an evening. Devastatingly cruel and funny, this film is ultimately, in the words of one character, "sad, sad, sad."

25 **THE WILD BUNCH** (dir. Sam Peckinpah, 1969) A has-been pack of renegades execute one last heist south of the border before they pack it in. All the mythical elements are in place: stoic bad guys following their twisted code of honor, vengeance-fueled law enforcers determined to bring them down, and ammo-happy feuding Mexican warlords. Peckinpah elevates this standard stuff with groundbreaking violence and beautifully choreographed shoot-outs. A visually stunning film, and an obvious inspiration for all action movies that have come since.

2 COMEDIES:
From Low-Brow to Hi-Jinx

Poor comedies. They're considered the dopey goofball younger sibling of the classier, smarter movie genres like drama, thriller, and romance. Often when people say "comedy," you think food fights, jockstraps as headgear, fart jokes, and fat guys falling down. And, well, yes, if **Animal House**, **Sixteen Candles**, and the work of John Belushi, John Candy, and Bill Murray are considered key examples of this genre, then bring on the fake vomit and clown cars.

Just because funny movies tend to be rather low-budget, low-concept affairs doesn't mean they're easy to do well; a good comedy is hard to find. Sure, a comedy can be easy to make (think **Bio-Dome** or **Naked Gun**), but a good comedy—one that works, delivering either belly laughs or smart satire or both—that's hard to do. So when a comic movie nails it, what could be better?

Comedies are about more than fun; they should be shocking, subversive, and smart. A good comedy should leave the viewer physically wrecked; the stomach aches, tears roll down the face, the mind races to remember the best lines. A great comedy always features at least one perfect performance—think of Dustin Hoffman in

Tootsie, Lily Tomlin in **Nine to Five**, and Mike Myers in **Austin Powers**. Funny people are incredibly charming; in fact, Andrea was seduced by the rather offbeat stylings of Leslie Nielsen in **Airplane!** (Don't tell her other true love, Richard Pryor.)

Show us the person who truly doesn't like comedies and, well, we'll show you a sourpuss. We Girls know that comedies, like people, come in all shapes and sizes, and not every comedy is right for every viewer. Take **Kingpin** (dirs. Peter Farrelly and Bobby Farrelly, 1996). For Sibyl, that flick was two hours of horrible, beyond-gross jokes about a loser with a prosthetic hand (Woody Harrelson) and a nice, oversize Amish bowling prodigy (Randy Quaid). But Lise liked it; it was gross, ridiculous, and featured the always brilliant Bill Murray, so for her rental money, that flick paid off. In fact, Lise's family worships at the alter of the low-brow comedy (e.g., **Better off Dead**, **Caddyshack**).

See, that's the funny thing about comedies: One person's yuk-fest is another person's personal hell. Clare's engaged in a lifelong debate with her parents about which classic Woody Allen comedy is better, **Annie Hall** or **Manhattan**. Jim Carrey, master of the rubber face, is loved by many and loathed by many, too. Though

GUILTY PLEASURE COMEDY FLICK

LISE: *Kingpin.* Yeah, you heard me! Observe the insanity that is Bill Murray's hair.

SIBYL: *The Little Shop of Horrors*—Steve Martin is a sadistic dentist, and there's a singing plant, too!

ANDREA: *My Fellow Americans.* Watching warring politicos James Garner and Jack Lemmon bicker like an old married couple made me laugh, a lot.

CLARE: *Parenthood.* Man, that flick delivered for me on so many levels. For more Steve Martin, I'd also go with *All of Me.*

Ace Ventura was pretty good, **Liar, Liar** made Andrea and Sibyl want to claw their eyeballs out. In comedy, there seems to be an especially fine line between the good and the god-awful.

Sibyl is a big fan of classic comedies of the thirties and forties. Often inhabiting both the worlds of comedy and romance (hence the subcategory "romantic comedy"), these flicks rely heavily on the razor-sharp banter between male and female leads and are great showcases for actors with timing and style. Katharine Hepburn and Spencer Tracy trade barbs with perfect rhythm in a classic series of flicks including 1952's **Pat and Mike** and 1957's **Desk Set**—so dry, so classy—there's nothing better.

Of course Hepburn and Tracy aren't the only great comedy team. There's Lemmon and Matthau (**The Odd Couple**), Aykroyd and Belushi (**The Blues Brothers**), and, um, well, Farley and Spade (**Black Sheep**, **Tommy Boy**). Andrea loves those old dudes Jack Lemmon and Walter Matthau; their comic patter works so well after all these years that they even made a hit out of **Grumpy Old Men**. And Sibyl has come to grips with Chris Farley and David Spade; sure, she didn't love **Black Sheep**, but just between us, she did giggle when Spade obsessively tried to get a dial tone on his cell phone.

The challenge with comedies is that they have to push the limits of taste and dark humor without pushing too far. As Alan Alda said in **Crimes and Misdemeanors**, "If it bends, it's funny; if it breaks, it's not funny." The Coen brothers' brilliantly dark film **Fargo** (1996) sits on that fine line between funny and disgusting. **Fargo** is supremely cool (so cool that hats with earflaps became all the rage); it boasts a great lead performance by Frances McDormand (she won the Academy Award for it), perfect writing, and a story that's not afraid to bend and bend and bend (leg in a wood chipper, anyone?).

We Girls were introduced to black humor when we saw

Heathers (dir. Michael Lehmann, 1989) as teenagers. With Christian Slater working a weird Jack Nicholson voice and Winona Ryder fulfilling every teenage girl's dream of revenge (she eliminates all the most popular girls from her high school), it's a classic black comedy, pushing the edge of propriety. Sadly, it may not seem quite as funny now that the problem of violence in schools has become so real.

Some comedies are so dark, so weird, and so whacked-out that a lot of people just find them downright offensive and disgusting. Director John Waters is not afraid to showcase a huge transvestite, the late actor Divine (**Female Trouble, Polyester**) or to tell the story of a June Cleaver type of mom who's so addicted to being perfect that she kills her neighbors for not sorting their trash and recycling (**Serial Mom**). Waters laid the groundwork for movies like **There's Something About Mary**, which features some great gags (a dog on drugs getting mouth-to-mouth) and some gags that drag (Ben Stiller and his zipper problem).

It's okay to be dumb and goofy, that's our mantra at Girls on Film. And that's never more true than with movies like **Airplane!**, **Caddyshack** (featuring a dancing gopher), or **Wayne's World**. These are the kind of flicks that make you sick from laughing too hard. You laugh, you cry, you go see it again. These great comedies are so popular they're often followed up by lesser sequels that pale in comparison.

Comedies can do way more than deliver laughs: Satire can make hard-hitting points about politics, the entertainment biz, and pretty much anything else. There are tons of great satires in the mockumentary style (you know, it's a "mock documentary"): **This Is Spinal Tap** brilliantly skewered the rock 'n' roll scene, **Bob Roberts** went after politicians, and **Waiting for Guffman** shows small-town America at its most wacky. The political satire **Wag the Dog** (dir. Barry Levinson, 1997) has become a part of our recent cultural language, since its story, of a president diverting the nation's attention from an inappropriate dalliance by concocting a fake war abroad, served as an eerie parallel to President Clinton's real-life activities.

Comic genius—that's what people say when they see a really funny movie, and there's a kind of comic genius for everyone. Maybe you like those hawking-up-a-loogie **Uncle Buck** kind of movies, or the old-school slapstick of the Marx brothers. Or maybe **Beverly Hills Cop**'s Eddie Murphy tearing it up is your thing, or maybe you love those fish-out-of-water flicks like **Private Benjamin**. Who knows? The good news is, everyone likes to laugh, and you can have a secret obsession with some off-the-wall flick like **Revenge of the Nerds** (uhm, that'd be Sibyl), and just rent it to your heart's delight. You've got to love comedy; it'll make you laugh, cry, and maybe even hurl all at the same time—that's comic genius.

GEE, SORRY YOUR MOM BLEW UP

By Lise

Every now and then, my family likes to sing a couple of lines from a song that my sister made up when she was about five, called "Being a Model"—it embarrasses her and reduces the rest of us to giggles. (It's also easy to remember, because the only words are "Being a model! Being a model! A great big model tooooooooooooo!" I have no idea what this means. No one does.) Every family has their own folklore, their own secrets, and their own language. You may call your grandparents "Grammy" and "Grampa," but your friends may call their grandparents "Bup" and "Nonnie," or something crazier that they made up during the crawling years. I'm sure you have specific books that your parents read to you when you were young (our favorite was **Big Bad Bruce**), and you certainly have family stories that are retold forever ("Remember Rob's imaginary friends?").

The same is true of movies. Take any family of movie watchers, and they'll have some comedies that became classics just within the family. Sibyl mentions her mom's love of **Earth Girls Are Easy**; in Andrea's family, it was **The In-laws** (dir. Arthur Hiller, 1979). She reminisces about sneaking sandwiches into the theater with her mom on one of those rainy New York afternoons. Starring Peter Falk and

UNINTENTIONALLY FUNNIEST MOVIE

LISE: *The Scarlet Letter.* The bird, the candle, and Demi—how this idea got past so many executives is beyond me.

SIBYL: *Fire Walk with Me*—David Lynch at his absolute worst; I laughed, then I fell asleep.

ANDREA: I can't say enough about the snickerfest that is *Showgirls.* Talk about laughing through tears.

CLARE: *Chain Reaction.* Keanu Reeves plays some kind of *scientist-genius.* (*HA HA HA HA HA.*)

Alan Arkin, the movie is, according to Andrea, hilarious. And to this day, Andrea knows that she'll like someone if they recognize the line: "Serpentine, Shelly, serpentine!" (Don't tell Andrea, but I can't remember what that means!)

In my family, the comedies we watched over and over were **Airplane!**, **Caddyshack**, and, the ultimate, **Better off Dead** (dir. Savage Steve Holland, 1985), which became one of our holiday traditions, just like turkey and Christmas trees. Starring a young John Cusack, whose charm had already fully developed, **Better off Dead** is the story of Lane Myer, his family, and his cohorts. At the beginning of the film, Lane's girlfriend dumps him for a feathered-haired skier named Roy Stalin, telling him "I really think it's in my best interest to go out with someone more popular." Nicely put.

The attention to detail and characters in **Better off Dead** is remarkable. Lane's younger brother, Badger, usually sports a weird leopard-print bathrobe, despite the fact that he is seven years old. Lane's friend Charles sports a top hat and says things like "I've been going to high school for seven and a half years, Lane. I'm no dummy." And the whole family lives in fear of both the paper boy and of the mother's cooking (one dessert actually slithers away when Lane pokes it). But the best thing about **Better off Dead** may be its PG rating. This movie, which still cracks me up after all these years, proves that a comedy can rely on a wacky family (remember the Griswalds?) and a cute love story. In my family, we'll be saying "Gee Ricky, sorry your Mom blew up" for years to come.

Certainly, to appreciate off-the-wall comedies like **Better off Dead**, **Airplane!**, and **Caddyshack**, it helps to have an off-the-wall family like mine. Example: One time we were talking around the kitchen table when our kitten jumped on it and walked by a candle, lighting its tail on fire; my mom just shoved the flaming beast under the faucet, all the while continuing with the conversation. No one flinched. Even the cat seemed to have a "just go with it" attitude; it just licked its tail and went outside to kill, kill, kill. I think we can all agree that **Airplane!** (dir. Jim Abrahams, David Zucker, Jerry Zucker, 1980) is not the right comedy for an uptight family, with Captain Oveur (Peter Graves) asking a young boy whether he's ever been in a Turkish prison. And then there's Barbara Billingsley as an elderly woman who speaks jive. And a sick girl whose IV is pulled out by an acoustic guitar—wielding flight attendant. The team that made **Airplane!** went on to make not only **Airplane 2**, but also **Top Secret** and **Ruthless People**, but none of them came close to matching the comic timing and sheer mass of jokes that makes **Airplane!** one of my family's comedy classics. And yet, there is one thing, or should I say one person, that **Airplane!** is lacking . . .

It would be impossible, or just dumb, to talk comedy without talking Bill Murray. His career has spanned three decades and has included not only brilliantly funny films like **Stripes**, **Ghostbusters**, **Where the Buffalo Roam**, **Kingpin**, and **Rushmore**, but also his genius work on "Saturday Night Live" in the late 1970s. Bill Murray inhabits his characters, no matter how insane they may be. For me, the funniest Bill Murray role of all time is in one of my family's comedy classics, **Caddyshack** (dir. Harold Ramis, 1980). Murray plays Carl Spackler, the groundskeeper at the golf course whose primary responsibility is gopher control, although he also dabbles in caddying for priests during lightning storms and draining the pool after a floating candy bar is mistaken for a "doody." (In the latter scene, which we rewound and played about five thousand times, Carl then eats the faux-doody, saying, "What? It's not so bad.") I was eleven years old when **Caddyshack** was released, possibly too young to fully grasp Chevy Chase's Ty Webb, the womanizing golf pro, but something about Carl, well, it spoke to me. So I got that goin' for me, which is nice.

While my family was watching Carl try to blow up gophers, Clare's family was having a slightly more highbrow comedy festival of their own, playing flicks like **Annie Hall** and quoting **Dr. Strangelove**. It just illustrates the point that no two families are alike. So whether it's **Blazing Saddles**, **The Pink Panther**, or something far more obscure, I'll bet your family has a few comedy classics in the comedy classic closet. Why not arrange a little film festival? It could be a fun, and funny, walk down memory lane.

MY MAIN MAN, WOODY ALLEN

By Clare

Some families debate over politics, books, philosophy, or religion. Some families, like Lise's, forgo such banter altogether to watch **Better off Dead**. When my family has a debate, though, it's about one thing: whether **Annie Hall** or **Manhattan** is the better movie.

My parents are especially confrontational about this subject. Because of my father, I've committed almost all of **Annie Hall** to memory. My mother, a little less fanatic about her preference, quietly insists that she prefers **Manhattan**, but Dad can't get past the fact that the fortysomething Allen's character has an on-screen affair with Mariel Hemingway's precocious seventeen-year-old. Eeeww. Life imitates art.

Now that Woody Allen's life and art have proven to mesh so nicely, I certainly feel like I know the guy. I grew up with him; I watched the progression of his movies from zany to sweet to serious to a mixture of all three, from way, way out there to a little too close to home. (Who didn't squirm with discomfort by the time Allen released **Husbands and Wives**, in which his character seduces the much younger Juliette Lewis and his ex, Mia Farrow, plays a total manipulative witch?)

I'm not the hugest fan of the early, madcap Allen films like **What's up, Tiger Lily?** (a spoof of badly dubbed Japanese films, in which competing spies battle over the recipe to the perfect egg salad) or **Bananas** (in which a consumer products tester becomes a South American dictator for the sake of a lady). But I do like his early stuff in general, before he got a little meaner and more lecherous, casting his old, toady little self opposite such knockout young actresses as Elisabeth Shue, Julia Roberts, and Mira Sorvino.'

No matter what I think of his casting practices, I can't deny that the guy's responsible for some of the best comedy around: not only **Manhattan** and **Annie Hall** (P.S., I like **Annie Hall** a little better, don't tell my mom), but **Love and Death**, a spoof of the Russian novel that's just hilarious; **Broadway Danny Rose**, about a sweet New York talent agent who gets caught up with Mia Farrow's carelessly charming gun moll; and the brilliant **Bullets over Broadway**, which proved to me that Allen could still make a beautiful, funny, semiserious comedy after the bloodbath of **Husbands and Wives**.

I'm going to talk about just three of my favorites here: **Play It Again, Sam** (1972), which Allen wrote and starred in but Herbert Ross directed; **Stardust Memories** (1980), a rumination on the failure of Woody's fans to appreciate his superdowner serious attempt **Interiors** (1978); and finally, **Crimes and Misdemeanors** (1989), which is, to me, Woody Allen's perfect blend of farcical comedy and grim, psychological drama.

I love it when Woody casts himself as the ultimate misfit, which is why I've always had a soft spot for **Broadway Danny Rose** (unlike Andrea, I found the Thanksgiving scene sweet and

FAVORITE WOODY ALLEN COMEDY

LISE: *Annie Hall.* Yep, sorry I can't be more original, but Diane Keaton's performance was so on the money.

SIBYL: *Bullets over Broadway*— John Cusack and Dianne Wiest are great. "Don't speak!"

ANDREA: I'm partial to the lighter-than-a-feather *Manhattan Murder Mystery*, especially the scene where Woody has a panic attack in an elevator. It's so perfect.

CLARE: I'll go with *Stardust Memories*, just to be different.

funny, not heartbreaking). So how on earth had **Play It Again, Sam** flown under my radar for so many years? It wasn't until my brother-in-law recommended it to me last year that I discovered this gem, in which Allen is nothing if not a misfit. In it, he plays Alan, a writer for a film magazine in San Francisco whose wife of two years has just left him.

Play It Again, Sam opens on a slack-jawed Allan, watching the end of **Casablanca** for what we can only assume is the hundredth time. We soon find that this neurotic movie enthusiast keeps counsel with a rough-and-tumble Humphrey Bogart, who tells him that he should just slap women around and drown his sorrows in bourbon. Unfortunately, Alan tries bourbon once, only to spew it out all over a bar, gasp, and drop his head with a thud (one of the many physical comedy bits that I loved in this movie; this scene literally made me guffaw).

Alan's married friends Linda (Diane Keaton) and Dick (Tony Roberts) immediately start trying to set him up with women they know. But every time he's put in a social situation, he gets so nervous that he sabotages himself, posing, tripping, stuttering, strutting, and basically striking out. The one woman he can be himself around is Linda, who shares his love of Darvon, Valium, and other pharmaceuticals. She also shares his insecurities; her husband, Alan's best friend, doesn't pay enough attention to her, stopping at phones everywhere they go to inform his office where he can be reached for the next fifteen minutes. Alan finds himself falling in love with Linda, and of course, the film ends with a riff on the famous last scene in **Casablanca**—except this time the plane's to Cleveland, not Lisbon, and Linda is leaving willingly.

Alan's desperate, repeated attempts to woo the ladies in **Play It Again, Sam** had me laughing aloud, by myself. When Linda and Dick set him up on his very first date, he begins to dance around the room with a huge smile on his face: "I really have mixed feelings about this!" He then goes home "to shower and douse his body in Canoe," after which his alter ego reprimands him: "For Christ's sake, kid, you're gonna smell like a French cathouse!" When it turns out that their outdoor dinner might be ruined by the rain, Allan pontificates in an attempt to impress his date: "I love the rain; it washes memories off the sidewalk of life."

Despite its sometimes cheesy score and the fact that it's not as lovingly shot as the films that he later directed himself, **Play It Again, Sam** remains one of Woody Allen's sweetest, funniest films. Rent it. If you don't rent this movie you're gonna regret it. Maybe not today, maybe not tomorrow, but soon and for the rest of your life. (Oh, sorry. It's catching.)

When **Interiors** opened in 1978, Woody Allen was recognized by the Academy (with five nominations), but reamed by die-hard comedy fans (including my family) for making such an unapologetically dour film. He was accused of ripping off Ingmar Bergman. So after he bounced back with **Manhattan** the following year, he got to work on **Stardust Memories**, which begins with—get this—an Ingmar Bergman rip-off scene, followed by producers reaming this "serious" filmmaking attempt by the movie's main character, filmmaker Sandy Bates (Allen).

A woman and a man (who looks scarily like Roger Ebert) start blasting Bates's latest work immediately. "He's pretentious! His filmmaking style is too fancy! His insights are shallow and morbid," the woman rails. "I've seen it all before; they try to document their private suffering and fob it off as art!" To which the Ebertesque guy responds, "What does he have to suffer about? Doesn't he know that he has the greatest gift that anyone can have? The gift of *laughter*?!"

But Bates doesn't feel funny anymore. At a weekend retrospective of his films at the Stardust Hotel, he grapples with fame, love, and existential angst. He confronts fans who keep repeating the refrain: "I love your movies—especially the earlier, funny ones."

He is hounded by people pitching story ideas (a "comedy" about "that whole Guyana thing") and asking for autographs ("Will you sign my left breast?"). He ruminates on his first true love, Dorrie (Charlotte Rampling), who was gorgeous and smart but tragically crazy, and receives a visit from his beautiful, blond, and *stable* girl-friend, Isobel (Marie-Christine Barrault), to whom he can't commit.

Shot in magnificent black-and-white by director of photography Gordon Willis, **Stardust Memories** culminates in an encounter with a group of nutcases waiting for a UFO (which turns out to be a bunch of weather balloons; the sight of them hovering in the sky is one of the more breathtaking shots in the film). In one of the movie's many fantasy sequences, Bates asks the aliens about the meaning of life; he asks how he can continue to make funny movies when there's so much suffering in the world. "You wanna do mankind a real service?" An alien asks him. "Tell funnier jokes!"

Well, in **Crimes and Misdemeanors** he does. The jokes in this movie still make me laugh, and I've seen it at least a dozen times. Once again, Allen plays a filmmaker—this time, a documen-tarian named Cliff—whose financial troubles force him to take up the offer of his officious brother-in-law, Lester (Alan Alda, in a bit of inspired casting), to document Lester's life as a comedy TV pro-ducer. On the set Cliff meets Hallie (Mia Farrow), for whose affec-tions both he and Lester are competing.

In a parallel story line, successful eye doctor Judah (Martin Landau) is being hounded by a cast-off lover (Anjelica Huston), who threatens to expose not only their affair but Judah's financial indis-crepancies if he doesn't leave his wife. When Judah's thug brother, Jack (Jerry Orbach) offers to "take care of the situation," Judah's left in a dire moral dilemma. Both stories dovetail nicely in the end, when Cliff and Judah end up at a wedding together.

The humorous aspects of **Crimes and Misdemeanors** are wickedly funny—Cliff's sister takes out a personal ad to disastrous results, and Cliff's finished film compares Lester to both Mussolini and Mr. Ed—but its serious aspects are just as strong, thought-provoking, and delicately structured. Bucking the tendency of comedies to allow for only broad characters, **Crimes and Misdemeanors** gives each person a rich inner life and complex motives.

Throughout, Allen juxtaposes scenes from old, melodramatic films from the forties with present-day scenes to draw a sly humor even from the most morbid of circumstances. And the score, including a stirring Schubert violin symphony, perfectly builds dramatic tension. This is just such a great film; I'd say it's one of my top ten favorites of all time.

No matter that Woody Allen's got more dirty drawers hanging out than a Chinese laundry, or that I'm sometimes made uncomfortable by his take on women—the man is easily one of the most brilliant filmmakers of the century. And whether you prefer **Manhattan** or **Annie Hall**, his earlier, funny, films or his later accomplishments, he's certainly worth a debate or two.

THEY DON'T MAKE 'EM LIKE THEY USED TO

By Sibyl

Food fights are funny. A dog on drugs getting mouth-to-mouth is funny. And mockumentaries are funny. But, sometimes, just sometimes, I'm in the mood for something a little more restrained. Something elegant, even swellegant. A movie with dashing men in tuxedos, women in evening gowns, drinking cocktails, bantering, with the occasional perfectly timed pratfall. Yes, sometimes I want gorgeous black-and-white (colorized versions are lame! Demand the real thing from your video store!), no curse words, no fart jokes. Just pure wit with a dash of romance thrown in. And when I do, it's classic comedies of the thirites and forties for me.

These films are lovely and witty, but they also feature really great roles for actresses. It seems like these days, there aren't nearly enough good roles for women in movies. It's either young hotties or nasty old hags—that's a shame, particularly since there are so many great actresses out there who are too old to play teenybopper bimbos. Not so in the classic comedies; the women are always tough and funny. Occasionally they're airheads, but rarely—imagine Katharine Hepburn playing dumb, or watch **Bringing up Baby** to see for yourself the rather disastrous results. Aside from great female characters, these flicks tend to have certain elements in common: weddings, nosy reporters, social differences (usually the woman is an heiress), and lots of coincidental encounters. But it's the women (and of course their dashing escorts) who make classic comedies so great.

I SAY THIS LINE ALL THE TIME

LISE: "If it bends, it's funny." Alan Alda as the self-centered cheesy TV producer in *Crimes and Misdemeanors.*

SIBYL: "I'm the host with the most, I'm hot as toast, and hung like a post." *Eating Raoul.*

ANDREA: "Looks like I picked the wrong day to stop sniffing glue!" and just about every other line from the brilliant *Airplane!*

CLARE: "Get the machine that goes 'PING!'" from *Monty Python's the Meaning of Life*

Claudette Colbert is a bride on the run in **It Happened One Night** (dir. Frank Capra, 1934). Considered one of the greatest screwball comedies ever made, the film won all five major Academy Awards. Colbert is an heiress who leaves her rich dullard of a fiancé at the alter. She runs away into the unlikely arms of sexy muckraking reporter Clark Gable. It's amazing that Colbert manages to be so delicately beautiful while she's being so funny and bawdy, too—check out the notorious hitchhiking scene.

Speaking of fickle brides, Katharine Hepburn is all over the place in **The Philadelphia Story** (dir. George Cukor, 1940). She's a society girl (as usual), Cary Grant is her ex-husband, and Jimmy Stewart is a buttinski reporter sent to cover Hepburn's wedding. Hepburn is a coltish tomboy type determined to take no flack from her meddling ex-husband—but who could resist Cary Grant? Fortunately, meddling Jimmy Stewart and sassy Hepburn guzzle endless bottles of champagne together, and she realizes that Grant is the right man for her. Abundant banter keeps this movie funny, while the coupling of Grant and Hepburn provides plenty of swoons.

For an earlier taste of Katharine Hepburn in the heiress role, check out **Holiday** (dir. George Cukor, 1938). Cary Grant is engaged to Hepburn's sister. But it's Katharine, of course, who steals the spotlight. She's a smart, opinionated, quirky girl, and wow, what a fast talker. This film really showcases Hepburn's signature quicksilver eloquence, particularly in her conversations with hopeless dreamer Grant. With a fancy party as the background, Hepburn and Grant teach each other circus tricks (like walking on their hands). Grant is the epitome of elegance somersaulting in a tuxedo. They've got great chemistry and can handle physical comedy, too.

Obviously, Grant and Hepburn are meant to be together.

In Preston Sturges movies, the women are looking for one thing (well, maybe two, but one is foremost in their minds): money and how to get it. That leads them of course to men—sounds kind of dated and pathetic, but not with these amazing characters. His women are part sly devil, part angel, and all smart-ass. In **The Lady Eve** (1941), the leading lady (Barbara Stanwyck) is a con artist. She travels around with her cardsharp dad, duping guys with his clever scams and her great legs. Once she meets Henry Fonda, as a rich but dopey scientist, she actually falls for him. Of course, nothing goes quite as planned, and Fonda wrongs her. So she seeks revenge by fooling him into marrying her (only—get this—he thinks she's some-body else). Payback time comes when, as the other bride, Stanwyck regales the naive Fonda with all of her previous sexual escapades. Horrified, he demands a divorce. It's hilarious, and Stanwyck is amazing—funny and beautiful, but also tough and edgy.

Watching these movies may make you kind of sad. These films are so completely different from the modern comedy; the pace is relaxed, there are no huge yuks, just lots of little laughs resulting from great dialogue and brilliant performances. In the classics, tim-ing was everything; actors couldn't rely on gross-out sight gags, they were *acting*. Of course, they had great directors like Frank Capra and Preston Sturges to guide them.

There are no cheap laughs in the classics. It's the restraint and elegance that make them both funny and glorious. There's just not much grace in **The Naked Gun**. And there certainly aren't smart, clever female roles, the kind that Hepburn or Stanwyck played. Sigh.

Still, the classics are out there, ready for you to rent them. If these flicks appeal to you, then you might also want to check out some great bubbling romantic comedies like **The Awful Truth** (dir. Leo McCarey, 1937) and **The Palm Beach Story** (dir. Preston Sturges, 1942). Or enjoy the quiet, graceful flicks of Ernst Lubitsch, like **Ninotchka** (1939) and **The Shop Around the Corner** (1940). **The Shop Around the Corner** was such a good idea, in fact, that Nora Ephron recently remade it into **You've Got Mail**, with Meg

Ryan and Tom Hanks. Now, if you think Ryan and Hanks live up to the legacy of Margaret Sullavan and Jimmy Stewart, more power to you. But I think I'll pass on that one and just stay at home, sip some champagne, and slip into the light, courtly world of old-time comedy.

THE FASTEST WAY TO MY HEART ...

By Andrea

During my high school years, I tended to fall for the "rebel without a cause" type of guys. They were surly. They smoked cigarettes. They wore dark colors. They were strong, they were silent, some might say they veered toward the sullen.

Being with them was like pulling teeth, but I persevered. I believed that their behavior was masking depth, wisdom, and a shy, timid little heart yearning to burst free and love someone just like me. Uh-huh. Right.

In my very last week of my very last year of high school, I attended a party with a bunch of the students who worked on the school newspaper. They were kinda nerdy. I mean that in the best way: They were witty, irreverent, willing to poke a little fun at themselves, willing to act silly, have a good time. They made me laugh, they brought out the best in me, and best of all, I felt like I could be myself with them, not having to pretend to be cooler-than-thou. I went home and kicked myself repeatedly, hard, for not noticing these people until it was too late.

Now, I'm the world's biggest sucker for a person who provides some serious laughs. One time I threw myself (humiliatingly) at a

INSTANT PARTY MOVIES

Austin Powers

Strictly Ballroom

Beat Girl

Beetlejuice

The Big Lebowski

Alladin

Swingers

House Party

Rush Hour

Velvet Goldmine

Canadian stand-up comic I'd met through work. The guy wasn't afraid to wear strangely patterned clothes, or to work in clubs called "Chuckle's House of Yuk Yuks." Still, he was super sexy because he was so hilarious. Sadly, he had other plans for spending his leisure time. Besides having a girlfriend, I think the crazed look in my eyes when I asked him to tell the one again about how he just flew in from the coast (and, boy, are his arms tired) got him sorta nervous.

Oh, well.

The one place we can always satisfy a comedy craving is in the movies. There's a lovin' spoonful of wonderful performances out there from people who have cracked us up and therefore become the recipients of our affections. Whether it be Clare's love of Meg Ryan (of the romantic-comedy oeuvre—check out her ode in the Romance chapter), Lise's affection for Bill Murray, or Sibyl's appreciation for the tall, gangly, jug-eared Jeff Goldblum, all of us have fallen for people because they make us laugh.

Here are some of the sexiest funny performances around:

JOAN CUSACK IN *IN AND OUT* (dir. Frank Oz, 1997) Emily Montgomery could have been an awful role. A faithful fiancée discovers that her lover is gay, after waiting years for him to marry her? And nada nookie that whole time? Urk! However, the talented Cusack pulls off the role with aplomb, causing the audience to totally fall for her, especially when she freaks out in her puffy wedding dress.

BENICIO DEL TORO IN *THE USUAL SUSPECTS* (dir. Bryan Singer, 1995) Comedy is not the word that comes to mind when you think of this elaborately plotted thriller, but Benicio Del Toro's performance in this flick was true comic genius. Playing a mumbling, heavy-lidded crook, Del Toro almost managed to steal this picture away from the rest of the killer cast (forgive the pun).

JOHN GOODMAN IN *THE BIG LEBOWKSKI* (dir. Joel Coen, 1998) Goodman's Walter is a Vietnam vet who sports Ambervision sunglasses, wields a wicked temper, and lives a devout Orthodox Jewish lifestyle in this wacky Coen brothers flick. His explanation of why he can't go out on Friday nights ("Shomo fucking Shabas!") had all us Girls in stitches for about a month.

CARY GRANT IN *ARSENIC AND OLD LACE* (dir. Frank Capra, 1944) Cary Grant is the ultimate sexy leading man, but rarely has he been so goofy as in this cute classic, playing a man leaving town with his new sweetie, who first stops in to wish adieu to his beloved aunties. Whoopsie! Turns out these sweet old ladies have a tendency to poison lonely men (mercy killing, they say) and bury them around the house, and Grant twists himself into a pretzel trying to protect the dear old biddies when he finds out their sinister secret.

HOLLY HUNTER IN *HOME FOR THE HOLIDAYS* (dir. Jodie Foster, 1995) Hunter's Claudia rules; she is my idol. During this flick, she freaks out about ninety-seven times while at home visiting her family for the Thanksgiving holiday, degenerating into her usual dysfunctional daughter role perfectly. What I have always liked about Holly Hunter is her ability to seem like a real person, albeit a really crazy person sometimes, and here she is at her most awesome and adorable.

MIKE MYERS IN *AUSTIN POWERS: INTERNATIONAL MAN OF MYSTERY* (dir. Jay Roach, 1997) The shagadelic Mike Myers wrote and stars in this silly spy-thriller spoof, and his adorableness runs free playing Austin Powers, an out-of-touch secret agent. The opening sequence, with him doing a dance through swinging London, is terrific, as is the supporting role his rocking chest hair plays. Yeah, baby!

LESLIE NIELSEN IN *AIRPLANE!* (dir. Jim Abrahams, David Zucker, Jerry Zucker, 1980) Swoon. Leslie Nielsen's Dr. Rumnack is perfectly ridiculous, right in keeping with the rest of this brilliant, way juvenile spoof. Everything he does, from wearing his stethoscope at all times, to replying to someone who says "Surely you're joking," that he's serious, "and don't call me Shirley," is adorable. It takes a tough man to make a tender comedy.

RICHARD PRYOR IN *STIR CRAZY* (dir. Sidney Poitier, 1980) Richard Pryor is one of those people who can make even the smallest little throwaway stuff funny, always, and particularly in this goofy flick about two totally nice guys who are thrown in the pokey for a crime they didn't commit. My fave scene is when Pryor struts down a prison hallway with the equally dorky-looking Gene Wilder by his side, trying to look tough: "That's right, that's right, we bad, we bad." I particularly love how warmly he acts toward Wilder, both on a character level, and as far as not hogging the limelight. Cool.

CHRISTIAN SLATER IN *HEATHERS* (dir. Michael Lehmann, 1989) Christian Slater channels Jack Nicholson here as a rebellious teen who convinces popular girl Winona Ryder that the world is a better place without her bitchy friends in **Heathers**. In fact, I fell for my first serious boyfriend because he reminded me of Slater here. Dark, twisted, yum, just the way I like 'em.

So there you are. Plenty of funny fish in the sea. Which leads me to the moral of this story: If you want to have serious dating success, perhaps you're wise to spend time working on your funny bone, not on your pecs.

25 Comedies to Rent

1 **AIRPLANE!** (dirs. Jim Abrahams, David Zucker, Jerry Zucker, 1980) Every line's a gem in this silly, zesty spoof of disaster flicks. An airplane's going down and the only fella on board (Robert Hays) who can fly that puppy home has some serious mental problems. As does every other character around, played with the right amount of gonzo lunacy by the game cast of Julie Hagerty, Lloyd Bridges, Kareem Abdul-Jabbar, and of course, spoof-meister Leslie Nielsen.

2 **ANNIE HALL** (dir. Woody Allen, 1977) The perfect introduction to Woody's world. Allen plays Alvy, a neurotic, paranoid, Jewish comedian with women troubles. (Sound familiar?) Alvy's on-again-off-again romance with Annie (Diane Keaton, sporting the bespecta-cled preppy bohemian look she made famous) is tragicomedy at its finest. Allen's riffs on New York, L.A., showbiz, psychotherapy, and politics are the themes he has continued to pursue in almost a film a year since *Hall*.

3 **AUSTIN POWERS: INTERNATIONAL MAN OF MYSTERY** (dir. Jay Roach, 1997) Yeah, baby! This supermod spoof of James Bond manly action flicks is raucously funny. Mike Myers dancing through the streets of London in a frilly blouse and hip huggers is shagadelic. Myers also plays bald Nehru-jacket-wearing bad guy Dr. Evil. Full of quotable lines. ("Do I make you horny?")

4 **CADDYSHACK** (dir. Harold Ramis, 1980) Absolute vintage Bill Murray as Carl, the wacko groundskeeper at a prestigious country club, whose main quest is to kill those pesky gophers with plastic explosives. Still, this is an ensemble piece; Chevy Chase ("Be the ball, Danny") and Rodney Dangerfield ("Looks good on you, though") definitely pull their weight. Just ignore the Danny-and-Maggie pregnancy/romance story and wait for Carl to caddy for the priest in a torrential downpour.

5 **CLUELESS** (dir. Amy Heckerling, 1995) As if!! Zany, funny, sweet, and full of jargon, this California-style eye-candy is a pop reworking of Jane Austen's *Emma*. Alicia Silverstone manages to infuse self-centered rich girl Cher with a certain lovable quality. And as her liberal-arts-school step-brother, Paul Rudd sneers and smolders to perfection.

6 **DUCK SOUP** (dir. Leo McCarey, 1933) It's slapstick and satire and a classic. Groucho (sporting the eyebrows, mustache, and cigar) is the new leader of Freedonia. He's got bumbling spies (Chico and Harpo) following him and a plot to unseat him, so he declares war on neighbor Sylvania. Madcap Marx Bros. at their best; Harpo jumping in a bucket of lemonade, a zillion Groucho zingers, and great political commentary—as Groucho says, "If you think this country's bad, wait till I get through with it."

7 **DR. STRANGELOVE** (dir. Stanley Kubrick, 1964) Brace yourself for a wild, weird ride straddling a nuke warhead. This black, bleak, funny attack on American politics, nationalism, and warmongering amazingly reflects current affairs as well our involvement in Vietnam and the arms race. Peter Sellers displays his comic genius playing a buttoned-up officer, a wishy-washy president, and a crazed German scientist, and George C. Scott proves that he can do comedy in addition to *Patton*.

8 **EATING RAOUL** (dir. Paul Bartel, 1982) The Blands are an aggressively straight couple who start inviting swingers over to their place, then killing them with a swift conk on the head with an iron pan. See, they're trying to rid the world of loose people and get money to fund their dream restaurant. Black comedy doesn't get much darker or funnier. The swinger-party scenes are great—hot tubs, hot hosts, great one-liners.

9 **HAIRSPRAY** (dir. John Waters, 1988) The king of shock is pretty subdued in this period piece. Set in the sixties, *Hairspray* is the story of a dance show (like "American Bandstand") and the struggle to racially integrate the cast of dancers. Ricki Lake is a teen with a dream; Sonny Bono and Deborah Harry are her parents. Funny, at times a little gross, with a great soundtrack of classic sixties tunes. Do the mashed potato!

10 **MONTY PYTHON AND THE HOLY GRAIL** (dirs. Terry Gilliam, Terry Jones, 1975) This brilliant, bawdy riff on the story of King Arthur makes us cry laughing; its many memorable scenes include a witch-hunt ("She turned me into a newt!"), a surly French knight ("I fart in your general direction!"), and a political naysayer who questions King Arthur's rule ("Oh, but you can't expect to wield supreme executive power just because some watery tart threw a sword at you!"). The best of Monty Python's hilarious movies.

11 **LA CAGE AUX FOLLES** (dir. Edouard Molinaro, 1978) Forget the limp remake (*The Birdcage*), the original French farce is laugh-packed. With domesticated middle-aged boyfriends—one owns the drag club, the other is a performer there—attempting to play it straight for their right-wing future in-laws, things take a campy turn. Claude, the giggly afro-sporting houseboy who can't walk in his shoes, is particularly great.

12 **THE LADY EVE** (dir. Preston Sturges, 1941) Perhaps the most perfect comedy ever. Barbara Stanwyck is a beautiful con artist. Henry Fonda is a naive scientist with a fortune. They fall in love. He learns her true identity. She seeks revenge, and marries him with a different identity. She gets her revenge. Then they fall in love again. Every line zings. Scenes from this flick have been stolen for zillions of lesser comedies. This is genius.

13 **LIVING IN OBLIVION** (dir. Tom DiCillo, 1995) Thinking about making an indie film? Watch this brutal skewering of the process first. Steve Buscemi is the perfectly put-upon director. James LeGros is the Brad Pitt–esque star who thinks an eye patch is acting. Then there's the crew: sleepy, stoned, temperamental, and not that talented. A gut-wrenching nightmare—mean, tuxedo-wearing dwarf included.

14 **MARRIED TO THE MOB** (dir. Jonathan Demme, 1988) The most amazing thing about this mob movie spoof is that it came out two years before Scorsese's *Goodfellas*, yet it mocks that flick at every turn. The other amazing thing is Michelle Pfeiffer looking skanky as a mob wife. Plus, Mercedes Ruehl plays a deranged and possessive wife of the don, Dean Stockwell. Demme keeps it moving with great music by Talking Head David Byrne.

15 **PARENTHOOD** (dir. Ron Howard, 1989) This comedy about the pleasure and pain of parenting raises the question, Can one bad scene (the epilogue) ruin an otherwise laugh-filled, perfectly cast, dead-on movie? Well, almost, but Steve Martin as an imperfect dad and Dianne Wiest as a single mom struggling with rambunctious daughter Martha Plimpton and Plimpton's airhead boy-toy Keanu Reeves redeem one bad, stupidly sappy directorial choice.

16 **THE PLAYER** (dir. Robert Altman, 1992) Dark insider psy-chothriller/satire on Hollywood dealmakers, *The Player* is classic Altman, with a zillion characters (and as many celebrity cameos, from Cher to Bruce Willis) floating around cutthroat movie exec Tim Robbins. Bitter writers seek revenge and sellout writers suck up. Cell phones and designer water just add to that creepy L.A. vibe.

17 **THE PRINCESS BRIDE** (dir. Rob Reiner, 1987) It's a fairy tale. It's a spoof of fairy tales. It's an action-adventure. It's a romance (with gorgeous damsel Robin Wright and kind prince Cary Elwes). But above all, it's comedy, with perfect performances by Mandy Patinkin as Enigo Montayo, Billy Crystal and Carol Kane as witchy forest dwellers, and Christopher Guest as the bad guy.

18 **THE PRODUCERS** (dir. Mel Brooks, 1968) Two losers (Zero Mostel and Gene Wilder) find Broadway success with the most unlikely production ever: a musical about Hitler. This movie is so mod, madcap sixties. Great perspective on the theater world. Who can resist a casting session where dancing Hitlers are stage right, singing Hitlers stage left? The "Springtime for Hitler" number is brilliant.

19 **RAISING ARIZONA** (dir. Joel Coen, 1987) The greatest Coen brothers comedy. Nicolas Cage and Holly Hunter (he's an ex-con, she's his parole officer) snatch a baby since Hunter is "barren!" They're pursued by a crazed jailbird (John Goodman), an evil, Harley-riding bounty hunter, and the baby's cheesy furniture salesman daddy. Perfect blend of heist and slapstick.

20 **SOME LIKE IT HOT** (dir. Billy Wilder, 1959) One of the few films that knew what to do with firecracker Marilyn Monroe (hint: she's funny, everyone). In this classic flick from director Billy Wilder (*Sunset Boulevard*, *Double Indemnity*), Jack Lemmon and Tony Curtis don wigs, dresses, and hideous makeup in an attempt to pass for ladies, albeit ugly ones. Risque, smart, and just absurd enough, *Some Like It Hot* is fun for the whole family.

21 **STIR CRAZY** (dir. Sidney Poitier, 1980) Gene Wilder and Richard Pryor are sweet New York goofballs (just go with this premise) who set out to find some sexy babes in California. Uh-oh! After performing at a bank in woodpecker suits, they're framed for a robbery. They get sent to jail, befriend some jailbird freaks, and scheme to bust out. This flick is a perfect vehicle for Gene Wilder's sweet befuddlement and Richard Pryor's manic misery.

22 **THIS IS SPINAL TAP** (dir. Rob Reiner, 1984) Do these go to eleven? That's the question in this rock mockumentary. A has-been classic rock band tours with disastrous results. They've got a sleazy manager, drummers who catch on fire, and a miniature Stonehenge set. The definitive mockumentary.

23 **TOOTSIE** (dir. Sydney Pollack, 1982) Dustin Hoffman is a surly, out-of-work actor who snags a job playing a woman on a soap opera (so he's secretly cross-dressing, then playing a woman). He makes a surprisingly nice woman, and she's kind of attractive in a matronly way. The soap opera cast and crew includes sleazy director Dabney Coleman, tall ingenue Geena Davis, and sexy star Jessica Lange. The weird premise works brilliantly with Hoffman's legendary performance.

24 **WAG THE DOG** (dir. Barry Levinson, 1997) Great political satire. Spin doctor De Niro is brought in to distract the nation from a president's improper relations. He hires Hollywood producer Dustin Hoffman (big-haired, smoothie-drinking, tanning-bed-addicted egomaniac) to create a distraction. These two acting greats are a perfect pair. Eerie precursor to Clinton's zipper problems.

25 **WOMEN ON THE VERGE OF A NERVOUS BREAKDOWN** (dir. Pedro Almodóvar, 1988) Set in Madrid—which, in director Almodóvar's hands, is easily the most Technicolor, wacko-filled city in the world—this is a great Euro screwball comedy. Three women (all nutty) pursuing one man, plus some political terrorist intrigue, propel this madcap flick, with a batch of tranquilizer-laced gazpacho and the young Antonio Banderas thrown in for comedic perfection.

3 INDEPENDENT FILMS:

Off the Beaten Path

I ndependent films, or "indies," as they are affectionately called, are films made outside the realm of the Hollywood studio system. These films can be harder to find, both in theaters and in video stores. Still, we Girls champion independent films; when we're tired of seeing the same old McMovies, it's a godsend to find a personally crafted work from a filmmaker who is working outside of the mainstream.

However, the phrase "independent film" had different connotations twenty, and even ten, years ago. A lot of this is due to one man who has become a walking, talking American icon. His name is Robert Redford, and his friends call him Bob. But none of us even know him, so we'll continue to call him Robert. Anyway, in 1984, Robert Redford began to lend his support to what had until then been called the U.S. Film Festival. What he renamed the Sundance Festival had previously been known as a showcase of truly independent films; it has since (and we're not blaming it on Bob—Robert! Robert!) turned into a week-long schmooze-and-sell-fest, where some of the biggest movie deals are made. Let's put it this way: If you're in movie acquisitions, you can't not go to Sundance (or Telluride, or Toronto, for that matter), so strap on your gigantic fur hat, grab your cell phone (oh look, it's already attached to your ear!), and look like you're having fun.

COOL CAREER: I THINK THIS DIRECTOR IS BOLD

LISE: Allison Anders, for never being afraid to go out on a limb.

SIBYL: Gus Van Sant (*Drugstore Cowboy, To Die For*) Cool movies even when he misses.

ANDREA: John Sayles. I think this indie director (*Brother from Another Planet, City of Hope*) is all that. He's rumored to be incredibly nice, to boot.

CLARE: Hal Hartley. Always mannered, always quirky, always shoots his movies on Long Island. Loved *Trust, Amateur, Henry Fool*, etc.

It's hard to define what an independent film is anymore. It once meant any film that was made outside the studio system, with money that was raised by a starving artiste who wanted nothing more in life than to see his/her vision on some grainy film with bad sound. But now that Disney owns Miramax, and gigantic corporations like Twentieth Century Fox have established little satellite development and distribution companies with cute names like Fox Searchlight, it's a whole different scene. For example, here's the name of a so-called independent film that may give you pause: **Pulp Fiction** (dir. Quentin Tarantino, 1994). See?

The good news is that indies like this—and **The Piano, Big Night, Hoop Dreams**, and **Eve's Bayou**, to name a few others—are getting larger theatrical releases, critical acclaim, and awards aplenty. The bad news is that they often get pulled from theaters when they don't make a fraction of the money that an

Independence Day or a **Men in Black** would make; worse yet, many independent films don't make it to major theaters at all. And the somewhat silly news is that pretty much every foreign film becomes an indie when it is distributed here in the United States, despite the fact that the film may have been wildly popular in its country of origin—like the Miramax release **Ridicule**. This is due to a widespread fear of subtitles and unfamilar actors. But don't worry, Andrea is going to take us on a tour of must-see foreign films later.

So what's a girl to do? Get thee to the video store! Presumably, that's why you bought our book in the first place— because you love movies and need more, more, more to watch—so what we're talking about here should amount to some very exciting news for you. If you've sat in a movie theater at the megaplex any-time recently, eaten your $12 nachos and thought, "I think I already saw this movie, but it had George Clooney instead of Nicolas Cage and Michelle Pfeiffer instead of Sandra Bullock," than you should be very inspired and encouraged by the news that there are hundreds of remarkable movies that you have not yet seen, all waiting for you in your local video store or library. Okay, stop the conga line for a minute while we discuss some particulars.

You know what a very wise girl named Andrea said the other day? She said, "You can't hide a bad script with a huge budget." Indie film directors often base their stories on real-life experiences, since their small budgets don't allow for monsters as tall as buildings or futuristic cars or a cast of billions. No matter, because a quirky character or creative cinematography can go a long way. Take **Flirting** (dir. John Duigan, 1989), an amazingly charming Australian film starring Thandie Newton and Noah Taylor, two wonderful actors that you may never have heard of. They play Thandiwe and Danny, boarding-school students who have an interracial first-love affair that grows more complicated because of the political situa-tion in her native Uganda, where her father is a diplomat. Sure, this was a "small" film; it was also one that, quite literally, made us laugh, made us cry, and made us think.

In the best of independent films, nothing is taken for granted. Again, because of budget concerns—we're talking about people who have maxed out their credit cards, spent all the money that their generous relatives were willing to give, and may actually be eyeing a certain elderly grandmother—every frame counts. In a film like **Heavy** (dir. James Mangold, 1995), this is interesting because, in traditional narrative terms, very little actually transpires. The quiet landscape and surrounding hills in which the movie is set actually become another one of the characters (along with Pruitt Taylor Vince, Liv Tyler, and Shelley Winters) in a way that rarely happens in big-budget Hollywood flicks.

Speaking of which, is it stars you want? Are you afraid of having separation anxiety, of watching an entire film and not recognizing any of the key players? Fear not, because part of the fun of watching older (as in a few years, not fifty years) indie films is seeing what your favorite actors were doing before they made the A- or even B-list. **Flirting** featured a slightly younger Nicole Kidman (who is, of course, featured on the video box even though she plays a minor part); and a great little flick called **Five Corners** (dir. Tony Bill, 1988) stars Jodie Foster, John Turturro, and Tim Robbins. Set in the Bronx in 1964, **Five Corners** is the story of a pretty psycho guy named Heinz (Turturro) who returns to his old neighborhood after a stint in jail, only to pick up where he left off, stalking his old obsession, a nice but tough neighborhood girl named Linda (Foster). The film also features a dog named Buddha, a stolen penguin, and a memorable elevator-riding scene. Or check out **sex, lies, and videotape**, starring Andie MacDowell and Peter Gallagher; or **Heavenly Creatures**, starring the heavenly Kate Winslet in a somewhat darker role than she had in **Titanic** (now there's the understatement of the decade).

We're asking you to trust us here; we're not talking about ten-hour-long, Russian subtitled, black-and-white silent films (oh, wait, Andrea does discuss **Potemkin**). We're talking about movies that you may not have heard of, not because they're not good movies, but because they didn't have a billion-dollar marketing budget. It's interesting to note that we can't even remember who first told us about Hal Hartley's **Trust**, but read on to see what a major role this film now plays in Clare's life. Then there are other exceptional films like Boaz Yakin's **Fresh**, Paul Thomas Anderson's **Hard Eight**, and Allison Anders's **Gas, Food, Lodging**. There's something rousing about the idea that we all found these movies without the ad campaigns, without TV commercials, and without the cover of **Entertainment Weekly** telling us that they were "the movie" to see. When you see a good indie flick, it's like choosing to eat at the Southern home-cooking restaurant down the road, instead of at the McDonald's right across the street.

Chances are your catch-of-the-day will be fresher than the Filet-o-Fish, too.

EIGHT FILMS TO DISCUSS AT YOUR NEXT COCKTAIL PARTY!

By Andrea

The whole arthouse indie scene would be nothing without foreign films. Long before Quentin, eons before Spike, hipsters would don a beret and flock in droves to see the latest subtitled masterpiece from overseas. Not only are these films usually above par (they have to go through such an intense filtering process to even make it

I HATED, EVERYONE ELSE LOVED

LISE: *Before Sunrise* with Ethan Hawke and Julie Delpy. Booooo-ring! I never want to spend another night with those two.

SIBYL: *The Unbearable Lightness of Being*—endless saga that everyone loves for the cheesy sex scenes.

ANDREA: *Trainspotting.* Too trendy to be believed, and not particularly pleasurable to sit through.

CLARE: *I Shot Andy Warhol.* I felt like such a grump and a loser not liking this flick starring Lili Taylor, whom I love without reservation. But I just didn't like it. I just didn't.

to the United States that you know *someone* thought they were good), but they can also make you look really smart at a cocktail party. So you can kill two birds with one stone.

Remember that scene in **Good Will Hunting** where Matt Damon's character shows up a snotty (and unfortunately ponytailed) intellectual who's not one-tenth as well read as he makes himself out to be? Wow, I can still taste how satisfying that was. Just like when Woody Allen busts out the media critic Marshall McLuhan in **Annie Hall** to quiet some pontificating wisenheimer on a movie theater line. Ah, the joy!

You've got to know what I'm talking about. Haven't you ever been at a party, quietly talking with a buddy, maybe admitting to how much you liked **While You Were Sleeping** or **House Party II: The Pajama Jam** when suddenly, out of nowhere, Mr. Film Snob Weasel sidles up to you and says, "How can you say that was a great movie? Now, Jean-Luc Godard, he made great movies." Flustered, you stammer something like, "Godard, yeah, he's great." But you feel like Ben Affleck without your own personal Matt Damon. Lousy. Trod upon. And annoyed, to boot!

But ho! Fret no longer! That's why I'm here, that's why you bought this book! (Well, maybe.) I'm offering you that magic one-two punch: the opportunity to learn about a smattering of the greatest movies ever, the kind of films that have inspired artists, changed lives, moved audiences around the globe—and the opportunity to put Mr. Film Snob Weasel firmly back in his place. Once again, two birds with one stone. Yesiree.

It's as easy as the hokeypokey. Read the following brilliant manifesto, learn about the movies, decide what you want to rent, rent it, learn it, live it, love it. Before you know it, you'll be a graduate of Andrea's Film History 101 Course.

You gotta know about: *Potemkin* (also known as *The Battleship Potemkin;* dir. Sergei M. Eisenstein, 1925)

Why: Famous for its structure and most of all, its brilliant editing (which heavily influenced later filmmakers like Godard), *Potemkin* falls into the "Soviet Montage" film category. It's the story of workers and revolution set in 1905 Russia. To be honest, there are a few dull moments here (argh, the shame I feel in admitting that!), but what's cool is director Eisenstein's editing technique, montage. He used rapid cuts, editing high-contrast scenes back and forth, all in order to generate a powerful, visceral response in the viewer. This was groundbreaking, and it's influenced cinema—as well as commercials and MTV—ever since.

How else this will help you at a cocktail party: Trivia alert: Did you know that Brian De Palma ripped off *Potemkin*'s famous baby-carriage-in-peril scene for 1987's *The Untouchables*? Well, he did.

Should you really rent it? If you can handle the thought of watching an eighty-six-minute silent film, you could find *Potemkin* really rewarding. If not, just memorize the words "Soviet Montage" and "baby carriage in peril" and you'll be fine.

Why: Ich bin ein Berliner? Sure, I may know German like I know how to play the tuba (that means not at all), but I do know that German Expressionist films (made pretty much from 1917 to right around when the Nazis took power in 1933) are freakin' cool. German Expressionist films actually strongly influenced the look of films noir (check out the drama chapter to find out how much I love those!). They used unique camera angles and pushed the boundaries of how films looked and felt. Within the ranks of this genre, few films hold up better than M.

M is a totally creepy flick about a child murderer named Franz Becker (Peter Lorre) who's recognizable by his whistle. Becker is being hunted both by the police and the criminals of Germany, who, angry that the police are out in force, take matters in to their own hands with harsh vigilante justice. It's one of those "everybody is creepy" movies, a harsh indictment of German society during that era.

How else this will help you at a cocktail party: It's a good political conversation starter, for it's a nifty reminder that when government sponsors filmmakers and gives them artistic freedom (as the German government did during this time), then some wonderful art can happen.

Should you really rent it? If you're like me (smart, inquisitive, always wanting to learn more about film), the answer is "rent." If you're more like Sibyl (silly, impatient, lover of the slapstick comedy school), the answer is, Stay away. Far away. It could drive you to drink.

You gotta know about: Rashomon (dir. Akira Kurosawa, 1950)

Why: Because it's so brilliant, with director Kurosawa turning the linear narrative film structure on its head. Rashomon is the story of a crime, told in flashback from the perspective of all the different participants: a bandit, the husband and wife he attacks, and the supposedly "objective" woodcutter who observed the entire event. Each version is different that the one before, and Kurosawa's exploration of the subjectivity of truth is masterfully explored.

How else this will help you at a cocktail party: It'll be cool to mention that this film inspired the structure for *Courage Under Fire*, the Meg Ryan flick.

Should you really rent it? Quite honestly, you might enjoy *Akira Kurosawa's Dreams* or *Ran* better, especially if you're a relative novice at this whole foreign film thing. But you've got to, absolutely have to, know about Kurosawa's brilliant feat in presenting a story that changes with each person's perspective.

You gotta know about: *La Strada* (dir. Federico Fellini, 1954)

Why: Because Fellini is the *Man!* Oh, sorry. But why *La Strada*, when it's his *8½* and *La Dolce Vita* that are considered his true masterpieces, you ask? Well, it's always a personal choice, but I think most people will respond to the wonderful performance of Giuletta Masina (Fellini's real wife) in this movie. Masina plays this sweet little waif, the sad-eyed Gelsomina who works for an overbearing, tough performer named Zampano (Anthony Quinn). The dynamic between the two of them is fascinating, and this film's a total heartbreaker.

How else this will help you at a cocktail party: You get to use the term "Felliniesque" as much as possible.

Should you really rent it? Rent. Absolutely.

You gotta know about: *Breathless* (dir. Jean-Luc Godard, 1959)

Why: Because every yutz and every yutz's sidekick claims to understand Godard. Whoopie for them, except 10 to 1 they're lying like rugs, since Godard can be tough to digest. I suggest starting with his first film, the very viewer-friendly *Breathless*.

Michel (Jean Paul Belmondo) is a French criminal on the run, but he's not willing to run too far from Patricia (Jean Seberg), an American girl who's selling newspapers and studying at the Sorbonne. This is an homage to American tough guys like Bogart, as well as a cool, albeit twisted, love story. Plus, it's got those Godard tropes (like talking to the camera), but without being too intrusive to the viewer. Ooh, this film is great!

How else this will help you at a cocktail party: Maybe you can take a page from Jean Seberg's awesome gamine look and spice up your wardrobe. Or throw around great terms like "French New Wave," a movement of which Godard was a part, along with François Truffaut and others, which was a new wave of young French filmmakers, often inspired by American directors, who were interested in doing things differently than had been done before. Also feel free to bust out the auteur theory, which is a school of film criticism that believes that filmmaking is less a collaborative team effort, and more about the single, solitary vision of the director alone.

Should you really rent it? Rent it. You'll like it. Also highly rentable is Truffaut's *The 400 Blows*, another French New Wave fave whose style was heavily influenced by Hitchcock.

You gotta know about: *Cries and Whispers* (dir. Ingmar Bergman, 1972)

Why: Slow-moving, quiet, and often depressing, Bergman's films have been copied and spoofed, and spoofed and copied. *Cries and Whispers* is about a woman dying, surrounded by the other women in her life. It is totally gorgeous to look at. And so subtly acted, too.

How else this will help you at a cocktail party: It'll remind you that no matter how glum you're feeling, standing alone by the spicy guacamole, at least you're not as depressed as the people in a Bergman film.

Should you really rent it? Everybody's got to rent a Bergman sometime; it's just inevitable. Start with this one—it's the most accessible.

You gotta know about: The Apu Trilogy (dir. Satyajit Ray, 1955–59)

Why: Because everyone talks about Satyajit Ray, and no one I know has ever seen any of this famous Bengali's films. The Apu Trilogy, a coming-of-age tale about a boy named Apu, consists of three parts: *Pather Panchali* (1955), *Aparajito* (1956), and *The World of Apu* (1959). And yes, I'm admitting it, I saw *Pather Panchali*, but have yet to delve in to the rest of this trilogy.

Considered one of the last humanist filmmakers, Satyajit Ray is beloved by directors and editors around the world (and in fact became friends with legendary French filmmaker Jean Renoir when Renoir filmed *The River* in India), but when he won an honorary Academy Award before his death in 1992, the show's coordinators found that a lot of Ray's work was in horrible shape due to neglect. Since then, the producing/directing team of Ismail Merchant and James Ivory (*A Room with a View, Howards End*) have started a crusade both to save Ray's work and to promote its appreciation outside of the musty halls of academic cineastes.

How else this will help you at a cocktail party: You can talk about "Bollywood" (the term for Bombay's filmmaking center) and how India produces more films than any other nation yearly. [NEED STAT HERE] Oh, and a bit of trivia: In a goofy homage to Ray, Matt Groening named his Indian convenience-store worker "Apu" on his hit TV show "The Simpsons."

Should you really rent it? If you can find it, rent it. The quality may be poor, and you may have better luck finding *The Home and the World* (1984), but if you can dig up the Apu Trilogy, grab it. And invite me over.

You gotta know about: An Angel at My Table (dir. Jane Campion, 1990)

Why: There's been a whole lot going on over in Australia and New Zealand in recent years. Along with Campion, there's the work of Peter Weir (*Gallipoli*), Gillian Armstrong (*My Brilliant Career*), George

Miller (*Mad Max*), and Lee Tamahori (*Once Were Warriors*) to consider. And this is just the tip of the Australia/New Zealand iceberg!

An Angel at My Table is based on the true life story of New Zealand poet Janet Frame (here played in her adult years by Kerry Fox). It's a bittersweet film about a truly unusual woman, directed by the gifted and inquisitive Jane Campion (*The Piano, The Portrait of a Lady*).

How else this will help you at a cocktail party: You won't be reduced to lame *Crocodile Dundee* references if you meet someone from "Down Under."

Should you really rent it? I loved this film; Clare, on the other hand, a self-professed admirer of Jane Campion, found it very slow-moving. If you have as little patience as Clare does, you should seek out 1993's *The Piano* instead—if you haven't seen it already.

This is just the beginning of a very long list of great movies by great directors from different periods of cinema. I hope I've proven my point that arrogant, skinny-wristed film buffs do not have the lock on foreign-film appreciation. They may act like you don't have what it takes to understand these flicks, but they're wrong. They're just trying to keep something special for themselves.

TO BE REAL

By Lise

Like Andrea, I strongly believe in actively seeking out lesser-known films. Along with the foreign films she discussed, another true indie favorite of mine has got to be the documentary. Why? Let me toss this curve ball at you: Documentary films are often more captivating, fun, and fulfilling than any big-budget blockbusters playing at the local megaplex.

Still with me? 'Cause I'm not joking around here. If you're thinking "Look, I watch movies to be entertained. If I want to learn a bunch of facts, I'll go to the library," then you may want to rethink your stance. Take 1994's **Hoop Dreams** (dir. Steve James), the story of two high school boys and their dreams of being professional basketball players. **Hoop Dreams** was a spectacularly entertaining and well-crafted human drama; its emotional power was due, in large part, to the fact that the characters and the story were real.

Even within the changing world of independent film, the role of documentaries in particular is metamorphosing. First of all, cable television has opened up a new world for us; whether we watch MTV, the History Channel, E!, the Pet Channel, BET, the Discovery Channel, or any of the hundreds of other choices out there, we clearly have inexpensive options that may prevent us from actually renting a documentary film. And a lot of documentary-style programming on television—from A&E's "Biography" to HBO's **From the Earth to the Moon** to the Discovery Channel's "How'd They Do That?"—is very well produced.

But even before we had what seems like a million channels to choose from, documentaries were always relegated to one dusty

12 MAGNIFICENT DOCUMENTARIES

Best Boy

Fast, Cheap and Out of Control

Harlan County, USA

Looking for Richard

Manufacturing Consent

Microcosmos

Paradise Lost

Sick

The Thin Blue Line

Truth or Dare

Visions of Light

When We Were Kings

shelf in the back corner of the video store; in fact, in major video chains today, there are almost no documentaries at all.

This, if you will pardon my language, is a damn shame.

Because people who make documentary films are certainly not in it for the money; no sir, these passionate directors and producers make documentaries because of their dogged dedication to the telling of one particular story. And this personal touch often makes for movies that are not just entertaining, but may just teach you something or make you think about your own life. Believe you me, more uplifting and heartbreaking events occur in real life than in the minds of a thousand highly paid screenwriters. . .

The documentary film sometimes takes the form of an in-depth portrait, like **Anne Frank Remembered**, or **Carmen Miranda: Bananas Is My Business** (which is a favorite of Sibyl's), or **The Times of Harvey Milk**, about the first openly gay elected politician, a member of the San Francisco Board of Supervisors. Narrated lovingly by Harvey Fierstein, **Harvey Milk** was one of the first documentaries I ever watched and, to this day, it remains one of the most meaningful stories I have ever seen unfold on film. I really urge you to seek this film out.

Even if the topic of the film is someone in whom you had no previous interest, as was the case with me when I popped in **The Line King: The Story of Al Hirschfeld** (dir. Susan Warms Dryfoos, 1996), a skillful documentary will draw you into a life by dangling a carrot on a stick. In the case of Al Hirschfeld, that carrot was the fact that he hides the name "Nina" in almost all of his caricatures. When the film was over, I felt like I had met and talked with an absorbing and worldly man. An hour and a half with Mr. Hirschfeld was certainly better than small talk at a stale cocktail party!

Sometimes the documentary film introduces us to a group of people who serve to represent an overarching theme. One of the indisputable masters of documentary film, Errol Morris, does this in his recent film **Fast, Cheap & out of Control** (1997). A perfect example of a brilliant film that fits neatly into no category, **Fast, Cheap & out of Control** is a portrait of four fascinating men: a lion trainer, a topiary gardener, a mole-rat specialist, and a robot scientist. Like all of Morris's films, **Fast, Cheap & out of Control** works on more than one level in that it is also about the random and synchronous connections among all people in this life. But to really understand Morris's vision, we'd have to go back to 1978's **Gates of Heaven**, a film about a man's lifelong dream to build and maintain a pet cemetery.

As you can see, I am partial to Morris's films; I admire their deceptive simplicity of style (Morris developed a special piece of camera equipment that enables interviewees to talk directly to him, but to appear to be speaking into the camera). I love the way his topics are highly specific and all-encompassing at the same time. But there are many other established documentarians, including D. A. Pennebaker—who, like many established documentarians, is an accomplished director, cinematographer, and editor—and the award-winning Barbara Kopple, who directed 1976's **Harlan County, U.S.A.**, about a coal-miner's strike in Kentucky.

Whatever your passion, trust me, there is some intrepid film-maker who has researched and documented that topic for years. Is it rap music? Check out **Rhyme and Reason**, directed by Peter Spirer. Interested in insects? Rent 1996's **Microcosmos**, an award-winning film in which directors Claude Nuridsany and Marie Perennou used special microscopic cameras to actually enter the tunnels and habitats of tiny bugs.

But, truth be told, the absolute best situation is "documentary kismet," when you take a risk on a renter, or somehow find yourself drawn into a story you knew nothing about. This was the case when a friend loaned me a copy of **Brother's Keeper** (dirs. Joe Berlinger, Bruce Sinofsky, 1992); it's the story of an elderly man named Delbert Ward in a small town who is accused of murdering his brother. The film examines not only the effect of the second-degree murder charges on Delbert, but the impact the whole event had on the small, upstate New York community in which it took place. (Berlinger and Sinofsky went on to make another great, dark documentary called **Paradise Lost**, which I also recommend.)

Or, if you can find it, check out a film that Clare and I discovered years ago, a documentary from 1979 called **Best Boy**, in which director Ira Wohl films the day-to-day struggles of his cousin, Philly—a fiftysomething man whose mental capacity equals that of a five-year-old. As Philly's parents, who are his caretakers, get older, Philly focuses on his efforts to become independent.

If you are still feeling a little nervous about the concept of spending your hard-earned cash on a documentary, or if you just feel that you should start with something that'll really blow you away, allow me to suggest 1996's Academy Award-winning **When We Were Kings** (dir. Leon Gast), the true story of Muhammad Ali and George Foreman's "Rumble in the Jungle." The combination of amazing archival footage, an electrifying personality, numerous interviews, and a great story landed **When We Were Kings** on my permanent list of favorites.

And, best of all, it really happened.

I AM CURSED TO WALK ALONE

By Clare

Hey, Lise, I'll tell you about something else that really happened: Your ex-boyfriend passed the test.

Oh, wait. Let me back up here. We're talking about indie films. And we're talking about how unique they are; how they take a little more work to find and sometimes even to enjoy, but how they can reach into those narrow, twisted corridors to occupy a tiny, priceless space in your heart that big-budget films just can't squeeze into.

Indies are intensely personal that way.

And I take my movies more personally than some—okay, maybe more than most. My best-loved indie films are more than just movies—they're a litmus test, a test by which I pick a real-life guy and decide whether or not he's **the One**.

It goes like this. Say I've got a new boyfriend. (Hey, back off, it happens.) I sit him down, pop in a video, and watch—not so much the movie as his face. Does he *get it*?! Does he *see*?! Can he *pass the test*?!

It's tough competition, I know. And some people just don't get it. I'll always remember renting **Witness** (dir. Peter Weir, 1985) with this guy and his parents. (Now, it's technically not an indie—in fact, it's listed in our Romance chapter—but I'm trying to give an example of just how tetchy and snooty I can be.) A moody film about a tough cop (Harrison Ford) who has to protect an Amish woman (Kelly McGillis—what happened to her?) and her son (Lucas Haas) because her son witnessed a murder, **Witness** is a nice blend of romance and suspense. The cop and the Amish woman come to an understanding. They fall in love. When the bad guys come, it's all really tense and scary, and then Harrison Ford has to leave the

WANT TO BE MY FRIEND? BETTER FIND SOMETHING TO ENJOY ABOUT

LISE: *Ma vie en rose*, about a little boy who is convinced that he was supposed to be a girl. So he dresses like one.

SIBYL: *Harlan County USA*, a classic documentary about miners strike in Kentucky.

ANDREA: *The Front*, a bittersweet comedy with Woody Allen and Zero Mostel about a writer during the McCarthy era. If you like it, your heart is definitely in the right place.

CLARE: *Baraka*. If you can't find something to love in this gorgeously shot 70mm film with no dialogue, then you should get your head checked.

Amish people because he doesn't belong. The Amish woman runs out after the cop into a field of wheat or something. They embrace. Music plays. Later, he says good-bye. It's all very sad.

As the credits started to roll, a silence fell over the room. It was abruptly broken by this guy's mom.

"So, did they *do it* or not?!"

Ack. I crossed the guy off the list. Guilt by association. I know it's unfair, but hey, I'm no freakin' monument to justice.

I was once talking about books with my doctor, of all people, and we were happy to find a kinship in our love of **A Prayer for Owen Meany**, by John Irving. My doctor firmly stated that the world should be divided into two groups: those who "get" **Owen Meany**, and those who don't. Those who don't could live on an isolated island, like lepers.

I feel the same way about **Trust** (Hal Hartley, 1991). This flick just delighted the pants offa me. I rented it all by myself back in

1992, when Lise and I were living together in Manhattan. **Trust** is a quirky love story by a quirky director who likes to work with a lot of quirky actors (Martin Donovan, Adrienne Shelly, and now Parker Posey and Elina Löwensohn) and almost always shoots in quirky but hideously normal-looking suburban locations on Long Island.

Adrienne Shelly plays Maria, a bratty, big-haired, heavily madeup teenager who, in the opening credits, flippantly informs her parents that she's pregnant by her jock boyfriend. They're dismayed. They ask her what the hell she's going to do. While applying her lipstick, she says that her boyfriend will get a "bitchin' job" working for his father and be raking in the money. Her father calls her a slut. She slaps him across the face. He drops dead. She goes shopping.

But Maria unwillingly transforms when things don't quite go as she'd expected. Tramping around in her orange miniskirt and white tights, she looks for a place to hide out. She runs into Martin Donovan's misunderstood genius, Martin, a technical wizard/misanthrope with a violent streak, and tells him that she's a murderer. He lets her stay at his place.

So much more happens, and yet *some people* (ex-boyfriends all) have the *gall* to find this movie boring. Just the deadpan dialogue alone—not to mention the perfect little touches that Hal Hartley gives his characters—is enough to keep me swooning for all of this movie's economical ninety minutes. Martin tells Maria that he carries a grenade around. "Why?" she asks him. "Just in case." "In case what?" "Just in case." A repentant, somber Maria starts wearing her glasses and Martin's dead mother's dress, pulling her hair back, sleeping on the floor, and carrying around a dictionary. (When searching for a certain man on a commuter train, she pulls this dictionary out. "He should look childish," she informs Martin. "Nave." He checks out the dictionary entry. "You mean naive." "Yes. Naive.")

When Lise got home from work that day, I practically jumped on her. *"Why didn't you tell me about this movie you knew about this movie and you didn't tell me Jesus what kind of friend are you God it was great!"*

She was all casual about it. "Yeah, I liked it. You know who really loved it, though? Jason."

Her ex-boyfriend. Ah, the bitter irony!

Later that week, Jason walked up to me at a party, grinning expectantly. "Your job is making you boring and mean."

Sigh! He even quoted **Trust**! I wanted to leap into his lap, give him a big smooch, run away and get married! But no! It was not to be!

Ever since then, I have wandered the Earth, searching for that perfect movie mate. Someone who will love and understand **Trust**. Someone who will love and understand me. I test them again and again. They fall asleep on the couch. They say they don't know what the big deal is. They laugh it off.

But I am not laughing.

I pull out other test movies. Did Ron Fricke's spellbinding, gorgeous, wordless documentary, **Baraka** (1993), fill them with a numinous sense of wonder and awe, as it did me? Do they think **Hard Eight**, directed by twenty-seven-year-old prodigy Paul Thomas Anderson (**Boogie Nights**) and starring a brilliant Philip Baker Hall, a gritty Gwyneth Paltrow, and a hilariously sad John C. Reilly, is a work of tragicomic genius, as I do? Do they *really* understand the heartbreak and beauty of 1994's **Fresh**, about an inner-city boy (Sean Nelson) who uses the basic rules of chess taught to him by his absentee father (Samuel L. Jackson) as a way to get out of the 'hood? For God's sake, are they thunderstruck by the strong characters and circular narrative in the breathtakingly original Macedonian film **Before the Rain**?!

No? Then get out! Go away! I break with thee!

I am cursed to walk alone.

WARNING: MY INDIE PICKS AREN'T FOR EVERYONE

By Sibyl

A fork in the cheek. Yes, that's what I said, a nice, fancy dinner fork impaled in the cheek of a diner. Sounds gross, but that's just one of many stomach-wrenching but weirdly amazing moments from **The Cook, the Thief, His Wife & Her Lover** (dir. Peter Greenaway, 1989). I remember seeing it the summer I lived in Boston. I'd read the reviews and was psyched for something freaky and visually lush. I got just what I ordered, plus my first encounter with the amazing English actress (Clare's absolute favorite) Helen Mirren. In my enthusiasm for the flick, I invited a friend along. We got a jumbo popcorn and soda to share (as was our ritual) and hunkered down. Well, after endless shots of kinky sex, rotting meat, and extradeviant violence (the fork thing is pretty mild), I noticed my friend wasn't eating her share of the popcorn. Then she left the theater, and she didn't come back.

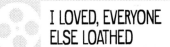

I LOVED, EVERYONE ELSE LOATHED

LISE: *187*, starring Samuel L. Jackson. Besides the unfortunate *Deer Hunter* ending, this was a compelling and well-acted film.

SIBYL: *The Hudsucker Proxy*. I thought the art deco look was cool, and Paul Newman is always cool, and Tim Robbins is, too.

ANDREA: *She's So Lovely*, with Sean Penn and Robin Wright Penn. I thought it was funny and sad and romantic. Everyone else thought it was dreck. Oh, well.

CLARE: *Dream with the Fishes*. David Arquette is so great. This movie snuck up on me, and I love it still.

When the credits rolled, I went to search for my friend. She was sitting in the lobby sort of leaning against the wall. I must say she looked a bit green. No need for me to ask if she liked the movie; I can safely say that she didn't. **The Cook** is not for everyone; in fact, I learned that it's not for almost anyone, since I recommended it to my gourmando stepdad and he only made it fifteen minutes into the flick before claiming queasiness.

Sometimes the movies I love the most are the ones I know I can't recommend to most friends or family. Like Clare said—and as we mentioned earlier in the chapter—small indie films can be intensely personal. Often they're quirky enough for me to enjoy, but just weird enough so that I'm not comfortable sending anyone else to see them. Fortunately, over the years, I've started recommending these movies with warnings.

So, keeping in mind I like some strange stuff, but also that I've got decent taste, I'll unearth some indie gems, with warnings:

BARTON FINK (dir. Joel Coen, 1991) **WARNING:** May cause panic attacks in the claustrophobic viewer: This film has lots of scenes in a small, scary hotel room. Also has been known to cause boredom in those easily bored. Just because you liked *Fargo* (1996) and *Raising Arizona* (1987) doesn't mean that this dark, strangely paced period piece will work for you. This underrated character study by the Coen brothers is about the life and struggle of a writer in 1940s Hollywood. John Turturro is a New York playwright transplanted to L.A. to make it big writing screenplays for the studios, but something is not quite right (for one thing, his hotel is suspiciously hellish—check out the dripping walls and the weeping wallpaper, creepy). John Goodman is amazing as a guy who's desperate to be an average Joe, but is obviously not quite right in the head. Great art direction in the ultimate dive hotel.

CITIZEN RUTH (dir. Alexander Payne, 1996) **WARNING:** May cause feelings of revulsion and shame. Not for the politically apathetic or those who shy away from sick humor. If you must have a likable, sweet heroine and a pat, sentimental ending, then don't even think about *Citizen Ruth*. This black comedy is all about the politics of abortion. Ruth (an absolutely brilliant Laura Dern), a paint-sniffing welfare mom in the family way, becomes the center of a tug-of-war between equally repulsive pro-lifers and pro-choicers. The flick drags a bit, but Dern's Ruth is the most riveting, repellent antihero I've ever seen.

HENRY FOOL (dir. Hal Hartley, 1998) **WARNING:** May bring on a severe attack of attention-deficit disorder or a case of "numb butt." Not for those sensitive to vomiting/diarrhea/unwashed hair. Also, if you haven't grooved on director-writer Hal Hartley's distinctive choppy-talky style, walk away now. *Fool* is Hartley's epic saga (clocking in at two and a half plus hours) about two outcasts, one a garbage collector, another a nutso vagabond, who become friends, create some award-winning poetry, and ponder the nature of writing, genius, culture, society, etc. Plus, there's the skank sister, some really gross bathroom scenes, and just lots of bizarre activity set in a dreary any-burb kind of existence. I thought this flick was brilliant; others I know were either puzzled or bored senseless.

LIVE FLESH (dir. Pedro Almodóvar, 1997) **WARNING:** May incite resentful feelings in fans of Almodóvar's signature madcap Euro-comic style. If you're expecting another insane comedic romp along the lines of Almodóvar's *Women on the Verge of a Nervous Breakdown* (1988), consider yourself warned: *Live Flesh* isn't a comedy, exactly. It's more of an exploration of how funny, as in strange, life can be. This time Almodóvar uses distinctive actors and bizarre plots to create an amazing drama. Where else can you see a love story involving an ex-con, a paraplegic basketball star, and a handful of insanely sexy Latin ladies? *Flesh* is a wild ride visually and in its twisty structure.

A PERFECT CANDIDATE (dirs. R. J. Cutler and David Van Taylor, 1996) **WARNING:** For political junkies only. Not recommended for the apolitical viewer. Also not advised if you only like fancy-looking art movies: This flick looks like an old CNN news report. It's a bit slow at parts but, if you're interested in politics, this tale of Oliver North's run for the Senate in Virginia is pure viewing satisfaction. There's lots of great insider stuff, with strategic angling among the various campaign managers, a tweedy liberal reporter, North's uber-patriotism, and the incumbent Senator's sexual peccadilloes.

TRUTH OR DARE (dir. Alek Keshishian, 1991) **WARNING:** Not recommended for viewers with divaphobia. If you don't like Madonna, or are offended by huge egos, entourages, and the despicably manipulative use of a parent's gravestone, then forget this flick. This highly stylized documentary is for the voyeur in you. If you like Madonna's music and are into a so-called all-access view of life on the road with a pop sensation, then *Truth or Dare* is fun. Knowing that Madonna called the shots (she produced the flick) makes the movie more interesting, since you've got to think that none of the spontaneous or private stuff really is either spontaneous or private. It also makes it a bit repulsive.

So there you have it: some of my personal favorites. If you rent them and find yourself breaking out into a rash, falling into a sudden, deep sleep, or suffering from an inexplicable, crushing feeling of ennui, don't say I didn't warn you. Take two and call a friend in the morning.

25 Indies to Rent!

1 **THE APOSTLE** (dir. Robert Duvall, 1997) "Love my neck!" That means give me a hug in the words of Robert Duvall's fire-and-brimstone preacher. Duvall wrote, directed, and starred in this story of a tragically human man of God. The Apostle seeks redemption after a violent incident. Of course you can't run from your past, a lesson he learns. This movie runs long and slow, but Duvall's performance is divinely inspired, a reminder that he's one of our greatest living actors.

2 **BEFORE THE RAIN** (dir. Milcho Manchevski, 1994) An amazing political drama focusing on the strife-torn Republic of Macedonia. In three seemingly unrelated stories; a young Christian monk protecting a Muslim girl, a London-based photographer, and a photojournalist returning to his Macdeonian homeland, a portrait of religious hatred, personal struggle, and an attempt to do good when the world had turned bad forms. One of the weirdest, most interesting narrative structures we've ever seen. Brutal and fascinating.

3 **BROTHER FROM ANOTHER PLANET** (dir. John Sayles, 1984) Joe Morton plays a sweetly befuddled alien who—aside from his clawlike feet—happens to look like a typical African-American male. On the run from alien bounty hunters, he arrives in Harlem and gets to sample good old American racism. Features some nice cameos from director Sayles, and from Fisher Stevens as a subway-riding card shark.

4 **DEATH AND THE MAIDEN** (dir. Roman Polanski, 1994) An intense and often unsettling psychological thriller set in an unnamed country in South America. Since it was based on a play, this film feels like a play and has only three characters. Sigourney Weaver plays Paulina Escobar, a woman who, by sheer coincidence, is reacquainted with a doctor (Ben Kingsley) by whom, she is convinced, she once was tortured and raped to the sounds of Schubert's "Death and the Maiden." She, uh, takes revenge.

5 **DOWN BY LAW** (dir. Jim Jarmusch, 1986) Deejay Zack (musician and sometime-actor Tom Waits) and pimp Jack (musician John Lurie, who also scored this film) end up in prison in large part because they're just too easygoing to avoid being framed for crimes they didn't commit. They end up sharing a cell with an eccentric Italian, Roberto (Roberto Benigni), who may not be able to speak English very well, but who knows an escape route. Vintage Jarmusch (*Stranger Than Paradise, Midnight Train, Dead Man*), this black-and-white film is quirky, funny, sweet, sad, and delightful to watch.

6 **DRUGSTORE COWBOY** (dir. Gus Van Sant, 1989) Matt Dillon is a drugstore cowboy hitting pharmacies for dope and other assorted narcotics in early seventies Portland. Along with his old lady Kelly Lynch, low-level burglar James Le Gros, and a young, weird-looking Heather Graham, he evades the cops and gets high. It's a grim, sensitive, surreal portrait of the seduction of heroin. William S. Burroughs (a notorious smack advocate) makes a cameo as an old priest with a habit.

7 **EUROPA, EUROPA** (dir. Agnieszka Holland, 1991) Suspenseful and sad true story of a Jewish teenage boy during WWII who passed as an Aryan to escape persecution. Marco Hofschneider turns in a brave and raw performance as the boy who struggles to protect himself and attempt to live some semblance of a life at the same time.

8 **EVE'S BAYOU** (dir. Kasi Lemmons, 1997) A powerful and personal directorial debut from actress Kasi Lemmons (she was in *Silence of the Lambs*), starring gorgeous child-actress Jurnee Smollett as Eve. This is a shocking family drama, with amazing performances from Lynn Whitfield and Samuel L. Jackson as Eve's parents. The steamy Southern bayou somehow becomes a character in its own right. This film feels like a handmade blanket in a world of synthetic comforters.

9 **FIVE CORNERS** (dir. Tony Bill, 1987) Wanna see some of your favorite stars before they made it big? Jodie Foster, John Turturro, and

Tim Robbins are three of the characters in this 1960s Bronx tale. There's a beautiful scene—which does nothing to further the story— featuring two of the neighborhood floozies who, with their boyfriends du jour, go for a joyride on the top of side-by-side elevators. See baby-faced Tim Robbins with a dog named Buddha. Good stuff.

10 **FRESH** (dir. Boaz Yakin, 1994) Michael (Sean Nelson), aka "Fresh," is a drug runner in New York City. He's also a really smart kid who would rather just go to school and hang out with his friends. His father (Samuel L. Jackson) teaches him the lessons of life, using chess as a metaphor. Unfortunately, his dad's not around enough to keep Fresh from getting into a major situation with the neighborhood drug lords. Great music and cinematography to boot.

11 **HEARTS OF DARKNESS: A FILMMAKER'S APOCALYPSE** (dirs. Fax Bahr, George Hickenlooper, 1991) Eleanor Coppola, Francis's wife, helped make this truly amazing documentary, which details the making of *Apocalypse Now*. What you should really do is rent both films and watch them as a double feature. You'll never believe what went into the making of *Apocalypse Now*, from the production disasters to the personal tolls the film took on all the people involved.

12 **HOOP DREAMS** (dir. Steve James, 1994) Documentary about two high school boys from Chicago, each of whom had dreams of being an NBA basketball player. What made this story so powerful was how close we felt to the subjects—there were extensive interviews with William Gates and Arthur Agee, the two boys, as well as with their coaches, their parents, and recruiters from various colleges. Ultimately, it is a story about facing the sometimes harsh realities and disappointments that we all encounter in life.

13 **HOUSE OF GAMES** (dir. David Mamet, 1987) One thing's for sure: If you're going to watch a Mamet film, you have to be prepared to listen to Mamet-speak. Real people don't talk that way, and that's not the point. Lindsay Crouse and Joe Mantegna star in this thriller about a psychiatrist who becomes obsessed with and personally

involved in the seamy underworld of con artists. If you like this flick, check out Mamet's more recent *The Spanish Prisoner*. You'll be a happy person.

14 **JESUS OF MONTREAL** (dir. Denys Arcand, 1989) Beautiful, lyrical, and surprisingly funny film about an out-of-work actor (Lothaire Bluteau, who was also stunning in Sean Mathias's 1997 film *Bent*) who agrees to play Jesus in a Passion Play. As he recruits his actor friends to play the other parts, the parallels between his life and the life of the character he's playing reveal themselves. He pulls together his apostles, provides gentle guidance to them, and suffers from persecution by the authorities because he's misunderstood. A truly touching and remarkable movie.

15 **MA VIE EN ROSE** (dir. Alain Berliner, 1997) We put this wildly original film on our Best of 1997 list. About a young boy who is con- vinced that he was meant to be a girl, so he does what seems most logical to him: He dresses like one. His grandmother understands and does some disco dancing with him, his mother does her best to hold the family together, and his father freaks out and tries to make him into a "normal" boy. Colorful, fantastic, hilarious, and touching.

16 **MRS. DALLOWAY** (dir. Marleen Gorris, 1998) Vanessa Redgrave is a brilliantly understated actress who only gets more beautiful over the years. This film tackles the always tricky Virginia Woolf and gets it right. It's one day in the life of Clarissa Dalloway (Redgrave) as she prepares to host a party in her London townhouse in 1923. She flashes back to her youth and the choices she made, while still pondering the current state of her affairs. How rare that a film explores love, death, war, loneliness, and regret with such sensi- tive accuracy.

17 **REPO MAN** (dir. Alex Cox, 1984) An amazing ode to the eighties. Emilio Estevez plays Otto, a belligerent dude who gets fired from his supermarket job and becomes a repossessor of used cars (aka "Repo Man"). Along the way, he meets Laila, a total freak who gives him the scoop on some kidnapped aliens in the trunk of a car. Generic

food items, Harry Dean Stanton, bad special effects, and a killer soundtrack, featuring such classics as "Pablo Picasso Was Never Called an . . ." well, you know.

18 **RESERVOIR DOGS** (dir. Quentin Tarantino, 1992) The favorite movie of most guys we know. Regardless of whether this film is the rip-off that many seem to believe it is, *Reservoir Dogs* is still Tarantino's best film (according to Lise, anyway). A black comedy and botched-crime caper featuring great performances from Harvey Keitel, Michael Madsen, and Steve Buscemi as the unforgettable Mr. Pink. And that wily Tarantino has the soundtrack thing down pat.

19 **SEX, LIES, AND VIDEOTAPE** (dir. Steven Soderbergh, 1989) This award-winning film studies the relationship among four inhabitants of 1980s Baton Rouge. When self-centered husband John's (Peter Gallagher) college friend Graham (James Spader) comes to town, he has an immediate impact on John's goody-goody wife, Ann (Andie MacDowell), and her supersexual sister, Cynthia (Laura San Giacomo). Definitely a "who's zoomin' who" situation among the four of them. A little dated, yes, but this film was groundbreaking in its frank discussion of sexuality and its use of video.

20 **SMOOTH TALK** (dir. Joyce Chopra, 1985) A deceptively simple story of one's girl's harsh initiation into adulthood. Laura Dern captures the awkwardness and confusion of small-town teen Connie unbelievably well. Connie's main concerns are how to get to the mall, boys, and her annoying mother; when a dangerous older man puts the moves on her, Connie wishes she could be a sheltered little girl again. Mary Kay Place is great as Connie's confused mother.

21 **SWIMMING TO CAMBODIA** (dir. Jonathan Demme, 1987) You should know what you're getting into with this film: It's a one-man show, folks, a monologue by the hilariously funny and engaging megalomaniac Spalding Gray. Gray tells of his adventures in Thailand while filming *The Killing Fields*, in which he had a very small part. Covering both Gray's obsessions (with sex and psychedelics) and the

history of the Khmer Rouge in Cambodia, this flick beautifully meshes the serious with the silly, the sad with the sublime.

22 **THE TIMES OF HARVEY MILK** (dir. Robert Epstein, 1984) A riveting documentary on the first publicly elected gay official, Harvey Milk, who served on the San Francisco Board of Supervisors in the seventies. The story, narrated by Harvey Fierstein, says a lot about community and politics—and unfortunately it has a tragic ending. If you don't know about this true story, seek out this film ASAP!

23 **TRUE LOVE** (dir. Nancy Savoca, 1989) Contains possibly the greatest wedding scene ever, in which bride Annabella Sciorra sits in a toilet stall, her poofy dress up around her ears, and her bridesmaids in gaudy dresses cram in the stall to commiserate about her butthead husband (Ron Eldard), who just left the reception to go out partying with his buddies. A comic look at wedding preparations and romance in a boisterous Bronx Italian setting.

24 **THE UNBELIEVABLE TRUTH** (dir. Hal Hartley, 1990) This is classic Hartley, which means strangely alienated regular folks talking in strange, choppy sentences with lots of measured pauses. In *Truth*, Adrienne Shelly (a Hartley regular) is a doom-mongering teen coping with her irksome parents and butthead boyfriend in the 'burbs of Long Island. An ex-con moves to town and wreaks havoc on everyone's simple but twisted lives. Jangly music and surprisingly scenic vistas of suburban New York are just extra bonuses to an already excellent low-budget flick.

25 **WINGS OF DESIRE** (dir. Wim Wenders, 1988) This life-affirming, poetic story posits a world (or at least a Berlin) densely populated with angels in black trench coats who hang out on top of enormous gargoyles and make their home base a public library. Starring Bruno Ganz as a restless angel who wants to become human (and Peter Falk as himself!), *Wings of Desire* was the basis for *City of Angels*, which turned this intensely spiritual, philosophical journey into an intensely cool love story.

4 ROMANCE FILMS:

Dancing Cheek to Cheek

Innnn your eyes...

Love, true love. What a joy it is to find everlasting love. And what a pleasure it is to find it in the movies, too. Romantic films hold a special place in our hearts (forgive the pun) because they've given us hope and spurred our fantasies since we were but wee. Sometimes these films are incredibly sad, other times humorous and light, but at their core, all romances provide confirmation that we're not alone in our search for everlasting love, and that the search for that special someone to care for, or the quest to learn to care for our mate in a better way, is a heroic one.

It's easy to be confused about what defines a romance, since there are plenty of movies that have a love story as part of the plot, but aren't primarily romances, at least we don't think so. **Raiders of the Lost Ark** had some serious chemistry between Karen Allen and Harrison Ford, but at its core, it's an adventure film. **Ghostbusters** charmed us with a cute Bill Murray/Sigourney Weaver tryst, but that movie is a comedy. But when we feel like turning to a romance, we're

STEAMY ROMANCES FOR A HOT SUMMER NIGHT

Grease

As You Like It

Roman Holiday

Out of Sight

The Princess Bride

Ever After

The Wedding Singer

Bull Durham

Mississippi Masala

The Flamingo Kid

hoping it's going to show us a powerful love between two people, a love that's brimming with the sort of passion that alters lives. That love defines the plot and what the characters choose to do throughout the story.

We always thought it was weird that people insisted on calling these movies "date movies." We think they're great to see alone, or with a platonic pal, so that we can become fully immersed in the story without having to look at our sweet pea next to us and compare them to the fantasy up on-screen, or be embarrassed that we're crying in our popcorn while they're snickering madly at our foolishness. Not only that, but it can be awkward watching a steamy sex scene when you're hyperaware of the person sitting by your side, especially if you don't know them as intimately as the characters know each other, wink wink, nudge nudge. Once in a while, seeing a "date movie" on a date can lead to the sort of seat-shifting embarrassment that scars you for life, like when Sibyl saw **The Lover**, about a young French woman's sexual awakening, on just such an outing, not knowing it was about 97 percent sex scenes. She still blushes when she thinks about it.

What is it that makes a romantic film successful? They give us hope, and they make us feel. But they're not easy films to make, because if we don't buy them, we become excruciatingly aware of the sometimes corny dialogue, or of the silly soft lighting that bathes everyone in a filmy glow; we might even start to wonder why it is that no one in a romantic movie ever seems to need to go to the bathroom or why their noses don't run when they cry.

It's important, therefore, that we're along for the ride. It's key that the chemistry between the two people supposedly in love is there, and how. Many a romance has been ruined when the heat between the leads is about as fiery as a New England winter. (For instance: 1993's smashing dud, **Boxing Helena**, directed by Jennifer Lynch—argh.) This chemistry isn't because of how the actors look, or because they're famous, or even because they're really talented. It's just some strange, inexplicable phenomenon. People spark off of each other, or don't, and, as the saying goes, it takes two to tango. Madeleine Stowe with Daniel Day-Lewis in **The Last of the Mohicans**? Wowee! Madeleine Stowe with Aidan Quinn in **Blink**? Yuck.

Not only must there be that all-important chemistry, but there must be some powerful opposition to the love between the two people we just know are meant to be together. This hindrance keeps the two people apart, at least for a good hour or so. Class differences in **Wings of the Dove** spark a series of betrayals. In **Sleepless in Seattle**, not only are Meg Ryan and Tom Hanks separated by a few thousand miles, but they've never even met. This tension produces some of the most satisfying movie-watching in the world. Most of us aren't too fired up watching two totally happy, angst-free, complacent, already-been-together-for-eighty-years people. Nope, we want confusion! Pain! Obstacles! Mix-ups! We demand suffering!

There are two broad romantic film subgenres. Remember, we're saying broad here, but you can keep on breaking it down— man and woman, man and man, woman and woman, woman and ghost, woman and man and man, man and car, et cetera, et cetera. Ahem, sorry, back to our two categories: romantic comedies, and Serious Romances (which are often sad to boot.) Both have their place, and complement each other quite well.

Romantic comedies are the light, fluffy films. Even when they're a bit formulaic, there's a true joy in sitting back and knowing exactly where they're going to take you, and enjoying the entire ride nonetheless. **While You Were Sleeping**, that cute little Sandra Bullock film, is a fave of both Clare and Andrea, who, though loathe to admit it, have each seen it more than once. What made this film so enjoyable was seeing the nice, shy, mousy yet gorgeous girl (a strange, movies-only phenomenon) find true love and get embroiled in a totally unbelievable but charming mix-up that we're sure is going to work out from almost the first second we see her on-screen. But don't get us wrong—just because it's a comedy doesn't mean it can't be a great, quality flick. One of Lise's favorites is **Moonstruck**, because it's so well written and acted, and most of all, she likes the funny, quirky, off-the-wall characters who aren't like most of the ones we see in movies.

And then there are the Serious Romances, which are hard to make compelling. We have to fall for a love between the two leads that's so powerful that people are willing to make the greatest sacrifice for it. 1942's **Casablanca** is the definitive romance film, or at least one of them. Those marvelous lines, those leads, that intricate and wonderful plot! Swoon-o-rama.

In any good romance, the characters are profoundly changed by the love they've been blessed enough to find. Maybe they grow infinitely more confident about themselves (**The Truth About Cats and Dogs, Roxanne**), or maybe they risk it all for a moment with the one they love (**The English Patient, City of Angels**). Regardless, no one walks away from the affair the same. And, if the movie works, neither do we.

THOSE SIX MAGIC WORDS: AND THEY LIVED HAPPILY EVER AFTER

By Andrea

At a young age, my mother got married. Soon after, she got divorced. Then she met my father, and they were married. And then they divorced. My dad then married another woman, which again ended in—you guessed it—a divorce. In total, four divorces and no lasting marriages between the two most important role models in my life.

I am as jaded as they come about the state of true love.

Except, that is, at the movies, where I let go of all my cynicism, and live for those magical words "and they lived happily ever after."

I have never fully understood why that is. I fought it, oh, yes, I did. I would snicker and snort and roll my eyes when my friends and I discussed "romantic comedies," speaking with the same disdainful, disgusted tone that most people reserve for discussions of head cheese or ingrown toenails.

But, much to my shame and consternation, I found myself going to see these romantic comedies again and

A FABULOUS ON-SCREEN COUPLE

LISE: Noah Taylor and Thandie Newton in *Flirting*. Man, they are cute!

SIBYL: Katharine Hepburn and Cary Grant in *The Philadelphia Story*—the epitome of sophistication.

ANDREA: Hands down, Bogie and Bergman in *Casablanca*. Talk about chemistry.

CLARE: Matthew and Maria in *Trust*. Or Horst and Max in the heartbreaking *Bent*.

again. Oh, I'd skulk my way in, hoping no one would recognize me. And I'd make up some excuse about why I was going: It was the only thing close by that was playing (not true), or I just wanted to know what everyone was talking about (blatant lie).

But really, to sit in a darkened theater, and spend a few hours watching two adorable actors with great chemistry stumble around and finally fall into each other's arms and lives? Sigh, I just love it.

And not just the high-quality romantic comedies. No siree. I like the good, the silly, and the utterly daft of this genre—happy to watch them all, just so long as it all ends well.

In the "good" category, you can check out **love jones** (dir. Theodore Witcher, 1997). This classy flick has a lot to offer, even for a more discerning viewer than myself. It opens on Nina (Nia Long), as she mopes around her fabulous apartment after a devastating breakup. Love is "played out like an eight-track," she explains to her best bud, saying that she'll "never make the same mistake twice," meaning she won't fall in love again. Sure, Nina.

Nina goes to a local bar, where she strikes up a conversation with the sweet and endearingly named Darius Lovehall (Larenz Tate). Turns out this guy isn't just cute and funny, he's also a talented writer, and he goes up to the mike and busts out a poem that he's titled "A Blues for Nina," right off the top of his head. Swoon.

Nina, though, is unimpressed by his telling the entire bar that he's the "blues in her left leg, and wants to be the funk in her right." What about love, she asks him, shooting him down in front of his hip urban buddies (who play an important role in this flick). But for Darius, hope springs eternal, and he pursues her, finally getting her to acquiesce to a first date, which leads to a night of passion.

But neither of them will admit that perhaps it's a bit serious. No, each of them tells their respective friend, "this ain't no love thing, we're just kickin' it." Sure, kids.

Anyway, pain and angst and mix-ups and past loves keep our

two lovebirds apart. Through it all, though, they manage to look fabulous (she wears cute, close-fitting tops and a nice jacket, even a sleek little cap in one scene; he sports elegant sweaters and perfectly faded jeans), and live in gorgeous apartments (with huge kitchens!). They each keep up a stream of friendships with other smart, attractive people, who all say smart and funny things, and who comment on love and dating with much wisdom and wit. The entire movie just glows with good looks and good lines. It can be funny, and sort of sad, and sexy, too. This is a movie of the high caliber. And it ends well.

Entering into that nebulous midrange comes one of my most beloved picks, a guilty pleasure which we mentioned at the beginning of this chapter: **While You Were Sleeping** (dir. Jon Turteltaub, 1995). Like **Love Jones**, this film is also set in Chicago, but for the most part, that's where the similarities end. It's more of a family film than **love jones**, and it's a sappier and a bit dorkier, too.

In **While You Were Sleeping**, Sandra Bullock plays Lucy, an orphaned, lonely young woman who works as a subway token booth clerk. Each morning, she gazes dreamily at Peter (Peter Gallagher) as he waits on the platform for his train to arrive. Lucy worships Peter, and somehow decides that this perfect-looking man is just perfect for her. She's in love. One day, some muggers push Peter onto the subway tracks, and Lucy jumps in after him, saving his life.

Then, at the hospital, a series of mix-ups occur (the kind that only happen in Hollywood), and all of Peter's family gets the mistaken idea that Lucy is his fiancée. Oops. Lucy's so nice that she doesn't want to burst their bubble, and since Peter's in a coma (good grief, what a great plot device!), what harm is there in her pretending?

The harm comes in the form of the tasty Jack (Bill Pullman), Peter's older brother. He favors work boots to Peter's slickly polished shoes, and flannel shirts to Peter's expensive suits. He is, basically, a Real Man. A carpenter, no less! (Peter's a, yawn, snore, lawyer.

Always bet on the guy who works with his hands, kids.) Anyway, turns out Lucy's got a heck of a lot more in common with Jack, and it's obvious that he's digging her, too, except that he thinks she's his baby bro's fiancée.

What will happen? Um, a lot of cute things, like Lucy and Jack slipping around on the icy Chicago sidewalks and almost kissing, and Lucy being so nice to everyone, and wearing floppy dresses and pushing the hair out of her eyes. Nice stuff about family, too, and why we all want somebody for ourselves. It's all very sweet. And it ends well.

Dipping well below average into the nadir of romantic comedies comes one honking guilty pleasure, **The Cutting Edge** (dir. Paul M. Glaser—a.k.a. Starsky!—1992), starring Moira Kelly as Kate, a spoiled, turbo-competitive figure skater who's frightened away all of her partners with her sharp tongue and brutal workouts. Enter Doug (D. B. Sweeney, where is this guy now? Yowsa, what a hottie!), a pro hockey player who's just suffered an injury to his eye that's going to keep him off the hockey ice permanently. Except that he's somehow still able to skate well enough to be an Olympic-caliber figure skater—something about not seeing the puck but being able to catch the girl twirling around in his arms. Yeah, whatever, stop with the exposition, we believe ya, fortheloveofgod!

Phew, thank goodness, faster than you can say "reverse salchow," these two get paired up and argue more than Lemmon and Matthau in **The Odd Couple**. It's the ideal formula for love: from opposite sides of the tracks, the two react like oil and water, initially loathing each other. Except that they're stuck together in an isolated setting with no hope of escape, and they each have one last chance for glory. And of course their sharp words for each other are but a feeble cover-up for their growing attraction. Wow, this is some good cheese!

Anyway, after lots of angst and bickering and confusion (and much skating—this is a skate-o-phile's delight), it all ends well.

So there you have it: the good, the bad, and the ugly. I guess it's official. I'm out now, for good. An admitted romantic comedy lover, willing to sit and watch just about anything for some good old-fashioned escapism. Don't bother telling me about our society's divorce rates (I know!), or how hard it is to have a successful relationship (no, really?), or how happily-ever-after is a foolish schoolgirl's dream (yeah, yeah, sing me another one)—let me have my fantasies, okay?

And then I'll live happily ever after, too.

ODE TO MEG RYAN

By Clare

I'm with Andrea here: Guilty, guilty, guilty as charged! Love a cheeseball romantic comedy, yes I do. Don't get me wrong, I'm all for romance of the tragic kind as well, but nothing lifts me up to a place where I belong better than a romantic comedy. It's all about love. A love that dare not speak its name—at least not around my more jaded friends. Love of melodrama, love of cute outfits, love of a perky gal. One perky gal in particular.

Yes, I love Meg Ryan.

Meg may not be ready for the world to know about our love, but I am here to tell you about it, and baby, it's intense.

Okay, so we've never met. I did actually see her—eek! in person!—at a party once, laughing and dancing with hubby Dennis Quaid, but I kept my distance, lingering creepily around the periphery of Meg, just happy to know she was there.

I should of course be more accurate and say that I love the on-screen Meg—especially when she's in romantic comedies written by Nora Ephron. I'm honestly not interested in Meg's personal life; I don't devour magazine articles about her, I don't want to know about her marriage, I don't burn to discover her favorite color. And I'm not planning on stealing her mail (which a friend of mine did to Madonna once), or penning an unauthorized biography of her or anything. I just dig her. Love can be simple that way.

To my knowledge, our eyes first met across a crowded theater in Boston, circa 1990. I was visiting Lise, who lives outside the city in nearby New Hampshire, and we'd gone to see **When Harry Met Sally** (dir. Rob Reiner, 1989). At the time, I didn't think the movie was so great (sorry, Nora). I think I was mostly irked by that now-famous scene of Sally (Meg) sitting in a diner, faking an orgasm. The crowd roared. I sighed. I mean, the scene is okay, but it's not by any means my favorite part of the movie. I get kinda testy when other audience members make me feel pressured

MY GUILTY PLEASURE ROMANCE FLICK

LISE: *Pump up the Volume*, with Christian Slater and Samantha Mathis. Some of it is embarrassing, but the romantic parts are so sweet.

SIBYL: *The Big Easy*. You can't go wrong with Dennis Quaid.

ANDREA: *The Matchmaker*, with Janeane Garofalo and David O'Hara—I couldn't believe more people didn't enjoy this film. I thought it was funny and find the leads completely appealing and great.

CLARE: Please refer to the entire Meg Ryan oeuvre. Oh, and I also liked the even more embarrassing *Untamed Heart*, with Christian Slater and Marisa Tomei.

to laugh, and I feel maybe everyone was just floored because they found a representation of a female orgasm, real or fake, to be so risqué that their guffawing came from an inner embarrassment about the scene. But I guess a lot of good comedy hinges on sexual hang-ups, so whatever. Still, it continues to irk me.

When Harry Met Sally has been beaten so soundly into our cultural consciousness that I probably shouldn't bother with a plot synopsis. Suffice it to say that Harry (Billy Crystal, who is charming, yes, but not truly worthy) and Sally meet in college in the seventies. Their styling is fantastic: She's wearing walking shorts and knee socks with blue eye shadow and feathered hair (actually, she's got those big, weird, hot-roller curls that kind of swell from the front of her head and crash to the back, like waves—what a hideous time for hair!). He's got huge sideburns and a smarmy grin. They drive to New York together, then part ways. Years later, they meet again: He's engaged, she's dating seriously. Then, once again, their paths cross: He's divorced, she's broken up. They finally become friends and— guess what?!—oh, I won't give it away!

One of the important things to note about my friend Meg is her clothes. I am convinced that she has a say in her wardrobe on every film, because she's always perfectly dressed. At the beginning of **When Harry. . .** , she wears the seventies and eighties getups required of her (the early-eighties scene involves a preppy, floppy, paisley bow tie and a shiny woman-suit—yikes!), but then she comes into her own. She sports all the best clothes of her time: cute hats and blazers, fake wire-rim spectacles when she's reading or writing, casual jeans and mock turtlenecks for everyday, even some great formal wear. She continues this impeccable fashion trend in later films, including **Sleepless in Seattle, Prelude to a Kiss, French Kiss, When a Man Loves a Woman, Addicted to Love,** and **City of Angels**. (Gee, do these titles tell you anything about Meg's movies?)

A great thing about Meg—and a quality that makes her perfect for romantic comedy—is that she really does look like the girl next door, only a little hipper, a little prettier. Unlike the absolutely stunning Michelle Pfeiffer, whose razor-sharp cheekbones and flawless lips and eyes betray her, Meg looks like someone you could know. And like. Her high and warbly voice of yesteryear, which has become deeper and smokier of late, makes her seem more real, not like some slick, over-voice-coached, overtrained, overspa'd, over-nipped-and-tucked, -plucked and -tweezed plastic doll. (In other words, not like Demi Moore. Meow!)

Okay, here's the best-kept secret about Meg, though: She can truly act. Comedy is hard, I think, harder than straight drama in a lot of ways. It requires such delicate timing. That's why Nora Ephron's writing suits Meg so well: She's allowed to be whimsical, ridiculous, serious, and heartbreaking all at once.

Ephron, in my humble opinion, has elevated the romantic comedy to the level of art. (Check out 1998's **You've Got Mail**, also penned by Ephron and reuniting Meg with **Sleepless** costar Tom Hanks, for further proof.) I believed in the end of **When Harry Met Sally** because Ephron got all the details right: Harry tells Sally that he loves that she gets cold when it's 70 degrees outside, that he loves that it takes her twenty minutes to order a sandwich, that he loves the wrinkle between her eyes when she's concentrating. Sigh! He doesn't just say she's smart and pretty; he basically says that she's a bundle of neuroses and a huge pain in the ass—and that he loves her for it. What chick wouldn't like to hear *that*?

Sleepless in Seattle (dir. Nora Ephron, 1993) gives Meg another opportunity to be neurotic and cute at the same time. She sits in an editorial meeting and suddenly wonders aloud about "all those cows" that got hit by lightning. She's brought to tears upon hearing Tom Hanks's voice on the radio, talking about how much he loved his dead wife. She barges in on her psychologist brother and demands to know the facts about cold feet, then sees a heart on the Empire State Building and impulsively decides it's a sign. It is, Meg, it is! Get away from sweet, unfunny Walter! Take a chance on love! It's always worth it!

I'm Meg's personal cheerleader, by the way.

I could go on and on about Meg's lesser-known accomplishments, especially in her "serious" romantic films—**When a Man Loves a Woman** broke my heart, and I saw **City of Angels** twice in the theater—but you must be sick of hearing me yammer on about Meg this, Meg that. Just rent the movies. Whatever the film, she's guaranteed to have a luminous smile, sassy hair, great clothes, and a smart screenwriter who loves her. Best of all, though, she's got me.

Rah rah.

LOVE HURTS

By Sibyl

Sorry, Clare, but happy, bubbly romances don't do it for me. I need misery, despair, treachery, and manipulation in my love stories. Sounds pretty twisted, I know. But come on, we all know that love is a game, and I want to see it portrayed that way on the big screen.

That's why the most satisfying love stories are the period pieces; they don't shy away from the pain and agony of passion. And, best of all, these movies are full of gorgeous costumes, beautiful locations, and intricate plots. This is not the stuff of giggly Billy Crystal and Meg Ryan, oh no! In the bodice rippers, look for vicious mind games, money-grubbers, people dying from sheer misery, and of course the wrath of God.

Dangerous Liaisons (dir. Stephen Frears, 1988) is one of my favorite movies; it's both dastardly and sexy. This Oscar-winner (screenplay, makeup, and costumes), set in eighteenth-century France, reveals all the games behind love, seduction, and betrayal. Glenn Close is a countess who takes enormous pleasure in manipulating others' love affairs. Of course she has plenty of lovers herself, including her friend and partner in deceit, John Malkovich. These two are twisted: They take great pleasure in others' pain, particularly in seducing others and then dumping them.

Close and Malkovich endeavor to pay back several enemies at once. Hence, Malkovich is simultaneously seducing Uma Thurman's young convent girl and the pious (and married) Michelle Pfeiffer. Meanwhile, Glenn Close keeps herself busy by observing Malkovich in action and amusing herself with the young music teacher, Keanu Reeves. Close's countess is a bitter, nasty woman; her veneer of elegance barely hides her venom. Watching Malkovich seduce the young ladies is amazing. He's not that great-looking; his power comes from language and gently unleashing these girls' pent-up desires, which drives them mad. This movie culminates in multiple seductions, a sword fight, death by heartbreak, and a nervous breakdown. Wow!

The Wings of the Dove (dir. Iain Softley, 1997) is an excellent companion piece to **Dangerous Liaisons**. Set in the early twentieth-century London and Venice, **Wings** is another manipulation-for-love story. There's a conniving woman of questionable social stature (Helena Bonham Carter), her working-class boyfriend (Linus Roache), and an American heiress traveling abroad with a mysterious illness (Alison Elliott)—typical Henry James characters. What makes **Wings** so intense is that Helena's character concocts a scheme in which her boyfriend will seduce the American and get her money, but, uh-oh, he falls for the American girl for real. All the while, they're wearing the most gorgeous costumes I've ever seen. **Wings** is about love and trust and crossing the line. It's brutal—deliriously, tragically brutal.

Many people felt that watching **The English Patient** (dir. Anthony Minghella, 1996), in all its two-and-a-half-hour-plus glory, was pure misery. Not for me. I swooned my way through it, crying, sighing, gushing. Tragic love, disfiguring accidents, the gorgeous, swirling desert, World War II—that's perfect misery. Kristin Scott Thomas is devastating as a dashing, witty woman of the world, married to a dolt but pining for the equally dashing bookworm/explorer Ralph Fiennes. These two have never looked better, traipsing around exotic locales in their Banana Republic finery. Of course, multiple tragedies befall them; fortunately, though, they find time to consummate their relationship in a slippery-when-wet bathtub scene before the war separates them. Look for betrayal, crushing loss, and—sniffle sniffle—dying alone in a cave to break your heart, if the romance and valor of the story haven't already done you in.

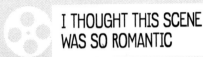

I THOUGHT THIS SCENE WAS SO ROMANTIC

LISE: When John Cusack holds the radio over his head and plays "In Your Eyes" in *Say Anything*. Cheesy? Yes. Romantic? You'd better believe it!

SIBYL: *Breaking the Waves*. When Bess (Emily Watson) finds out that her husband Stellan Skarsgård has been severely injured, and she wails with misery, very powerful.

ANDREA: I swoon every time Daniel Day-Lewis yells to Madeleine Stowe in *The Last of the Mohicans* to "Leave now! I will find you! Stay alive!"

CLARE: When the two leads in *Rhythm Thief* take the A train all the way to Rockaway Beach; weird reggae music plays as they stop between subway cars to kiss in the brilliant sunlight. Sigh.

Thomas Hardy specialized in misery (remember poor Tess of the D'Urbervilles?), and **Jude** (dir. Michael Winterbottom, 1996), the film version of his **Jude the Obscure**, is as sad and dreary as you'd expect. It's the late nineteenth century, and Jude (Christopher Eccleston) is a scholarly stonemason who happens into a bad marriage. He leaves his small village to pursue his studies in the city. He meets his cousin, Sue Bridehead (Kate Winslet, in a gloriously glowing yet understated performance), a confident, clever young woman, and falls passionately in love with her.

Aside from the fact that they're both kind of married to other people, and they're cousins, Jude and Sue are also doomed to fulfill their family curse of fateful love affairs. Argh. Throwing caution to the wind, they follow their hearts and embark on a rather nontraditional union. Of course they are severely punished—one might say they just have bad luck, or, as Sue comes to believe, that the wrath of God is crashing down on them, their love was wrong, and their hearts are justly broken. **Jude** is as grim as a romance can get, but its portrayal of such a fierce love is oddly uplifting.

These diabolical period pieces give me the best of two worlds. Most often, they're adapted from classic literature, so the source material is high quality. Yet there's also a certain amount of campiness inherent in the high costume drama. What a great combination of love, sex, manipulation, and the harsh judgment of a strict society upon these ill-fated lovers! This is the world of delicious misery. The big budgets, soaring scores, and great costumes—oh, catch me, swoon, swoon—love and tragedy all mixed up into one big corseted mess! Now that's a fine romance!

KEEP YOUR FAKE ORGASM AND PASTRAMI—I'M ORDERING IN

By Lise

In the spirit of honesty and disclosure, I have something to confess: I have been accused of being unromantic. Sure, it's true, I'm not one to go for the candlelight dinner and horse-drawn carriage thing; I'm more of a "let's grab a burger and rent a movie" kind of girl. Why? Well, I'm sure no one wants me to drag out my matching set of emotional baggage; suffice it to say that I honestly don't know one single person who hasn't been through some horrendous breakup or romantic disaster. So I like to be realistic (some call it "pessimistic") and maybe a little careful (that'd be "jaded"). Do I think I'm unromantic? Nope. Do I think I have different ideas about what true romance is? Well, yeah.

Let me put it this way: With the exception of an occasional Fred Astaire–Ginger Rogers romp—which I like mostly for the dancing—I'm not a fan of sentimental movie pastries like **Bringing up Baby** and **An Affair to Remember**. And if I never see that stupid fake orgasm scene from **When Harry Met Sally** again, it'll be too soon. (Sorry Clare, I hate to offend your best friends, Meg and Nora, but I know that even you understand how tragic that scene was.) And I'm not that big on the period-piece bodice rippers. I like a little reality in my romance. Give me an unconventional couple, some slightly neurotic characters I can relate to in some way (not that I am neurotic, but you know what I'm saying), or a romance that is half as complicated, crazy, or tragic as real life.

In 1996, Hettie MacDonald directed **Beautiful Thing**, which got almost no attention, yet is a charming, funny, and complicated coming-of-age story about a boy named Jamie Gangel (Glen Berry).

THIS MOVIE WEDDING IS GREAT

LISE: *The Godfather.* Duh. The dress, the cake ... How much money do you think a wedding like that would cost?!

SIBYL: *High Society* (Grace Kelly and Bing Crosby). Louis Armstrong plays the wedding march. Very glamorous and jazzy.

ANDREA: When Steve Guttenberg gives his bride-to-be a sports quiz in *Diner* before he'll agree to marry her. When they finally do walk down the aisle, it's all Baltimore Colts colors and decidedly un-romantic. Comic genius.

CLARE: Clare: The wedding at the end of *Crimes and Misdemeanors* rocks; that philosopher guy talks about things that make life worth living, while the blind rabbi dad dances with his just-married daughter.

He lives with his thirty-five-year-old chain-smoking mother (Linda Henry) in a generic high-rise apartment building in London. The Gangel's neighbors are just this side of believable—especially Leah (Tameka Empson), the atypical girl next door who is completely obsessed with Mama Cass (of the Mamas and the Papas). Jamie's mother has a boyfriend named Tony (Ben Daniels), a young painter who Drives a VW bus, sports stringy blond hair and a mustache, and ponders some serious questions between drags on his cigarette, like "What is age?" and "What is place?" It's a peculiar cast of characters.

Jamie falls in love with one of his neighbors, and there are several sweet, awkward scenes in which the two boys try to work through their feelings. Yeah, I said two boys. Jamie has fallen for Ste (Scott Neal), another teenager, who gets regularly beaten by his father. In one touching scene, Jamie rubs peppermint foot lotion onto Ste's bruised back. They go through some really tough times—being teased and all is bad enough, but add to that the confusion of being gay kids in this pretty closed community. When Jamie and Ste are finally able to experience a happy moment, at a gay bar that they sneak off to, I was so happy for them that my eyes welled up with tears. The soundtrack features the Mamas and the Papas, the acting is great—this is a really unsentimental and touching story.

Ju Dou (dir. Zhang Yimou, 1990), another story about an inconvenient and difficult romance, can be difficult to watch. Gong Li plays Ju Dou, a Chinese peasant woman who has been sold to Yang Jinshan (Li Wei), the owner of a dye mill in the 1920s. Ju Dou's new husband, nicknamed Uncle, treats her like an animal. Sadly, we find that this beastly, infertile man has already tortured several wives, some to their deaths, for not bearing him children.

Ju Dou is trapped, and turns to the only other person around, Yang Tianqing (Li Baotian), who is the adopted, but not beloved, nephew of Uncle. Uncle also treats Tianqing like a dog, working him night and day. Ju Dou and Tianqing fall in love, and conceive a son that Uncle believes is his own. It's a very rueful story, which grows increasingly more complicated after Uncle is paralyzed from the waist down. Despite all of the story's tragic elements, **Ju Dou** is a true romance—a story of the lengths to which people will go to be together. **Ju Dou** is also one of the most gorgeous films I've ever seen. The movie takes place in a dye mill, where bright scraps of fabric are forever blowing in the wind. It's hard to imagine that such horrible and tragic incidents could occur in a place where everything looks so colorful and bright. This is one of those movies that took me far away from my everyday experience; what brought me into the story was the emotion, the love between Ju Dou and Tianqing.

In stark contrast, Woody Allen's **Manhattan** (1979) is much lighter in tone and subject matter. (It's also Allen's best film, according to Clare's mom! See Clare's comedy section.) Not only are there several doomed romances between friends, ex-wives and lovers, and a high school student, but there is also Allen's undying love affair with New York City, which is filmed in beautiful black-and-white and featured prominently throughout.

This is a movie that really shows how complicated, crazy, and messed up things can get in the world of romance. Isaac Davis (Allen) is hanging out with seventeen-year-old Tracy (Mariel Hemingway), taking her to museums and old Veronica Lake movies. He is constantly trying to convince Tracy not to fall in love with him, and she is constantly getting mad that he won't take her seriously, "just because I'm seventeen." Mariel Hemingway is Ivory-girl beautiful and has this tiny mouse voice, but she is pretty fierce. (Of their sex life, Isaac comments, "As long as the cops don't burst in, I think we may break some records." Geez.)

As if that weren't complicated enough, Isaac then meets Mary Wilke (another hilarious performance by Diane Keaton). I love the way Mary keeps saying "I'm from Philadelphia," as a way of explaining why she doesn't discuss certain subjects, like orgasms, in public. She also busts out with such doozies as "I'm both attracted and repelled by the male organ," which annoy Isaac to no end—at first. Of course, he ends up falling for her, which isn't so great for Tracy, or for his married friend, Yale (Michael Murphy), who is also in love with Mary, unbeknownst to his wife, Emily (Anne Byrne).

There's a lot going on here, and most of it is not good.

There are so many precious moments in **Manhattan**. When Isaac breaks up with Tracy in an ice-cream parlor, she just looks at him over her milkshake and says, "I can't believe that you met somebody you like better than me." Whoa, I mean, I have said that—and not that long ago. It's one of those heartbreaking moments where you think, you know, it doesn't matter whether you're a gay teenager in England, or a Chinese wife in the 1920s, or a Manhattan teenager, because the pain that comes with love knows no spatial or temporal boundaries. Damn! Isaac finally realizes that he was happiest when he was with Tracy, but by the time he tells her this she is about to depart for London.

Watching **Manhattan** reminded me of my younger sister, Kelly—not that she is having an affair with a neurotic, twice-divorced forty-two-year-old, just that she has reached the age where she actually has some life experience and can dish out some good advice. Since part of my mind has Kelly permanently stuck at six years old, it can be disconcerting when she says, "It sounds to me like you're a little jealous," or "Yeah, I went through the same thing." Part of me wants to shout, *"That seems a little unlikely since you were just sitting under the clothesline clutching your blanky for three hours while it dried!"* Ahem, sorry. Then I remember, that was years and years ago—and I was wearing a Sting concert T-shirt and purple eye shadow at the time, so who am I to judge? My point is that I don't mind taking advice from a teenager, especially if, like Tracy, she seems to be the most together person around. As Tracy says to Isaac at the end of **Manhattan**, "You have to have a little faith in people." I think that's true, and my sister would probably agree, but boy is it scary.

Well, girls, I can't think of a bodice ripper starring Meg Ryan that, although tragic at times, turns out completely happy. So, if we're ever going to watch a romance together, I think we'll have to settle for the old standby **Breakfast at Tiffany's**. And, yes, I think it's romantic. What kind of a brute do you take me for?!

25 Romances to Rent!

1 **BABY IT'S YOU** (dir. John Sayles, 1982) Rosanna Arquette's a sheltered, middle-class Jewish girl who falls for Vincent Spano's tough, working-class Italian boy (with the nickname of "Sheik," oy). It's definitely not all sweetness and light in this moving, opposite-sides-of-the-tracks tale from indie superstar director Sayles.

2 **BEAUTIFUL THING** (dir. Hettie MacDonald, 1996) A truly touching romance between two teenage boys in a housing project in London. Jamie pretty much knows that he is gay, but his neighbor and love-interest, Ste, has a very difficult time coming to grips with his homosexuality (his abusive father doesn't help). Some wrenching and some tender moments, quirky supporting characters, and a great Mama Cass soundtrack come together to make a beautiful thing.

3 **THE BIG EASY** (dir. Jim McBride, 1987) This light, sexy thriller set in New Orleans is a bit dated (Ellen Barkin sports a suit larger than the one David Byrne wears in *Stop Making Sense*), but it does boast some highly charged chemistry between Barkin's uptight DA and Dennis Quaid's police officer who knows how to bend the rules. Nice soundtrack to boot.

4 **BOUND** (dirs. Andy Wachowski and Larry Wachowski, 1996) Instead of a guy and a moll, it's two dames (Gina Gershon, Jennifer Tilly) who generate white-hot heat in this fine, bloody update on the noir tradition. Gershon finds trouble and then some when she gets involved with her next-door neighbor (Tilly) and crosses Tilly's temperamental crook of a boyfriend, played by Joe Pantoliano.

5 **BREAKFAST AT TIFFANY'S** (dir. Blake Edwards, 1961) Doesn't everyone want to look as magnificent as Holly Golightly (the radiant Audrey Hepburn) as she charms her way through Manhattan's nightlife, snaring the heart of a writer (George Peppard) as well as

the rest of us? We do, for sure. Truman Capote wrote the story upon which this great flick is based.

6 **BREAKING THE WAVES** (dir. Lars von Trier, 1995) Gorgeous, nutty, willful Bess (Emily Watson) lives in an isolated, highly religious community in 1970s Scotland, where she raises the suspicions of her neighbors by marrying a strange outsider, Jan (Stellan Skarsgård). To complicate matters further, Jan gets in an accident, leaving Bess to carry on her two-way conversations with God (uh-huh, she thinks he talks back) all on her own. Funny, strange, tragic, ironic, and amazingly shot by Robby Muller, this flick delivers a powerful, romantic, and completely original story.

7 **CASABLANCA** (dir. Michael Curtiz, 1942) A perfect movie in every way, *Casablanca* won the top Oscars for 1942—Best Picture, Director, and Screenplay. Wonderful acting from Humphrey Bogart and Ingrid Bergman, as former lovers who meet again in Bogie's nightclub in Morocco, makes this film a joy to behold, as do the great supporting performances from Paul Henreid, Claude Rains, Peter Lorre, and Sydney Greenstreet, as well as dialogue that sticks with you for life. Here's looking at you, kid.

8 **HAROLD AND MAUDE** (dir. Hal Ashby, 1971) Talk about off-the-beaten-path: This quirky film features Harold (Bud Cort), a twenty-year-old who's depressed and obsessed with death, attends funerals for fun, and stages fake suicides in front of his mother. Enter Maude (Ruth Gordon), a seventy-nine-year-old who has all the youth and happiness that Harold seems to lack. Harold falls in love, and things get even wackier and more complicated, and even a little sad. All-around great flick, this.

9 **JU DOU** (dir. Zhang Yimou, 1990) The shockingly beautiful Gong Li plays Ju Dou, a young woman who is married off to a horrible brute who owns a dye mill in 1920s China. Ju Dou falls in love with his adopted nephew, Tianqing; it's a heart-wrenching love triangle. She's trapped in an awful situation; the beauty of the brightly col-

ored, newly dyed fabric blowing in the wind is a cruel contrast to her daily existence.

10 **JULES AND JIM** (dir. François Truffaut, 1962) A girl and a guy. And another guy. This moving French film is refreshingly open-minded about things like sex and commitment, especially in its depiction of the elusive Catherine, played by Jeanne Moreau. How come things are always sexier when they're said in French?

11 **LADY JANE** (dir. Trevor Nunn, 1985) Could this historical romance be any more sad? No. Dour and bookish sixteen-year-old Jane (Helena Bonham Carter) is swept up in her parents' schemes to make her the next Queen of England. They force her to marry drunken buffoon Guilford (Cary Elwes) as part of their plan to manipulate the throne. But love conquers all, the two fall in love, they make radical changes. The leads are so young, fresh, and naive. Their faith in God and each other is so huge. Prepare to sob uncontrollably.

12 **THE LAST OF THE MOHICANS** (dir. Michael Mann, 1992) Great storytelling from Mann, who makes this film as exciting as anything from his "Miami Vice" days. The gorgeous scenery (we're supposed to be in eighteenth-century America) is almost as eye-catching as the cast (including Daniel Day-Lewis, Madeleine Stowe, and Wes Studi). We're betting that this version is a whole lot sexier than novelist James Fenimore Cooper ever could have imagined.

13 **LOVE JONES** (dir. Theodore Witcher, 1997) Very hip love story for the nineties about two smart young Chicagoans (Larenz Tate and Nia Long) who set off sparks together, each claiming that it ain't no love thing. We know better. Poetry was never so sexy as when Tate performs his impromptu seduction riff on the stage of a nightclub.

14 **MANHATTAN** (dir. Woody Allen, 1979) Woody juggles the ladies (Mariel Hemingway, Diane Keaton, Meryl Streep) and his own neu-roses in this moving flick about just how easy it is to make a mess out of your love life. This is one of Allen's most romantic flicks, with depictions of loss that ring almost painfully true.

15 **MRS. BROWN** (dir. John Madden, 1997) Get out the hankies! This period piece focuses on the friendship between grumpy Queen Victoria, who mourns perpetually for her late husband, and sassy Scotsman John Brown (Billy Connolly). She's a Queen, he's a servant, yet he's the only person who can crack through her dour attitude. It's more about friendship than romance, but with Dench's and Connolly's nuanced performances and all that Scottish tweed, this is a truly heartwarming tale of star-crossed lovers.

16 **NOW, VOYAGER** (dir. Irving Rapper, 1942) This flick will satisfy the corny old-movie lover in you that, deep down, believes *Casablanca* was a little too subtle. High melodrama finds a scenery-chomping Bette Davis, "plain" at the movie's open (i.e., she has this horrific fake unibrow and spectacles); she comes into her own after spending time in a loony bin (she had a nervous breakdown because she was so plain). Costarring the ever-lovable Paul Henreid (*Casablanca*) as a man she meets on a cruise!

17 **OUT OF SIGHT** (dir. Steven Soderbergh, 1998) Wonderful Elmore Leonard adaptation starring George Clooney and Jennifer Lopez as a bank robber and a cop, respectively. Dialogue that snaps, crackles, and pops; gorgeous stars; and a soundtrack that sets a mood. This romantic crime story is, well, out of sight.

18 **THE PHILADELPHIA STORY** (dir. George Cukor, 1940) Katharine Hepburn's at her high society best as a woman attempting to pull off a glitch-free wedding. However, in between ex-hubby Cary Grant's reappearance, Jimmy Stewart's getting underfoot as a besotted reporter, and too much champagne all around, there's no way, no how. Enchanting. The perfect union of sophistication and screwball.

19 **SAY ANYTHING** (dir. Cameron Crowe, 1989) Young love hurts, friends. John Cusack turns in another superb performance as the slightly daft Lloyd Dobler, a kick-boxer and general flake who falls for his high school's valedictorian (the luminous Ione Skye). Their courtship is extremely sweet, and the story is both amusing and moving. You will fall in love with either one or both of these two leads. Trust us.

20 SENSE AND SENSIBILITY (dir. Ang Lee, 1995) A wonderful adaptation of the Jane Austen novel, penned by and starring Emma Thompson, who plays the eldest of three impoverished British sisters (the other two are Kate Winslet and Emile Francois) trying to find a way out of their money woes. Set in a time when women weren't able to just say what they felt or do what they wished, *Sense* is chockablock with cool lines and strong female role models. Plus lots of romantic intrigue.

21 TRULY, MADLY, DEEPLY (dir. Anthony Minghella, 1991) Think *Ghost*, only smarter, funnier, more original, and more touching. Director Minghella (*The English Patient*) brings us this romantic fable about a woman (Juliet Stevenson) who's filled with unbelievable despair over the death of her beloved husband (Alan Rickman)—until he reappears at her apartment and won't go away. Funny bits, like Rickman's continuing political involvement in the afterlife ("I still go to meetings") are woven in well with the film's big-hearted story.

22 THE WAY WE WERE (dir. Sydney Pollack, 1973) The first time you see Barbra Streisand stroking Robert Redford's beautiful blond locks, you'll know you're in for some heart-string a-tugging. The story of a smart, lefty college firebrand who falls for the All-American guy is the sort you want to see with your girlfriends when you've just had your heart broken. Actually worth renting just to hear Babs sings "The Way We Were."

23 WEST SIDE STORY (dir. Robert Wise and Jerome Robbins, 1961) This incredible musical picked up the Romeo and Juliet story and placed it firmly in the working-class streets of Manhattan. Natalie Wood and Richard Beymer are the ill-fated lovers, and they, along with a talented supporting cast (including Rita Moreno, George Chakiris, and Russ Tamblyn) sing, dance, and break our hearts.

24 `WHEN HARRY MET SALLY` (dir. Rob Reiner, 1989) Wittily scripted (by Nora Ephron) tale of two New York friends (Meg Ryan and Billy Crystal) who see each other through life's good times and bad, all without ever mucking up their friendship with the dreaded "romantic entanglement." Until one day. . . Sweet and entertaining, this flick's a true cheerer-upper.

25 `WITNESS` (dir. Peter Weir, 1985) This thriller stars Harrison Ford as a Philly cop who has to go undercover in a close-knit Amish community in order to solve a grisly murder. There, he begins to fall for a young Amish widow (Kelly McGillis, way better than in *Top Gun*) who is, of course, off limits. Way off. The whole film is well acted, but the scene where they dance to "What a Wonderful World" is a stand-out.

5 HORROR FLICKS:
Eek! Sleeping with the Lights on!

REDRUM

Your heart races. The hair on the back of your neck stands up. Your palms get sweaty, and you think the person sitting next to you might suddenly turn around with a knife in their hands. Sounds like fun, huh? Why do we put our bodies through this, willingly, when we spend time and money to sit in a theater (or on our couch) and watch people get murdered in the most awful of ways? Or stalked? Or haunted? Lots of us choose to do just that when we watch a scary movie.

Movies that can cause you to sleep with the lights on for a week afterward come in all shapes and sizes. Some of them are consummate flicks that have entered that good old film-classics canon. Alfred Hitchcock's 1960 horror film **Psycho**, for example, changed the way people make movies forever, and it's studied in film schools around the world for its pacing, camera work, and the commanding way in which it manipulates the audience. But a lot of scary films aren't particularly high quality (**Witchboard II**, anyone?), and we still love 'em. It certainly doesn't seem fun—cowering in your seat, covering your eyes, maybe even having nightmares long after the movie's ended. Kind of sounds like the sort of thing you'd pay to avoid. Yet again and again we line up to see films whose clearly stated intention to scare the bejeezus out of us. Why?

One reason might be the sheer thrill of the experience. We get the heart-pounding adrenaline rush of being in the midst of a chase, yet we know (at least on one level) that we're safe and sound, unlike the poor schnooks on-screen who are being hunted by some knife-wielding madman (or a horned, fork-tailed beastie). It's like an aerobic workout without any of the work.

Plus, we get to feel superior to the characters that are in harm's way. Have you ever actually entered a deserted, creepy-looking, haunted house, alone, in the middle of the night, armed with only a flashlight? Yeah, we did-n't think so. Therefore, we can all feel smug and yell things like, "Don't go in there, you dolt!" to a screen character who can't hear us, and think to ourselves, "If I were them, I'd be running the other way. That fool!"

For a long time, people thought men were primarily the ones who went to see frightening films, but we can attest to the fact that women see them, too. You might con-sider it kind of a bummer that in a whole lot of these, there's an evil man stalking a young,

THE CREEPIEST VILLAIN IS

LISE: A real person—as opposed to a monster—like Billy Zane's character in *Dead Calm*.

SIBYL: Danny Devito as the Penguin in *Batman Forever*—those terrifying webbed hands and purple drool.

ANDREA: Michael Myers, from the *Halloween* series. Ooh, chilling. He stands the test of time: He's still scary.

CLARE: Of course, that would be Beelzebub himself. No matter what the movie, he always terrifies.

attractive woman. But what we found is that, oftentimes, it's the women who turn out to be the real shit-kickers here, whomping the bad guy's ass in movies like **Nightmare on Elm Street** and **Halloween**. Trust us, there's a real satisfaction in seeing someone who looks small and unassuming turn out to have more moxie and guts than a boat full of Navy Seals.

There's a whole wad of academics out there studying horror films in relation to gender issues (now that's a cushy job!), making astute comments about everything from how the camera is used (jerky, hand-held, sometimes from the perspective of the killer, even) to who you're supposed to identify with (the victim? The killer?). You've probably noticed yourself that there's a strong link between sex and violence in a great many of these films. For instance, in **Friday the 13th** (dir. Sean S. Cunningham, 1980), the teenage counselors at the camp had sex when they should have been watching after the kids, and one of those children drowned because of it. Then the counselors start dying, one by one, stalked by a killer who seems to go after them mostly while they're making whoopie. Even in a film like **Seven** (dir. David Fincher, 1995), the maniacal murderer goes after people who have committed one of the seven deadly sins, like lust. They're like little morality plays with clear-cut definitions of good and evil. You could say they're like fairy tales for our modern times.

One of the best things about seeing a scary flick is that we get to have a shared experience with the rest of the audience. These aren't usually the sort of films you see, or rent, when you're alone, unless you are superduper brave (or didn't know what you were getting yourself into). Part of the fun is in grabbing your friend's arm and hearing the rest of the people in the dark theater gasping along with you. People wind up laughing almost as much as they're screaming, which makes the whole experience fun, in a roller coaster kind of way. It's half "get me offa this ride," and half "I want to do it again!" It's pretty hilarious seeing a theater full of people jump or scream at exactly the same time; it gives us the feeling that we're all in it together, and we bond through this strange, shared, ritualized experience. It's also why we so appreciate the comic relief in a scary movie, like in **Scream** (dir. Wes Craven, 1996), which would have been too much to take without those great one-liners peppered throughout the film.

Scary films come in all shapes and sizes, don't forget. There's a whole world of them out there, not just slasher movies. There are stories about nature out of control, or a compelling vision of hell, or even of people who look nice but aren't, but they all manage to scare us in one way or another. A scary movie could even be lurking under the guise of one of those children's fantasy films that were supposed to make us so gosh-darn happy when we were little. Remember **The Wizard of Oz** and **Willy Wonka & the Chocolate Factory**, shown year after year on television as feel-good family fare? Yeah, right, an evil witch and swarms of monkeys (**Oz**) and a glass tube that sucks up a child who eats too much (**Willy Wonka**)—that makes us feel good. Harumph.

One of the most interesting types of scary movies—well, from a purely psychological point of view, at least—is the evil-from-within type. These can be more terrifying than just about anything, because what if the person sitting next to you, right now, watching this movie, turns out to be *totally insane?* **Sorry, Wrong Number**, about a bedridden wife who thinks her husband might be the one plotting to kill her, or **The Stepfather**, about a totally normal-seeming pappy who's a little more enamored of his power tools than the average dad, are two fine examples of people who look nice and normal and turn out to be anything but. What about **The Shining**, with a descent into madness by Jack Nicholson? All work and no play, eek! Even a cheesy film like **Children of the Damned**, with those sweet little blond children with the strangely piercing blue eyes, can be good and frightening, and not only because all the little darlings sport a hideous bob hairstyle that went out with Dorothy Hamill.

From the most-absurd sounding horror film (**Pumpkinhead, Leprechaun II**) to the more thoughtful, intelligent frightener (**Don't Look Now, Jacob's Ladder**), sometimes nothing beats a good scare. Even when these films are guilty pleasures that we're embarrassed to admit to renting, we still go back and see them again and again. In other words, strange as it may sound, it's fun to be petrified.

GOD, THE DEVIL, AND LITTLE ME

By Clare

Cursed with what my parents liked to call an "overactive imagination" from the time I was a wee tot, I have been plagued by nightmares my whole life. I was brought up in a pretty religious Catholic home, went to Catholic grade school, and learned all about spirits and such from day one. Now, religion brings comfort to many, but for me it brought restless, feverish thoughts of demons and Hell and eternity. It was supposed to be a happy day when I learned, at the tender young age of nine, that our souls never die, but dwell with God after our bodies die, happy for all of eternity.

I latched on, not to the "happy" part, but to the "eternity" part. It terrified me. I remember waking up my mother in the middle of the night, asking her, "Okay, after we die, we're with God forever and ever, right? When does 'forever and ever' end?" And my mom simply said, "Never." Spooky. Later, to comfort me, she tried to tell me to think of heaven as being full of roses (wouldn't I get sick of roses? What's so great about roses?), and when that didn't work, she told me to think about Santa Claus and the Easter Bunny. Yeah, right. A weird old man in a red suit? A preternaturally huge bunny that sneaked into my house to deposit my Easter basket in a hidden place? I don't think so.

And in sixth grade, I had a religion class with an old priest who used a traditional Catechism book, which explained the philosophical precepts of the Church. The book was in question-and-answer form, with stuff like, "Why did God create the world?" (Answer: "For His outward glorification." Ack.) One of the questions was pretty simple; it was about demonic possession, a subject that, although acknowledged by many wacko Catholics out there, is considered embarrassing by most (including, apparently, the priest who taught my class). So we just skimmed over it. But not me, I didn't. The fact that such a horrifying experience was considered mainstream enough to

SCARY HAIR SITUATIONS

LISE: Don Cheadle in *Boogie Nights*. It was a good distraction, but still ... (I am referring specifically to the scene where he had braided, Cleopatra-like hair.)

SIBYL: Samuel Jackson's ponytailed goatee in *Jackie Brown*.

ANDREA: The stylist on *The Lost Boys* has got some explaining to do. Coifs less fetching that that of the entire crew of eighties one-hit wonder band Kajagoogoo.

CLARE: This may sound obvious, but Christopher Walken's hair in *The Prophecy* was beyond distracting. It was...disturbing. It looked like a wig made out of Michael Jackson's hair. Michael Jackson's *ironed* hair.

be included in this book at all—whether we skimmed it or not—convinced me that it must be real.

Thus, the groundwork was laid for the development of a very twisted child (that would be me) who dreamed of the Devil and expected him to come knocking on her soul's door any day. I mean, the guy didn't care if you were good or not; he didn't care if you were just a child; he was just trying to get back at God. We were all merely pawns in this lofty struggle. Oh, great. I was doomed.

My fear of the Devil turned into a fear of ghosts (you can't see them/they are not hampered by cumbersome bodies), and then, when I got older and the dreams stayed with me, a fear of my own mind and all the terrible, fabulous, ghostly things it could concoct while I was sleeping. Slashers don't faze me, like they do Andrea; you can always outsmart a human killer, or run away, or grab a knife and defend yourself.

Not so the demon.

What fertile ground, then, for **The Exorcist** (dir. William Friedkin, 1973) to take root. When little Regan (Linda Blair) first tells her mom (Ellen Burstyn) that her bed is shaking during the night and she has trouble sleeping, her mom takes her to the doctor. When various tests (that take place in a hospital scarier than any Hell I'd imagined) reveal that nothing's physically wrong with Regan's brain, her mom takes her to psychiatrists. They can't pinpoint a diagnosis, either.

Regan's mother's pragmatic approach to the problem marks an element that's missing in most modern horror flicks; instead simply concluding, "Oh, that's it! *Satan* must be trying to possess my daughter's *soul!*" the mother seeks out all the answers she can find through science. Meanwhile, her daughter is turning green and talking in a voice several octaves lower than her own. Oops.

The Exorcist is actually a very well made film, with thoughtful character development and careful pacing. And though it doesn't scare me now as much as it did when I was young, it's got the best effects of any scary movie, ever. Music is used sparingly, to chilling effect, and the Devil's voice actually sounds like a chorus of voices, all speaking at once; Regan also growls and groans like a furious beast.

Most terrifying of all is the "death mask" that flashes briefly on-screen twice during the film, once in the middle of a dream sequence, and once as Regan is thrashing around on the bed. Taking only a few frames, the "mask" is actually just a shot of what looks like a woman's face, painted a skeletal white, against a black background; she's grimacing and wild-eyed. When I watched the movie recently and did a frame-by-frame, I got chills.

In addition to all the scary Devil stuff, and the fact that poor little Regan is innocent of wrongdoing, we've also got some wicked psychological mind games going on between the Devil and the two priests who finally come to exorcise it, Father Damien Karras (Jason Miller) and Father Merrin (Max von Sydow). The crafty spirit goads the guilt-ridden Karras by blaming him for his mother's death and saying that she's down in Hell with him. He even perfectly imitates her pleading voice: "Why do you do this to me, Demi?"

Nothing could quite match the terror that struck my heart when I watched **The Exorcist** as an eleven-year-old with my two sisters while my mother fell asleep—fell asleep!—on the couch. (I slept in a twin bed with one or both of my sisters for a few weeks after that movie.) But a few have come close.

When I saw the much sloppier **Exorcist III** in 1991 (dir. William Peter Blatty, author of the original **Exorcist**), it was laughably inconsistent with the first movie, though it does pretend that **Exorcist II: The Heretic** never happened, as should we all. But it still left me with lots of nightmarish images of desecrated holy statues, evil hooded chimeras lurching after people with huge shears, and grisly murders that are neither quick nor painless. If you really, really liked **The Exorcist**, I'd recommend this one; otherwise, I'd give it a big miss.

Nightmare on Elm Street (dir. Wes Craven, 1984) also deals with spooks and spirits and the terror of the imagination. **Nightmare** is one of the only "slasher" films that ever stuck with me—not just because of Johnny Depp's huge eighties hairdo, but because of its chilling premise: Teenagers are being killed in their dreams. (I know, scary.)

Apparently, Freddy Krueger (yup, the infamous Freddy) was responsible for murdering a bunch of children years and years ago; after discovering his crime, the parents of the town surrounded his house and burned it down, with him in it. Now, the surviving children are teenagers, and Freddy's a burn-scar victim from Hell, and he's come back to finish the job, complete with his very special glove that has knives attached to the fingers. (Innovative!)

Only one plucky girl (Heather Langenkamp) figures out what's happening, and warns everyone not to go to sleep. (My exact warning to myself when I've just woken up from a nightmare! Uncanny!) Of course, everyone does go to sleep (including her boyfriend, the hapless Johnny Depp), and they are slashed to ribbons and Cuisinarted and have their guts spewed out all over the damn place. On second viewing, almost fifteen years later, I see how cheesy—and, actually, formulaic—this flick really is, but it's still scary. Laugh all you want at the bad acting, the supercorny "alcoholic mom" story line, et cetera, but don't judge until you see how you feel later, alone in your room at night. If I were you, I'd rent it only with friends, in a lighted room, during the day. And don't go to sleep . . .

Lastly, Stanley Kubrick's **The Shining** (1980), while not keeping me up nights, has quite a kick to it. As a dedicated Stephen King devotee (in the same way that someone with a fear of heights might be prone to peeking over high ledges), I thought this was one of his scariest books. Most directors slaughter King (no pun intended) when they bring him to the screen, the most egregious error being that they lose his twisted sense of humor.

But Kubrick's got it right on target here. His Johnny (Jack Nicholson) has just the right amount of anger, sick humor, and desperation. A recovering alcoholic who once accidentally broke the arm of his young son Danny (Danny Lloyd) in a fit of rage, John is looking to turn over a new leaf with his wife Wendy (Shelly Duvall). So he takes a somewhat questionable job as caretaker of the Overlook Hotel, up in the Rocky Mountains, where he and his family will be snowed in for the entire winter. There's talk of the Donner Party and other instances in which people trapped in the snow for months have gone totally berserk, but this foreshadowing is lost on our characters. Good for us, bad for them.

So it seems as if the Overlook, despite looking barren and empty, is actually teeming with inhabitants of the spiritual kind. But the only people who can see them are Danny, who has "the shine" (kind of like an ESP inner-sight power), and his father, who may have an even stronger and more sinister version of it (sort of like a Windows 98 to Danny's Windows 95).

There are lots of unforgettable images in **The Shining**: little twin ghost-girls asking Danny to play with them; an old, green hag who rises from a bathtub with a cackle; an elevator door opening and gallons of blood crashing out of it into the hallway. But best of all, there's Jack Nicholson: "Wendy, give me the bat . . . I'm not going to hurt you . . . I'm just going to bash your brains in. Bash them right the f——k in." Both wickedly funny and downright discomfiting, **The Shining** delivers a satisfying scare. Especially if you, like me, fear the power of angry spirits, scary visions, and the human mind.

Remember, none of the ghosts and demons in these movies cares if you're young or old, innocent or guilty, carefree or troubled. They have your number, your home address, and they don't need a door to get in.

(Kind of like telemarketers. Scary!)

I STILL KNOW WHAT YOU DID ... IN 1973

By Lise

I have an irrational and pretty embarrassing fear of flying. Andrea doesn't like to fly either, but she seems to have the situation a bit more under control. Still, we always laugh when we remember Clare, who did extensive world traveling at her previous job, telling us that "the perfect length for a flight is twelve hours." Twelve hours?!? Clare says that she likes flying, that she feels like a "king," because it's a time when no one is asking anything from her, people bring her food and drink, she watches stupid movies without shame. I once started crying on a forty-minute shuttle flight from Boston to New York while a flight attendant looked at me in total disgust. Cut to Clare in her crown and robe, sipping from a flute of champagne.

What can I say? Different people have different fears, some less rational than others. And when it comes to scary movies, I prefer the slightly older ones, say from the sixties to the very early eighties, which just seem more serious and moody than today's horror flicks. I can only get truly freaked out (and isn't that the point?) when I'm watching a horror movie with a serious drama just beneath the surface. To me, movies like **Scream** and **I Know What You Did Last Summer** are more like fair-to-middling comedies—how can people get scared while watching teen superstars like Brandy or Jennifer Love Hewitt!?

10 MOVIES WITH AMAZING CINEMATOGRAPHY

Baraka
Blue Velvet
Dead Man
Akira Kurusawa's *Dreams*
Gone with the Wind
Lawrence of Arabia
Like Water for Chocolate
Portrait of a Lady
Saving Private Ryan
Touch of Evil

So, if you're like me and you need a really creepy story to set the mood, I have three older movies that you should check out: **Don't Look Now** (dir. Nicolas Roeg, 1973), **The Changeling** (dir. Peter Medak, 1980), and **Rosemary's Baby** (dir. Roman Polanski, 1968).

Don't Look Now is a real find. Nicolas Roeg was a cinematographer before becoming a director (among other things, he shot **Fahrenheit 451** for François Truffaut), and his skill shows itself in this original and compelling movie starring Julie Christie and Donald Sutherland, as a couple whose daughter has recently drowned.

The film's opening is amazing: With cross-cuts between the man and wife working indoors, and the son and daughter playing outdoors, Roeg shows us synchronous events, matching colors, and simultaneous gestures among the four family members. The husband, John, abruptly stands up and runs outside at the moment that we see the girl in a bright red coat submerged and still. It's as if he knows. In this one scene, Roeg shows us things, like puzzle pieces, that we follow throughout the movie, like a red coat, broken glass, water, religious iconography—and he plants the idea of a second sense, one of my favorite scary elements!

What is most fascinating to me about **Don't Look Now** is the way it unfolds. We are left wondering not only whether people can see things about people, and events before they happen, but whether they can somehow cause the events to happen.

The Changeling is more of a traditional horror story, involving a composer named John Russell (George C. Scott), whose wife and daughter have recently died in a horrible accident while on a road trip near their home in New York City. Seeking to escape his misery, Russell accepts a teaching position and moves across the country to the Pacific Northwest. Specifically, he moves into a huge mansion, which has been unoccupied for years (hel-LO?! Houses like that are unoccupied for a reason!). Even though it's pretty obvious, while you're watching the film, that the house will be haunted and Russell will be tormented by some presence, the ways in which the spirit makes itself known are bone-chilling.

As John Russell, George C. Scott completely captures the essence of a man who has lost everything that is important to him. because of this, he does not immediately run screaming in the street, like I would, when he realizes that he is not alone in the house. Instead, he investigates. Along with Claire Norman (Trish Van Devere), the woman from the town historical society who rented the house to him in the first place, he gathers information about the previous inhabitants of the house, one of whom was a small wheelchair-bound child.

Do not, I repeat, DO NOT watch **The Changeling** alone. I watched it with my best friend, lights out, in my new apartment. I was not yet familiar with the little noises that every apartment makes—the heat turning on, the little clock on the stove. The only way to describe my post-**Changeling** behavior is skittish. Worse yet, my friend who claimed that he would not get scared, was looking a little iffy himself.

In **Rosemary's Baby**, we are treated to a deliciously torturous waiting game, as we observe the pregnancy of Rosemary Wood (Mia Farrow). The entire movie is basically about waiting. We know something is wrong, from Rosemary's "dreams" (or are they real?), her husband Guy's (John Cassavetes) increasingly distant and cruel behavior, the freak show that is their neighbors Roman and Minnie Castavetes (Sydney Blackman and Ruth Gordon), and the unconventional prenatal care that Rosemary's receives, including some Satan's Smoothies that Minnie Castavetes brews—I mean, blends—for her.

The most amazing thing about this film is how undated it is compared to many movies made in the sixties and seventies, and even the eighties. **Rosemary's Baby** is brilliant in so many different ways; not the least of which, as Andrea pointed out to me, is its implication that your greatest danger may be the people you're the closest to. Creepy! Then there's Mia Farrow's Rosemary, who looks more and more disgusting as the weeks go by. Now, I know pregnancy can be difficult, but we're talking about someone who looks permanently gray and pasty, has dark circles under her eyes, eats a practically raw steak and some chicken livers, sits around clutching her stomach most of the time, and is losing weight.

Also, there's nothing like a good anagram, huh? After you watch this movie, you will definitely be dumping Scrabble squares on the floor and trying to see what the letters in your neighbor's name really spell. By the time Rosemary, whose baby is due that very week, starts talking to herself in a phone booth ("All of them. All of them. All in it together"), I was a bundle of paranoia. In fact, this is the only movie that I could not finish at night. I had to wait until the next morning while getting ready for work, when things seemed safe. (And I've seen it many times!)

Over the years I have discovered that everyone I know has some weird fear, from fear of being bitten by a rat to fear of the year 2000 (oh, wait, those are both me, too). Even Clare, Fearless Flier of the Friendly Skies, sometimes calls me after she's had a superscary nightmare. Unfortunately, some people seem to have an unfounded fear of movies made before 1985. If you are one of these people, I urge you to face your fears and check out these films. You may not know all the actors and directors, but if you are looking for a good scare, you won't be disappointed.

ALL I REALLY NEED TO KNOW ABOUT LIFE I LEARNED FROM WATCHING *HALLOWEEN*

By Andrea

Clare's obsessed with her Beelzebub watch and Lise needs to go back two decades to find something that scares her. What is wrong with this picture? Don't these girls know that the world is filled with ax murderers, that madmen are lurking in closets with hunting knives as we speak? That we should all be at the ready, armed with the knowledge garnered by studying the methods of the mass murderers who walk among us?!

Sheesh.

Well, what do they know, anyway? They haven't been researching this for as long as I have.

The year I turned eleven, the research began. That was the year my two best friends and I entered in to our very own twilight zone. Every Friday, like three zombies, Kate, Bev, and I would head for the local video store, Video Vault, where the clerks would put plastic bags on top of their heads and try to sell them to us as "hats." We wouldn't buy the, ahem, hats, but we would rent scads of horror movies.

We started with the classics of the genre, such as the killer who stalks nubile baby-sitters in **Halloween** (dir. John Carpenter, 1978) and the killer who stalks nubile camp counselors in **Friday the 13th** (dir. Sean S. Cunningham, 1980), but soon we'd exhausted the quality picks and were delving into the lowest caliber fare. We saw **Happy Birthday to Me** (dir. J. Lee Thompson, 1981), featuring Melissa Sue Anderson from "Little House on the Prairie" as a girl flipping out after an accident. In this cinematic masterpiece, one guy gets butchered while lifting weights, and someone else gets a shish kebab stick rammed down his throat. We gaped at **Maniac** (dir. William Lustig, 1980), about a psychotic killer who scalps his victims. By the by, we innocent little girls, the apples of our parents' eyes, were particularly excited to read on the box that the flick carried an "X" rating because of the level of gore. Woo-hoo!

One particularly horrifying film ended with such a turboscare that Kate opened her mouth to scream, but no sound came out. I had to slap her (lightly, okay?) on the cheek to get her breathing again. As we gasped for air, shaking from shock, we looked around for Bev, only to find that she was buried under the covers, screaming for help.

Since these experiences sound so pleasurable, I know you won't be surprised to learn that we spent the next two years scaring ourselves silly, and many years after that wrestling with our wildly overactive imaginations (a trait Clare and I share) and our fears of a very strong, very psychotic killer lurking in the shadows (a trait Clare and I don't share—she's way more concerned with ghosts and spirits). I was permanently scarred. We were all permanently scarred.

I grew older. I started to breathe easy, no longer as confident as I once was that every noise was someone clawing at the walls with his razor nails, à la Freddy Krueger. I began to sleep well again.

AN ABSURD PLOTLINE

LISE: *Child's Play.* "I'm Chuckie, wanna play?" No, go away, freak.

SIBYL: *Tremors.* Killer worms. Yeah, right.

ANDREA: I'm going with the crazed green Irish imp plotline of *Leprechaun.*

CLARE: I laughed so hard I nearly vomited when Andrea and I watched *Phantasm,* with those little dwarf dudes running around and that ball that sucks people's brains out.

And I thought to myself that maybe everything was going to be okay.

As if they were a dim, distant, shameful part of my past, I discontinued my research, and stayed away from these slasher flicks for a very long time—until I was handed the assignment to review **Scream** (dir. Wes Craven, 1996) for Girls on Film. "Why not?" I thought. "This looks fun, and besides, I'm not that little girl anymore. I can face my fears."

I went solo to see **Scream**, and I left the screening room in shock. How could I ever have turned away from these movies? This wasn't some weird childhood obsession with scaring myself in order to work out preadolescent angst. Oh, no, I was just preternaturally aware at a young age of the threats out there, and what I had to do to protect myself. By gum, these films are the only known way we have to learn the customs of the serial killer (similar to the way you need to watch a Dracula movie to find out the key points about the garlic/crucifix/vampire-can't-come-in-unless-you-invite-him-in stuff). There's a method to the serial killer's madness, and the best place to learn that method is in the movies.

Halloween is probably the most apt serial-killer/crazy-maniac handbook. If you study only one film for your own research, it should be this one, and then you're good to go. Scoff not. If you want to safeguard yourself and your loved ones from pure evil (Clare, you can defend yourself! Never fear!), then you'd better bone up. What did I learn from **Halloween**? What can I impart to you?

First of all, it is important to note, as Laurie (Jamie Lee Curtis) does in **Halloween**, that there is, in fact, a bogeyman. This is important. As your mother might have said, if you ignore the realities of life, life is going to bite you in the ass. Actually, she probably didn't say that. But I did. If you ignore the threat of the killer, then it is very likely that the killer will come after you first because you're such a chumpola. Remember in **Scream** how they kept saying you should never yell out "I'll be right back" as you walk backwards in to a dark room? Well, point taken!

(Oh, I know, the other point is that **Scream** made fun of all these little serial killer rules, which is fine if you're some hipster snark wiseass, but honestly, I think it's really dumb, because hubris = asking for it. But enough about that.)

Second, the bogeyman is very strong, very clever, and surprisingly resilient. He is hard to kill, and even if you kill him, he comes back from the dead somehow by sheer force of his evilness. Michael Myers, the young chap who stalks Laurie throughout **Halloween**, gets poked in the neck with a knitting needle, stabbed in the eye with a coat hanger, and shot. Repeatedly. With a gun. Yet still he lives. Lesson here: It's good to be prepared at all times to go toe-to-toe with a very strong person. Travel in crews. Pack heat. Carry around knitting needles, rope, perhaps a dash of arsenic. Take karate lessons. Kick ass like Buffy the Vampire Slayer.

Third, said killer likes young, attractive people. So try to age as ungracefully as possible so he'll steer clear of you. Don't even try to ward him off with a wacky hat or a Twisted Sister T-shirt—you gotta go whole hog. You have to look awful. Sadly, even our society's serial killers have tweaked views of beauty and body image. Sigh. Skip the lipstick, work on your ability to nail people with a croquet mallet instead.

What else can I offer you? Oh, nothing fancy. Stay alert at all times, don't sleep, do not have sex, and for the love of all that is holy, don't ever play "(Don't Fear) the Reaper" by Blue Oyster Cult. You know, the usual sensible precautions.

No need to worry, it's just that the warning bell of the dawning of the apocalypse is ringing, and if you don't listen to it, you'll be sorry. Remain calm, rent **Halloween**, and don't forget to take notes.

I AM A BIG WUSS

By Sibyl

Well, Andrea, I'm not going to be renting **Halloween** any time soon, so I guess I can't take notes. I prefer to keep my head in the sand as far as this whole demon/serial-killer thing goes.

Because Sibyl the Wuss is my name, and fear is not my game.

It's not easy being a wuss; let me tell you, I know. I've always been a lightweight when it comes to scary movies. Partly I've got Mom to thank for that; she definitely didn't encourage scary movie-viewing. As a child I was sheltered; I don't think I even knew what a scary movie was until I saw **Bambi**.

Yeah, I know, **Bambi** isn't what we consider a traditional scary movie, but come on, when Bambi's mom dies, and there's the forest fire, and the hunters? I was inconsolable after seeing that movie. Crying. Wailing. Covering my eyes. To me, that's a scary movie.

Perhaps Mom realized then that she had a rather sensitive child on her hands. So I blissfully grew up seeing musicals, **The Bad News Bears**, and classics like **The Black Stallion**. No scary movies for me. Until the inevitable happened: No man, woman, or child can avoid **The Wizard of Oz**.

Mom was out that night when the baby-sitter joined me in front of the TV for the annual broadcast of **Oz**. Yowza, that's a scary movie. A nice girl and her dog swept up in nightmares, tornadoes, singing midgets, witches bad and good, and creepy-looking men suited up in funny costumes singing and dancing? And as if that weren't scary enough, how can a child cope with those freaky flying monkeys? I get chills just thinking about them now.

I don't know whether that baby-sitter got the ax, though I kind of doubt it; in my house, it was considered important that we learn how to deal with all sorts of things. But how do you deal with flying monkeys and cackling women riding by your window on a flying bike?

I knew then that I didn't like to be scared by movies; it just didn't feel good. But what I didn't know was that lots of weirdos out there do like to be scared, particularly by movies, to the point of screaming, yelling, and going berserk.

Soon enough, though, came that most treacherous time in a girl's life: slumber-party time. In eighth grade, I went to a particularly memorable birthday slumber party. It involved all the usual activities: pizza, soda, too much candy, giggling to the point of massive headaches, and, of course, a movie. With our bowls of ice cream in front of us, we gathered around the TV to watch the movie selected by the birthday girl. I was hoping for **E.T.** or **Grease**. Well, no such luck—her choice was **Poltergeist** (dir. Tobe Hooper, 1982).

You can imagine my shock as I watched, terrified but somehow peer-pressured into gaping, horrified, at the screen along with everyone else. **Poltergeist** is terrifying, with that little blond kid disappearing into the television, and that pool filling with gross gunk. Sure, it's also a clever, fairly high-end horror flick, but at twelve, it really spooked me. Everyone screamed and giggled

PHEW! IT'S NOT AS SCARY AS WHEN I WAS A KID

LISE: *Willy Wonka & the Chocolate Factory.* It's still kinda scary though, right?

SIBYL: *Fantasia*—Remember how scary those dancing brooms were?

ANDREA: *The Amityville Horror.* The only thing scary was waiting around expecting to be frightened for an entire film.

CLARE: For some reason, just the idea of H. G. Wells's *The Invisible Man* scared the crap out of me when I was little—and I didn't even see it!

and ate ice cream, and they all seemed totally into it. That's the thrill, I guess—everyone enjoys that adrenaline rush of fright and fear. Except for me; I didn't like that feeling at all. I didn't sleep much that night, huddled up in my sleeping bag, afraid I'd have a nightmare.

All these years later, not much has changed. I am a horror movie lightweight. Here I am, an adult, and a huge movie buff at that, gingerly sticking my toe into the pool of horror movies. Andrea and Clare put me to shame with their vast knowledge of the genre. And I'm amazed by the pleasure they take in viewing these shriekfest flicks. I have seen a few scary flicks on their recommendation: **Scream**, **Scream 2**, and the whole Hitchcock oeuvre (which, to me, are more like thrillers, not gross, scary movies). Those were all good choices, not too scary.

But because I'm such rube when it comes to these flicks, I don't know how to act while watching them. I blurt out things like, "Don't open that door!" I hide my eyes behind the sleeve of my shirt. I grab the knee, hand, arm, or whatever I can reach of the person sitting next to me. I'm an embarrassment to any seasoned scary-movie viewer. I think Clare nearly slapped me when we watched **Kiss the Girls** together; that wasn't even a very good movie, but it was too scary for me.

Not all genres work for all people, and I think the key is to know yourself. I know that **The Silence of the Lambs** (which, as Lise mentioned, I saw with her) was probably as scary a movie as I'll ever see. I know that I'll probably never see horror classics like **The Exorcist** or **Halloween**. But that's okay. At least I have come to enjoy **The Wizard of Oz**, finally getting over the creepy monkeys and embracing its Technicolor genius.

I do know myself, and I'm proud to be a wuss.

25 Scary Movies to Rent!

1 **ARMY OF DARKNESS** (dir. Sam Raimi, 1992) It could be argued that this third installment in the *Evil Dead* series belongs as much in the comedy section as it does here, but the gore is graphic and there are enough dead people around to warrant its appearance on Ye Olde Scary Movie Liste. The plot's got something to do with the past, the future, and a whole lot of skeletons. Very fun.

2 **BLOW OUT** (dir. Brian De Palma, 1981) This thriller stars John Travolta as a sound technician who becomes embroiled in a conspiracy theory with a serial-killer plot. Lots about voyeurism and some clever spoofing of typical slasher flicks add a level of intelligence to the proceedings, as do smart performances from a creepy John Lithgow and a ditzy Nancy Allen.

3 **DON'T LOOK NOW** (dir. Nicolas Roeg, 1973) In order to recover from the shock their young daughter's death by drowning, a couple (Julie Christie and Donald Sutherland) go to Venice. But this beautiful and peaceful city here takes on an eerie, lonely quality, and the entire film becomes one long "what's about to happen next?" tension-builder. Interesting, moody, and well shot, this flick has the added bonus of a sex scene consistently listed by critics as one of the most erotic ever filmed.

4 **THE EXORCIST** (dir. William Friedkin, 1973) Directed by William Friedkin (*The French Connection*), this is arguably the best, scariest movie in the whole world (according to Clare); it swept both the People's Choice Awards and the Oscars in 1974. Linda Blair (Best Supporting Actress) plays a little girl possessed by the King of Darkness Himself. And use your frame-by-frame on that remote to catch the (eek!) death mask on a single frame, flashed right after the head-turning scene!

5 **THE FLY** (dir. David Cronenberg, 1986) Jeff Goldblum gives one of his best performances ever in this grossfest by the Master of Gross, David Cronenberg. A remake of the 1951 movie starring Vincent

Price, *The Fly* is about a scientist (Goldblum) who accidentally combines his DNA with that of a fly. Soon he's shedding various body parts, vomiting on his donuts to predigest them, and causing all sorts of grief for his sweet girlfriend (Geena Davis). Eww.

6 **FRIDAY THE 13TH** (dir. Sean S. Cunningham, 1980) Though it spawned a whole mess of dopey sequels (*Jason Schleps to Manhattan*? Come on!), this first in the series is still well worth watching. The gory, sex-and-carnage-at-a-sleepaway-camp slasher flick scarred just about everyone under forty—particularly with the jerky, killer's-point-of-view camera work, spooky, whispery soundtrack, and, whoa, that ending.

7 **HALLOWEEN** (dir. John Carpenter, 1978) This classic horror flick is chilling from start to finish, though we think the eeriest part is the freaky music, which director John Carpenter wrote himself. Of course, watching the mask-wearing, zombielike madman stalk a peaceful neighborhood ain't no walk in the park, either. It made teen star Jamie Lee Curtis's career, as well it should have.

8 **INVASION OF THE BODY SNATCHERS** (dir. Philip Kaufman, 1978) Foliage never looked so grotesque as in this "X-Files"-esque remake of the 1956 classic, where aliens attempt to take over San Francisco. Donald Sutherland plays a sensitive, New Age city health inspector who's one of the few people who seems to know something isn't right in the Bay Area.

9 **JACOB'S LADDER** (dir. Adrian Lyne, 1990) Tim Robbins plays a just-returned Vietnam vet slowly becoming unhinged—or is he being driven insane by sinister forces? It's paranoid, it's bizarre, it's extremely confusing. Unlike many horror flicks, it's also got great acting—from both Robbins and Elizabeth Pena, as his devoted but demonic-seeming girlfriend.

10 **JAWS** (dir. Steven Spielberg, 1975) *Chomp!* What a brilliant flick! A great white eats its way through the summer tourists on a small beach town. Turns out that all the cool film-trick stuff we gave Spielberg credit for, like hiding the shark and only showing us peeks for the first half of the film, wasn't genius so much as his working

around the lousy, low-budget f/x. Still, it's so scary you might not bathe, let alone swim, for years afterward.

11 **THE KINGDOM** (dir. Lars von Trier, 1995) This five-hour film originated as a TV series in Denmark, the home country of its director, Lars von Trier (*Breaking the Waves*). It's like "ER" on acid: Doctors and patients in a huge hospital (The Kingdom) deal with disease, incompetence, and ghostly spirits that just won't go away. Narrated by two Downs Syndrome–savant dishwashers, *The Kingdom* is both hilarious and incredibly creepy.

12 **NATURAL BORN KILLERS** (dir. Oliver Stone, 1994) Dark portrait of cultural infatuation with murder and mayhem. Woody Harrelson and Juliette Lewis are psychokiller newlyweds on a murdering rampage. It's hard to say what's more nauseating: the bloodshed, Harrelson and Lewis's creepy performances, or Stone's kinetic, jumpy, bad-acid-trip camera work and editing. Definitely terrifying (particularly the prison scenes and flashbacks), sometimes effective, this critique of the glorification of violence is certainly riveting.

13 **NEAR DARK** (dir. Kathryn Bigelow, 1987) This hip vampire-Western is sharply made and well-acted (a pre-*Titanic* Bill Paxton is a particularly passionate vampire named Severen, and the fine Lance Henriksen plays the leader of the pack). Best of all, it's further proof (as if any were needed!) of the greatness of one of our fave directors, Bigelow.

14 **NIGHT OF THE HUNTER** (dir. Charles Laughton, 1955) Robert Mitchum (*Cape Fear*) turns in yet another suburb performance as a preacher with not God but greed and murder in his heart. Spike Lee borrowed the cool hand-tattoo sequence for his own masterpiece *Do the Right Thing*. An eye-opener for anyone who thinks movies weren't scary way back when.

15 **NIGHTMARE ON ELM STREET** (dir. Wes Craven, 1984) Though it's dated (where did Johnny Depp get that midriff-baring crop top?), it's still such a smart concept: a killer, the evil, razor-fingered Freddy Krueger, strikes young people during their dreams. Talk about your worst nightmare.

16 **THE OMEN** (dir. Richard Donner, 1976) Something's amiss in the Thorn household: Little boy Damien doesn't play nice, and his long-suffering parents (Lee Remick, Gregory Peck) can't understand why. When the young boy mows his mother down in his tricycle, we finally know for sure that this kid can be no one other than Satan's son, prodigy of Beelzebub. Who will take Damien down? The answer, of course, is no one: *The Omen II* and *The Omen III* are soon to follow.

17 **POLTERGEIST** (dir. Tobe Hooper, 1982) The scariest thing about this ghost story, directed by the guy who brought us *The Texas Chainsaw Massacre* and written by Steven Spielberg, is that it's rated PG and we all saw it sans adult supervision. This flick, about a spirit that grabs a sweet little five-year-old girl through the TV, is full of smart touches that stay with you, like the creepy clown under the child's bed and the piece of steak that crawls across a countertop. Eek!

18 **PSYCHO** (dir. Alfred Hitchcock, 1960) This is the definitive slasher flick, one that changed the way films are made. Director Hitchcock just went nuts with this creepy, Oedipal tale of murder at the lonely Bates Motel. Anthony Perkins turns in a brilliant perfor-mance, which he reprised in three sequels. Oh, and for the fun of it, check out Gus Van Sant's 1998 *Psycho* remake, and see if you can catch the few spots where the two versions differ.

19 **ROSEMARY'S BABY** (dir. Roman Polanski, 1968) Just because you're paranoid doesn't mean they're not out to get you, kids. Mia Farrow, all waiflike and pregnant and innocent, is married to John Cassavetes (a great director in his own right), an ambitious business-man. Oh, and Mia's carrying around the Antichrist in her womb. Chilling beyond belief.

20 **SCREAM** (dir. Wes Craven, 1996) Director Craven and screen-writer Kevin Williamson turn horror film convention on its head with this witty, scary teen slasher film that mocks all those hokey tropes we'd gotten so used to (and so bored by!). Nice acting from stars Neve Campbell, Skeet Ulrich, David Arquette, and others.

Single-handedly revitalized the teen slasher genre, long dormant after too many sequels and too few original ideas.

21 **SEVEN** (dir. David Fincher, 1995) Beautifully shot and incredibly well edited, *Seven* refers to a twisted killer striking people who have committed one of the seven deadly sins. Brad Pitt and Morgan Freeman are police officers investigating the crimes, Gwyneth Paltrow plays Pitt's lovely and loving wife. It also sports an opening title sequence so slick it's shown in art-school classes around the world.

22 **THE SHINING** (dir. Stanley Kubrick, 1980) A Stephen King adaptation that gets it so right. Jack Nicholson plays a writer who takes on the job of caretaker for a freaky hotel during the off-season, and he brings with him his family and, oh, yeah, his burgeoning psychosis. All work and no play makes Jack a dull boy.

23 **THE SILENCE OF THE LAMBS** (dir. Jonathan Demme, 1991) Jodie Foster and Anthony Hopkins both won Oscars for their roles in this film. Foster is a highly motivated FBI agent who's been assigned the task of interviewing Hopkins, a serial killer named Hannibal "the Cannibal" Lecter, who may hold clues to a string of murders taking place. Incredibly tense and well-made, though it can take the edge off if you hear Clare do her funny imitation of the killer's voice.

24 **THE STEPFATHER** (dir. Joseph Ruben, 1987) He looks like the pappy next door, Terry O'Quinn does, but he's the furthest thing from a nice or normal guy. Nope, like a black widow, this guy mates and he kills, always searching for the next family to become a part of. Creepiest of all: Only the teenage stepdaughter seems to know who he really is, and let's be honest, since when has anyone ever believed a teenager in a horror film?

25 **THE VANISHING** (dir. George Sluizer, 1988) This Dutch film is a great example of the "less is more" rule—tension builds slowly in this tale about a man who spends all his time hunting for his missing wife. There's barely any gore or violence, but it's chilling and scary nonetheless. Skip the 1993 American remake (also directed by Sluizer) and get this version instead.

6 TEARJERKERS:
Truly Moving Moving Pictures

Catharsis is an emotional cleansing. You've been sucked into a story, sympathized with the characters, bawled your eyes out, and basically joined the ranks of the human. The ancient Greek playwrights hoped to bring about catharsis in their tragedies; they wanted the audience to "suffer into truth"—truth being, naturally, that the human condition basically sucks, that life is pain, et cetera. Aristotle liked catharsis. Of course, Aristotle also liked plays about men who sleep with their mothers and gouge out their own eyes, or women who hack their husbands to death—but, hey. To each his own.

Movies have been jerking our tears ever since they were born. Whether it's through the bleak tragedy of **Sophie's Choice**, the tragicomedy of **Terms of Endearment**, the sentimental joy of **E.T., The Extra-Terrestrial**, or the touching triumph of **Rocky** ("Adrienne! I did it!"), all of these films make us cry in slightly different ways. Crying at the movies has become a national pastime.

Especially—but not exclusively—for women. (Most guys who want to cry have to do it during a manly flick like **Cinema Paradiso**, and then go to their therapy group in the woods and bang on drums and have other men tell them it's okay.)

Some people like to cry at the movies; others balk at such naked manipulation, or complain that if they wanted "reality," they'd have walked out their front door. Some people simply can't take it—after seeing **The Champ**, in which a young Ricky Schroder cries over his father's dead body for approximately one full hour, begging him to wake up, our young Andrea said she sat on the curb outside of the movie theater and cried and cried, until her father finally coaxed her little despondent self into the car. And Sibyl says she cried so much during **Longtime Companion** that the front of her white shirt was soaked with tears.

But for the most part, it seems that crying is cathartic. For a brief moment, you, like President Clinton (squeezing back tears), "feel their pain." Whether you like it or not,

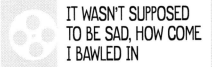

IT WASN'T SUPPOSED TO BE SAD, HOW COME I BAWLED IN

LISE: *Fly Away Home*, when cute-as-a-button Anna Paquin is flying in her homemade plane and the little geese are following her.

SIBYL: *Sixteen Candles*. At the end when the cute guy picks Molly up from her sister's wedding. Kleenex, please.

ANDREA: *The Nutty Professor* with Eddie Murphy. I felt so sad for his sweet, lonely character that I spent the film weeping instead of laughing like I was supposed to.

CLARE: I didn't bawl exactly, but I felt so, so bad for the misfit characters sitting at a table together in *The Wedding Singer* that Adam Sandler's character picks on; I thought that was really mean.

you've recognized something in these characters that resonates, be it through death, war, unrequited love, love that cannot be, or love that conquers all. Now, if there is to be one Master of the Tearjerker, it's got to be Steven Spielberg. Who didn't cry during **The Color Purple**, when Shug comes down the aisle of the church, singing to her estranged father? Or at the end of **Empire of the Sun**, when the boy (Christian Bale) is finally reunited with his mother after being trapped alone in a Japanese detention camp for two years? Who didn't need serious emotional support after Liam Neeson's heartbreaking scene in **Schindler's List**, when he rues the fact that he didn't save enough lives? Or especially after the actors walk down the hill with the real-life survivors and put rocks on the graves of the dead? Oh, help us!

Which brings us to a surefire method in tearjerkers. Attention, filmmakers: If you want to make someone cry—we mean, really open up those waterworks—how about just bringing back all those dead people for a reunion at the end? Works every time. That's why **Longtime Companion** had Lise so destroyed—that scene at the end, when all the friends who've died of AIDS come walking on the beach. The music is playing, you can't hear them talking, but they're all greeting each other, touching hands, hugging—ack. Gives us chills just thinking about it. Or the end scene in **Titanic**, when all the dead people come walking down the grand staircase in their finery—Andrea practically had to join a self-help group after that one.

Another classic bring-em-all-together-one-last-time scene was at the end of **Places in the Heart** (dir. Robert Benton, 1984). Sally Field plays a Depression-era policeman's wife in Texas whose husband is tragically (and accidentally) killed by a black teenager; she spends the rest of the movie trying to save her house from foreclosure by trying to grow cotton on her land. She takes in a blind boarder (John Malkovich) and hires a black man named Moses to help (Danny Glover), much to the ire of her local Klansmen. After all of this sad, sad stuff goes down—death and tornadoes and KKK attacks and Moses being forced to escape in the night—there's a final scene in her (segregated) church. At the end of the aisle we see Moses, returned; then we see her two children, then her. Then the camera pans to her left, revealing not only her dead husband, but the young black teenager, who was lynched. Clare remembers sitting and blubbering long after that film was over—the whole idea of a reunion after death is both sad and hopeful, looking towards a future when people can come together once again and be happy. Egad.

Of course, there's true human tragedy, and then there are the "tearsploitation" films, the ones during which you feel embarrassed to be crying, but you do it anyway. Like when you find yourself crying during a Hallmark commercial—pure, unadulterated sentimentality. **Steel Magnolias** has got to be one of those films: The characters are pure stereotype, the jokes are ridiculous, and yet the idea of a daughter (Julia Roberts) dying before her mother (Sally Field—again) is just wrong, a tragedy that strikes at the heart of every hormonally imbalanced person on the planet. The scene at the graveyard is a killer: Sally Field just won't stop crying. And crying, like laughter, is contagious: If somebody on-screen bawls for long enough, surely (unless you are made of stone), you will cry, too.

But the best kind of cry is the uplifting one. Sure, **The Killing Fields** (dir. Roland Joffe, 1984) left us devastated, but the end finds the two friends together again. One friend, American reporter Sydney Schanberg (Sam Waterston), had left the other, Cambodian reporter Dith Pran (Dr. Haing S. Ngor), to fend for himself in Cambodia after the Khmer Rouge started slaughtering everyone and putting them in Communist "re-education" camps. Pran witnessed countless atrocities and barely made it out alive; back in the States, Sydney won a Pulitzer for his coverage. When they're finally reunited, Sydney begs Pran to forgive him, and Pran says through tears, "There is nothing to forgive." They hug. "Imagine," by John Lennon, plays. We cry and cry and cry.

But why do we want to cry? Maybe it makes us feel better about our lives (Hey, no one I know is dead!). Maybe it makes us feel worse (What's the point?), and we like to wallow in it. Or maybe it makes us want to enjoy ourselves and our loved ones before it all gets snatched away. (As it most certainly will.)

Maybe what all these films get at is that the human condition, however painful, is one we share with everybody else. Clare and Sibyl were a little embarrassed to cry during **City of Angels** (dir. Brad Silberling, 1998), but then they saw a woman in the lobby after the film, weeping inconsolably, waiting for her boyfriend to come out of the men's room. When you see a fellow audience member losing it like that, it not only bonds you with them, it makes you think you may not have it so bad. It makes you want to help out somehow. You know, join the Peace Corps or something. Become a doctor. Help others. Of course, that fades, but it's nice while it lasts.

CRY ME A RIVER

By Clare

Some people just have a higher pain threshold than others. Now, I'm not bragging, mind you. I'm not proud of my inborn ability to watch hours and hours of other people's suffering on celluloid, but there it is. Take **Sophie's Choice** (dir. Alan Pakula, 1982), about a Holocaust survivor (Meryl Streep), her star-crossed lover (Kevin

Kline), a young writer (Peter MacNicol, now relegated to "Ally McBeal"), death, despair, and tragedy. I've seen this movie at least ten times, and I'd see it again in a heartbeat. Or **Midnight Cowboy** (dir. John Schlesinger, 1969), another longtime favorite of mine. For these two New York losers (Dustin Hoffman, Jon Voight), things just go from bad to worse. And I've seen *that* one about five times.

I was urging Andrea the other day to watch David Lynch's bleak, haunting, black-and-white masterpiece **The Elephant Man** (1980). Andrea asked what it was about—a simple request. I told her that, for one, it was based on a true story about a man in Victorian England whose body is covered in tumors so massive that they make a normal life impossible.

THE MOVIE I WANT TO LIVE IN IS

LISE: I'd like to live in *Strictly Ballroom*. Alas, I can't dance, so I should probably just stay right where I am, sitting at a computer. Sigh.

SIBYL: *Chariots of Fire*. Love the costumes, the champagne-drinking, the all-white running outfits, the Gilbert and Sullivan.

ANDREA: *Everyone Says I Love You*. This frothy Woody Allen comedy shows a Manhattan so idealized that it made me want to live there, instead of in the Manhattan I currently reside in.

CLARE: *Out of Africa*. Everything just looks so rough and wild and beautiful, and the people are all rich enough to not have to do much.

"No!" She drew back in horror. Oh, but yes. *And* his beloved mother died when he was just a boy. *And* he's been a *circus freak* his whole life, where he's been treated like an animal.

By this time, she was begging me to please, stop! But no. I continued, relentless, even telling her the part of the movie that gets me the most weepy. Dr. Frederick Treves (Anthony Hopkins!

Sigh!) takes an interest in the "elephant man," John Merrick (John Hurt! So good!), but thinks he's mentally, um, deficient. In an effort to convince his hospital director (Geez! John Gielgud! The hits keep coming!) to let Mr. Merrick stay in one of the rooms, Treves coaches Merrick, teaching him hello's and how-do-you-dos and even the Twenty-third Psalm. At the interview, Merrick fails miserably, and the director has just taken the doctor out into the hall when they hear Merrick, desperate, raising his voice, continuing on with the psalm. Suddenly, the doctor says, "Wait. I didn't teach him that part." (Chills.) Needless to say, Merrick is not only hideously deformed, abused, and maligned—but he hasn't even had the luck not to know it. He's an intelligent, sensitive man trapped in the body of a sideshow freak, eating maggoty potatoes for dinner and sleeping in a cage. His head is so huge that he has to sleep sitting up for fear of crushing his larynx if he lies down.

By this point, Andrea was clutching at her chest, muttering, "Ack! Ack!" She decided that she never wanted to see this movie. She asked me how it ended. I told her. I thought I was going to have to call 911.

What can I say? I'm morbid. I like to dwell on the awful and the treacherous. But I also like love, redemption, laughter-through-tears, choral music, and E.T. And I can get it all in just a few of the following flicks. Rent 'em and weep.

The lightest of my movie selections today is also the one I happened to cut my teeth on: **Ordinary People** (dir. Robert Redford). This movie was woven into the very fabric of my family life, as was a collective fear and loathing of New Yorker film critic Pauline Kael for tearing it to shreds when it opened in 1980. Her complaint: The film, about an upper-middle-class Chicago family coping with the accidental death of one son and the attempted suicide of the other soon after, was too dismal, grim, and obvious.

Dismal, grim, and obvious, you say? Why, thank you, I'll take that.

From the very open of **Ordinary People**, we're brought into an austere, somber place. The titles, white letters on a black background, flash in silence. Gradually, the black turns to dark blue as we hear the first piano notes of Pachelbel's Canon in D Major. Then the blue turns into the horizon of Lake Michigan, then cuts to a shot of a single bird swooping down to the water by the dock, then to a shot of fall leaves piled up on an isolated road. Finally, the tones of the piano turn into choral music, and we see Conrad (Timothy Hutton) singing in his school choir.

When he wakes up gasping from a nightmare in the very next shot, we know the poor guy is troubled. His father Calvin (Donald Sutherland), a kindly, absentminded tax attorney, desperately searches his son's face for signs of recovery. His mother Beth (Mary Tyler Moore) prattles on about her golf game and tries to pretend that nothing is wrong. Conrad finally seeks the help of a psychiatrist, Dr. Burger (Judd Hirsch), who mostly seems to make him feel uncomfortable.

Watching this movie as a young girl and then as a teenager, I certainly identified with Conrad, who, underneath it all, just wants to get better, score a date with a sweet, pretty girl (Elizabeth McGovern), and forgive himself and others for the past. When I watched it again for this book, I was surprised that the movie stood the test of time; other than the eighties styling, nothing about it seemed corny or irrelevant to me.

Redford, who won Best Director and Best Picture for **Ordinary People**, did a beautiful job with the actors (Hutton and Hirsch competed at the Oscars for Best Supporting Actor), the editing (complete with those ever-dicey, potentially cheesy flashback scenes), and the music (love that Pachelbel—me and every schlub who made a commercial five years hence).

Of course, the flick made me cry. We've got a dramatically unfolding story, tragic deaths, a blowout revelation in a psychiatrist's office, missed opportunities, forgiveness, failure, and of course, love. The last words of the movie are "I love you, Dad," and by the time they come, they're a welcome relief. Sniffle, whimper.

Usually, though, I tend toward the more heroically tragic in my search for the cathartic movie cry. You know, heroic and tragic in the true sense: characters doomed at the outset, a fatal flaw, lots of death (especially at the end), and ever-present Fate, frowning and frowning upon these people for reasons we can't quite comprehend. A historic backdrop helps give the tragedy weight, as does a sociopolitical agenda. When I watch movies this huge and sweeping, I am caught up not only in the characters, but in the issues: racism, classicism, lack of a clear moral structure, man's inhumanity to man, man's inability to cope with a hostile and unbending environment.

I think 1995's **Cry, the Beloved Country** (dir. Darrell James Roodt) covers just about all of those bases. Sibyl recently noted my weakness for films depicting the struggle against apartheid in South Africa—**Cry Freedom**, with Kevin Kline and Denzel Washington, and **The Power of One**, with Morgan Freeman and Stephen Dorff, are two others I adore—but this overlooked movie is, for me, the momma of them all.

Based on the 1946 book by Alan Paton, which I also loved, **Cry, the Beloved Country** follows the paths of two older South African men, one black, one white, who coexist for years in the sleepy farming province of Natal, before their respective sons in far away Johannesburg bring them together unexpectedly. James Earl Jones (yeah, I know, the Bell Atlantic spokesman, voice of Darth Vader) plays a poor, pious, old-fashioned *mfundisi*, or minister, at a Christian church, and Richard Harris plays Mr. Jarvis, a wealthy landowner who believes that the races are truly separate but equal.

When the *mfundisi* is summoned to Johannesburg, his journey of sorrow begins. I mean that—the guy does not get one break. The befuddled minister travels to this big, frightening, chaotic city and discovers the sad fates that have befallen his sister, his son, his brother, and his nephew. Meanwhile, urgent business also takes Mr. Jarvis to Johannesburg, where he finds that his son, a champion of civil rights for blacks, has been ashamed of his white heritage (i.e., his parents) and has been trying to set things right.

If you can handle Richard Harris's "ham on rye with extra cheese" performance (which, I swear, is nonetheless moving), the somewhat awkward use of slow motion for effect, and the mannered, almost biblical-sounding dialogue ("Go well, *mfundisi*." "Stay well, my brother."), this movie has a lot to offer, including no fewer than four separate scenes that get my tears a-flowing every time. The title is taken from one of the most beautiful passages in the book, and when it's used in voice-over—while we see black Africans being chased down, beaten, and arrested—it's some powerful stuff. Also powerful is the use of music, especially in a funeral scene during which "Amazing Grace" is sung by Ladysmith Black Mambazo. Oh, dear.

For a more unflinching look at an important social issue, check out **Dead Man Walking** (dir. Tim Robbins, 1995), which we mentioned in our Drama introduction, but which never fails to make me cry like a baby or a heartbroken teenager. Sean Penn, as an unrepentant rapist/murderer on death row, and Susan Sarandon, as the nun who tries to help him, turn in two complex, riveting performances that had me all twisted up with emotion. Robbins also uses terrific music (arranged by his brother), including the spiritual intonations of the late Nusrat Fateh Ali Khan, who sings along with—get this—Eddie Vedder from Pearl Jam.

As Penn's death draws near and he begins to weaken and unravel, we learn about forgiveness and love—and how many hankies it takes to staunch the flow of tears after witnessing capital punishment up close and personal. Thoughtful, effective, and mournful from the outset, **Dead Man Walking** is based on the true story of Sister Helen Prejean, C.S.J., who appears in cameo in the movie and attended the Oscars with Sarandon and Robbins the year the film was released.

You may prefer, like Sibyl, to cry during lighter fare (her favorites are musicals, especially **West Side Story!**), or you may prefer, like Andrea or Lise, not to cry at all. If so, you might be inclined to avoid the movies that I am most attracted to. But if you want a truly moving encounter, you don't need to look any further than the drama that springs from the sadness of true human experience: death, political injustice, and more death. If so, get thee to a video store! If **Sophie's Choice** or **The Elephant Man** are checked out already, you'll know who has them . . .

ONE IS THE LONELIEST NUMBER

By Andrea

On vacation with my friends Jen and Licia on the gorgeous Greek island of Corfu one summer, the conversation took a turn to things that make us sad (Woo-hoo! Fun holiday topic!). Licia and I each found ourselves confessing that we think the most unbearable sight in the world is a man eating solo at a restaurant. We're always positive the guy is lonely and sad. I taught Licia the little mind game I play to cheer myself up if I see a guy eating all alone. I make up a back-story for him. "Oh, he's just spent the day with his family and now he's getting a break from them, reading the paper, having a wonderful time, having a wonderful life. He's sooo happy to be alone right now. Oh, wow, is he ever *happy*!"

When it came time for us to choose what we wanted to write about for this chapter, it took me a while to figure out what really "got" me. The films that blow everyone else away move me just as much, but I can take it (although I'm no Clare, sheesh!). Sure, I cried in **Ordinary People**; good grief, I bawled before, during, and after **Schindler's List**. Oh, and Sibyl, **West Side Story** gets me every time, too. But I'm ready, I'm prepared. I may be moved, but then at least I'm capable of moving on.

It's the films that hold even a hint of loneliness that wreck me the most, and since oftentimes this is only a small aspect of these films, it's hard for me to prepare myself properly. I wind up walking in all unknowing and carefree. Bam! I get taken by surprise, and the pain hits me like a blow to the head. Films about loneliness might be billed as comedies, dramas, or thrillers, but I know better. Even a minor scene of loneliness in a larger, not-so-sad movie, means it's a sad film. Everyone else might be laughing, and there I am, crying all by myself.

MY THOUGHTS ON *TITANIC*

LISE: It sank. Can we stop talking about it now?

SIBYL: Sibyl: I was crying, because I wanted it to end. Sucks.

ANDREA: Cried, saw it twice, endured the mockery of the other Girls. Not ashamed to admit it, either.

CLARE: Some of the corniest, most simplistic dialogue I've ever heard. Gorgeous-looking, though. I cried, and was ashamed.

I still cringe with pain when I think of that scene in **Broadway Danny Rose** (dir. Woody Allen, 1984) when Woody Allen's character (he plays Danny Rose, a talent agent for rather "offbeat" types) has all his misfit clients over for Thanksgiving dinner. I kept wondering if they were as forlorn as they looked, if they'd have anywhere else to go if they weren't with the Wood-ster. Were there people in the world who loved them? That was it for me and that movie—it became tragic and I was truly bummed out by it. Any portrayal of loneliness in any manifestation is what stays with me, haunting me long after the film is over. When I tell friends that I think that movie is sad they always seem shocked by my admission. But sad it was.

Ditto for the thriller **Sea of Love** (dir. Harold Becker, 1989), with Al Pacino playing a hard-drinking police officer investigating a series of brutal murders. There are these woeful moments where he starts to hope again that he might find love, and he seems as nervous as a little kid, unsure of what to do. Sure, people call it a thriller, but really, I saw it as a story of a man alone in the world. In other words, sad.

My first experience understanding the tragedy of loss and loneliness in films definitely started when I saw **The Champ** (dir. Franco Zeffirelli, 1979) for the first time as a little girl. As we mentioned earlier, I couldn't stop crying afterward, not for a very long time. It was one of the most traumatic filmgoing experiences of my life, and it freaked me out to no end. If you haven't sobbed your way through this flick, you are missing out on one of the best all-time cries; I guarantee it will push just about anyone's buttons. Jon Voight plays Billy Flynn, aka "The Champ," a former boxer with a penchant for drinking and gambling who's down on his luck. He works and lives at the stables of a racetrack along with his little boy, T.J. (Ricky Schroder!), who worships his dad. The second you get a glimpse of T.J.—towheaded, eyes brimming with love and admiration for his father—you are going to cry. And cry. You'll continue to weep when little T.J. brags to the rest of the staff, "The Champ always comes through in the end," and you just know it's a harbinger of doom.

And of course it just gets sadder. T.J.'s long-absent mother Annie (Faye Dunaway) reappears in their lives, remarried and as rich as The Champ and T.J. are hard up. Annie wants a relationship with her son again, leading the Champ to do all sorts of stupid things in the name of doing what's right for his beloved boy, including, weepa-weep-weep, *pretending not to love T.J. anymore* so T.J. will go live with Annie and have a better life. That scene is brutal. I'm about to spoil the ending now, so skip this paragraph if you don't want to find out that the Champ decides to enter another boxing match to get money for him and T.J., against the advice of his old coach Jackie (Jack Warden), who reminds Billy that he took too many blows to the head during the last match. To sum it up, the Champ wins the match, but then dies afterward in the locker room as T.J. looks on in horror, left without the one person in his life who's been there for him. To this day, the sound of the Ricker screaming "Wake up, Champ! Wake up!" brings a tear to my eye.

Now, that film was at least intended to move its audience, but I cried about as much in **The Nutty Professor** (dir. Tom Shadyac, 1996), particularly during the scene in which Sherman Klump (Eddie Murphy), the sweet, smart, shy, overweight scientist, finally works up his nerve to ask out the lovely Carla (Jada Pinkett). He takes her to a club, only to be brutally humiliated by a sadistic stand-up comic played by David Chappelle. Sherman tries to laugh and go with it, but the smile keeps slipping off his face. Everyone is mocking him, and so he's in the awful position of being alone in a crowded room, feeling ashamed. Alone! Without anyone to take care of him and tell him it's okay! I can hardly bear it.

Oh, yeah. I also cried like a baby in **The Muppet Movie** (dir. James Frawley, 1979), when one of the Muppets got left behind at a gas station and was all upset, his eyes droopy and mouth turned down in that inimitable Muppet way. I'm almost crying just thinking about it. "Wait for me!" might be the three most tragic words in the English language.

As evidenced by **The Nutty Professor**, you can be pretty damn lonely even when you're not alone (that's a classic rock song, right?). A moment that really resonates with me is in **The Way We Were** (dir. Sydney Pollack, 1973), the love story starring Barbara Streisand as nice Jewish activist girl Katie Morosky and Robert Redford as her "gorgeous goyish guy," Hubbell Gardner. The first time the two spend the night together, Katie touches Hubbell's beautiful blond hair with a mixture of such affection and such a capacity for pain that you just know it's gonna hurt if it doesn't pan out for them. It's like Katie's all alone even though he's there with her, she's so in her own place with her own thoughts.

The portrayal of human frailty and loneliness isn't something I alone find painful. My mother once told me that her entire family nearly had a nervous breakdown after they went to see Arthur Miller's classic play **Death of a Salesman**, with its characterization of Willy Loman, the down and out salesman, husband, and father who wonders why he doesn't have the love and respect from others that he so craves.

I definitely think it's a testament to the power of films that they can move us to tears and stay with us. That they have so much power that sometimes you have to remind yourself it's "only a movie" in order to find peace with the feelings that they can evoke. I think sad flicks are hard—watching something that causes me pain is not easy, and I often wonder why I do it. I know I sometimes can't—if things in my life are sad, I steer clear of these films, which feel like opening up a barely healed wound. But they remind me of the lows, hopefully help me to appreciate the highs, and most of all, they allow me a good, wallowing kind of cry to remind me that I can feel deeply.

MAYBE LIFE *IS* LIKE A BOX OF CHOCOLATES

By Lise

In January 1995 I went to visit Clare, when she was living in Dallas. I think it's safe to say that the trip didn't go exactly as either of us had hoped. Clare had planned to take time off of work, and then got saddled with an unavoidable and huge project right before my arrival; then the heat went out in her house, and I basically watched movies all day, covered by blankets and one Italian greyhound, Walt. Me and Walt, under house arrest, watching movies in Dallas. It's actually pretty funny, when I think about it now. I feel like I starred in **National Lampoon's Dallas Vacation**.

Really, though, it wasn't all bad. Despite the cold and sleety weather, and the limited hang-out time, Clare and I actually had a few good laughs— one of them was a really good laugh. See, there's this movie theater in Dallas called the Granada, where they serve pizza and beer during the movies (you sit at tables instead of regular movie seats).

THIS MOVIE ROCKED MY WORLD

LISE: *The Times of Harvey Milk.* Not only is it an amazing story that I did not know, but it also made me realize how much I love documentary films.

SIBYL: *Funny Face.* Saw this Audrey Hepburn musical for my sixth birthday. Loved it. And am still loving Audrey.

ANDREA: Spike Lee's *She's Gotta Have It.* As a New Yorker, it was nice to realize that not all movies were made in Hollywood by some committee.

CLARE: *Once Were Warriors* really got me; I couldn't believe how powerful it was.

Going to the Granada was one of the events we had planned, so we were rather troubled to discover the movie that was playing: **Forrest Gump** (dir. Robert Zemeckis, 1994), which I had vowed not to see. But you know what they say about a "spoonful of sugar," and we figured that we could take on Gump with a pitcher of beer in front of us.

Cut to several hours later: We have eaten a pizza, finished several beers, and watched more Gump than I ever hope to see again in my life. How the words "My name's Forrest Gump. You can call me Forrest Gump" ever came to be considered an amazing turn of phrase is beyond me. And I won't even get into that whole "box of chocolates" thing. Really, I've got to hand it to Tom Hanks for even playing Gump with a straight face. Before we knew what had hit us, Momma had died and the whole place was sobbing—except Clare and me. We were ordering another pitcher and staring in disbelief. (Clare actually stood up and went to find a waitress, because we absolutely needed more beer if we were going to make it through the rest of the movie.) I mean, people were not only buying into this whole fake story, they were openly weeping for Gump! (If you are thinking while reading this about how cynical and embittered I am, please read on! Because I'm not, and this will hopefully become evident.)

I have thought of that moment many times. I now realize that it all boils down to something that Mrs. Weinhold, my elementary school English teacher, always taught us: It's important to drink a ton of beer at bad movies. No, just kidding. What she taught us was this: The specific is always better than the general. When you make up a character, give her some quirks and nuances, a nickname, a pet—these details are how we form attachments to characters we meet. Similarly, the key to making a moving movie is telling a real story (whether it is based on fact or total fiction doesn't matter), and presenting characters we care about and can relate to (whether they are housewives or princesses doesn't matter). To me, Gump was like the Wal-Mart of movies: there's so much stuff crammed in there that it's almost impossible to find one little thing to latch on to. I prefer films about very specific and detailed characters. Voilà Gillian Armstrong's 1994 version of **Little Women**.

I saw **Little Women** in the theater on one of those "possible new friend" dates, where you go out for the first time with someone from work or school. It can be awkward, leaving the usual surroundings with your possible new friend, and I certainly picked a doozie of a movie for us to see. Trying not to have a complete breakdown in front of someone you just met is hard! First of all, the acting in **Little Women** is so great. Susan Sarandon plays Marmee, a strong woman and the matriarch of the family. Marmee tells her daughters she won't have them being silly about boys, encourages them to run around and scream and express themselves, and embarrasses her oldest daughter, Meg, by talking to everyone and anyone about the annoyance of corsets. Just like in Louisa May Alcott's novel, Meg (Trini Alvarado), Jo (Winona Ryder), Beth (Claire Danes), and Amy (Kirsten Dunst when she's little and Samantha Mathis when she grows older) are sisters and best friends. They stage Jo's hilarious and melodramatic plays in the attic (in one scene, a cat in a bonnet is the love interest), publish their family newspaper, and are always following Marmee's example, trying to be generous to others and to better themselves. I love watching them interact, and although Winona Ryder gets top billing and the voice-over as Jo, Claire Danes is the real star of the movie. As Beth, the sweetest sister of all, Danes give s a wonderfully understated performance, really becoming the shyest sister who, unlike Jo and Amy, does not have the burning desire to go out and see the world or marry. Even knowing ahead of time that Beth will contract scarlet fever from a poor baby doesn't lessen the blow in **Little Women**. It almost makes it sadder, because knowing that something bad is going to happen doesn't stop it from happening, or stop the pain.

Unfortunately, my possible new friend and I went separate ways when **Little Women** ended, our faces too splotchy from crying to be seen in public, and the friendship never panned out. **Little Women** is definitely one to watch at home alone or with a good friend. It's a beautiful tale of family and love and friendship, as is **Shadowlands** (dir. Richard Attenborough, 1993), the true story of C. S. Lewis's (Anthony Hopkins) love affair with an American poet named Joy Gresham (Debra Winger) in the 1950s. I was undeniably moved by the straightforward direction and performances in this film; I immediately reread **The Lion, the Witch, and the Wardrobe** with new interest, too. What I loved was its simplicity and its distinction from generic love stories. Joy, a divorced American woman traveling around England with her son, is perceived by many as being brash or inappropriately forward. Still, Jack, as Mr. Lewis is known, finds himself somehow drawn to her. They begin an interesting and sometimes awkward friendship in which Joy challenges many aspects of Jack's controlled bachelor life.

Right around the same time that Jack accepts the fact that he is in love with Joy and allows himself to be truly happy, she is diagnosed with cancer. Her decline is rapid. Although this is so incredibly sad that I am about to cry while writing this, the movie manages to feel somewhat uplifting at the end. It's one of those movies that makes you think about the importance of living every day of your life to the fullest. I don't mean that you should sign up for bungee jumping lessons or make plans to hang-glide around the world, just that life's joys (pun intended) should not be taken for granted. I also have a soft spot for **Longtime Companion** (dir. Norman René, 1990), the story of how AIDS tears apart a group of friends in New York in the 1980s. Although we see man after man in this circle of friends succumb to the disease, the final scene in the movie brings them all back for one inadequate and imagined moment. Now, I see the argument that this moment is horribly manipulative, but I have to say that it really stirred me for this reason: Who has not fantasized a reunion with a lost loved one? Just to see them smile one more time?

When Clare and I walked out of the Granada the night we saw **Gump**, I was already developing some kind of theory along the lines of: "There's two people in the world, those who like Gump and those who do not." But I have since calmed down. Sure, **Forrest Gump** covered too much ground, and Forrest was everywhere—not because anyone is really like that, but because it afforded Zemeckis more opportunities to manipulate us. So to anyone who may have been in the Granada that night, thinking that Clare and I have shriveled and blackened little hearts because we weren't crying for Gump: I invite you to watch me dissolve into tears as Joy Gresham urges her new husband, Jack, to "let her go," as she dies next to him. Alas. It appears that I have revealed myself as the true softie that I am.

THEY'RE DANCING, I'M CRYING, WE'RE ALL SINGING!

By Sibyl

Okay, I guess it's important to say up front: I cry easily. If a movie is even halfway decent and kind of poignant, pass the Kleenex. I'm sentimental, and I love a movie that packs in all the classic tear-jerker themes: a love that knows no bounds, defying race and class divisions for love, triumphing over injustice, and love lost. Whoa, I'm getting choked up just thinking about this stuff.

Just add music to these classical tragic themes to really make the emotion hit home. Yes, the often disparaged movie-musical,

10 ROCKIN' MUSICALS

pooh-poohed by oh-so-many art snobs, is by far the most moving of films to me. What most people don't like about movie-musicals—that they're hokey and sickeningly sentimental—is what makes them great tearjerkers. See, it's the music that pushes me over the edge. Love, struggle, death, all with people singing and dancing to express their delicious agony.

Yes, it is true, most often musicals don't make very good movies. The transition from stage to screen usually results in a visually flat, overly staged production. And, worst of all, those ham-on-rye musical actors don't tone down their "every seat in the house" style emoting for the screen. So you've got actors mugging and belting into the camera and some goofy costumes, and flat direction—sounds bad. Well, not really, because, in a successful musical, it's the songs (and the dancing, and, oh yeah, some damn good stories) that jerk the heartstrings, that leave you humming and of course bawling.

West Side Story (dirs. Robert Wise, Jerome Robbins, 1961) is the **Godfather** of movie musicals. It's got everything going for it, most importantly the story of young lovers from feuding gangs; the Jets and the Sharks (an update of **Romeo and Juliet**). The music is by one of the greatest composers of modern times, Leonard Bernstein. **West Side** won tons of Academy Awards, including Best Picture, Best Director, Best Supporting Actress (for Rita Moreno as Anita), and special recognition for Jerome Robbins, the choreographer. This flick transcends the musical genre; it's a great film.

Emotionally, **West Side** is wrenching from the very first

note. Tony knows something's coming; he falls in love with Maria (played by the very pretty but not believably Hispanic Natalie Wood); then there's lots of dancing and the amazingly choreographed rumble scene. Of course everyone is doomed; the song "Somewhere" is so beautiful but eerie, as Tony and Maria dream of a place where they can live happily together. Mistakenly, Tony kills Maria's brother Bernardo, then as revenge, Tony is told that Maria is dead. Consumed with grief he surrenders to the bloodthirsty Sharks. The film culminates with Maria weeping over Tony's body as we hear "Somewhere." Argh. How brutal! How gorgeous! Anyone who doesn't cry at the end of **West Side Story** has ice water running though their veins.

Now, if love and death don't get those tears flowing, surely love and religious persecution will do the trick. Both **The Sound of Music** and **Fiddler on the Roof** use the impending cloud of war and oppression as the backdrop for singing, dancing, and—of course—romance. **Sound of Music** (dir. Robert Wise, 1965) is an annual event, shown every year on TV around the Christmas holidays. There's probably no musical more sickly sweet than this one, with its dancing children and singing nun. Despite that, it's a pretty touching story. Poor Maria, the failed nun (Julie Andrews), finds happiness with a family chock-full of children. She falls in love with the gruff widower Baron Von Trapp (Christopher Plummer), and brings song back into their glum lives, and then together they take a stand against the Nazis and flee to the hills. Julie Andrews is at her perky best belting the classic "The Sound of Music" and the nuns bring me to tears every time with the inspirational "Climb Ev'ry Mountain."

Fiddler on the Roof (dir. Norman Jewison) is also about a large family confronted with changing times and religious oppression, but with a completely different feeling. **Fiddler** was made in 1971, and the movie has sort of seventies look, though it's set in the tiny Russian village of Anatevka in the early 1900s. Tevye (played with vigor by Topol) clings to Old World tradition as his five daughters embrace new styles and gentile boyfriends. There are tons of great production numbers, like "If I Were a Rich Man." For tears, though, there's the mournful violin playing of Isaac Stern, the gloriously emotional wedding montage to "Sabbath Prayer" (with all of the leads singing, "May the Lord protect and preserve you"), and of course "Sunrise Sunset."

Of course there are many more great movie musicals; they're all sentimental, and if music gets your juices flowing, then any decent musical may move you to tears. Consider **The King and I**, **The Music Man**, **My Fair Lady**, and **Oklahoma** for some good romps—not quite as emotional as my guaranteed-to-make-you-cry top three, but they're still good. The key to enjoying these movie musicals is to embrace the inherent cheese factor. Let go of your haughty pride and let the music tingle your spine as you watch the love lost, the struggle of good against evil, and all those soaring ballads.

25 Moving Films To Rent!

1   **THE CHAMP** (dir. Franco Zeffirelli, 1979) Take a strong sedative before viewing this heartbreaking movie about a well-meaning loser of a dad (Jon Voight) who takes on a difficult boxing match to make his loyal son (Ricky Schroder) proud. "Champ! Wake up, Champ!" Sob.

2   **CITY OF ANGELS** (dir. Brad Silberling, 1998) Clare and Sibyl cried all the way through this recent film, which certainly requires a bit of suspended disbelief, but is enormously satisfying all the same. Based on the moody German film *Wings of Desire*, this movie finds a heart surgeon (Meg Ryan) with a crisis of scientific faith being courted by an angel (Nicolas Cage).

3   **THE COLOR PURPLE** (dir. Steven Spielberg, 1985) Based on the award-winning book by Alice Walker, this stirring film follows the trials of Celie (Whoopi Goldberg, in what should have been an Oscar-winning performance), an abused, downtrodden woman whose love for the glamorous Shug (Margaret Avery) lifts her up to a place where she belongs.

4   **DEAD MAN WALKING** (dir. Tim Robbins, 1995) This examination of the death penalty finds a nun (Susan Sarandon) ministering to an ignorant, unrepentant death row inmate (Sean Penn). Robbins wrote the script based on the autobiographical book of the same name by Sister Helen Prejean; the last half hour of the inmate's life, filmed in close to real time, is devastating.

5   **THE ELEPHANT MAN** (dir. David Lynch, 1980) A circus freak (John Hurt) with a rare birth defect causing tumors to grow over 90 percent of his body is befriended by a doctor (Anthony Hopkins) whose medical interest in his charge soon grows into a deep friendship. Set in the 1800s and based on a true story, this richly atmospheric black-and-white film is arguably Lynch's best.

6   **FIREWORKS** (dir. Takeshi Kitano, 1998) "Beat" Takeshi is a veritable jack of all trades: he wrote, directed and stars in *Fireworks*

(*Hana-bi*), the story of Nishi, a tough, violent former policeman. You won't believe how sad this Japanese film is, especially since it alternates among moments of surprising humor, incredible violence, and tender interactions between Nishi and the people in his life that he actually cares for, especially his beloved, dying wife.

7 **FLY AWAY HOME** (dir. Carroll Ballard, 1996) A preteen from New Zealand (Anna Paquin) must go live with her nutty inventor father (Jeff Daniels) in Canada after a tragic car accident takes the life of her mother. When the girl finds some orphaned baby geese in the woods, her father helps her teach them how to migrate. Bonding and tears ensue—as does a nice anti-commercial-developer theme.

8 **THE KILLING FIELDS** (dir. Roland Joffé, 1984) Again, a true story, about the friendship of an American journalist, Sidney Schanberg (Sam Waterston) and his Cambodian assistant, Dith Pran (Dr. Haing S. Ngor) on the eve of the bloody revolution of the Khmer Rouge. Sidney must live with the guilt when he is responsible for leaving Dith to fend for himself, and wins a Pulitzer for his coverage.

9 **THE LION KING** (dirs. Roger Allers and Rob Minkoff, 1994) It's funny. It's sad. It's *hakuna mattata*. The story of lion cub Simba's passage into adulthood as he avenges the death of his father, the Lion King, is packed with great songs (so great that the movie was made into a blockbuster Broadway musical). Cheech Marin, Whoopi Goldberg, and Nathan Lane lend their voices and some great comic moments to a story that is at times extremely scary and unbelievably sad. Jeremy Irons is evil Uncle Scar, terrifying as usual.

10 **LITTLE WOMEN** (dir. Gillian Armstrong, 1994) In this strong adaptation of Louisa May Alcott's beloved novel, smart, temperamental Jo (Winona Ryder) and her sisters, led by their transcendentalist, feminist mom (Susan Sarandon), deal with relationships, poverty, war, and scarlet fever. Claire Danes shines as Beth, the sweetest, shyest sister.

11 **LONGTIME COMPANION** (dir. Norman René, 1990) One of the first movies to deal with the AIDS epidemic, this film follows the

story of a group of friends whose lives are all changed—and many taken—by the disease. The men's reunion scene at the end, as they walk on the beach, young, happy, and alive again, opens the waterworks every time.

12 **MIDNIGHT COWBOY** (dir. John Schlesinger, 1969) Once again, Jon Voight plays a loser in this bleak but at times achingly funny movie about two friends, Joe Buck (Voight) and Ratso Rizzo (Dustin Hoffman), whose dreams of making it in the cold, hard city (why, New York, of course) have been unceremoniously dashed.

13 **ONCE WERE WARRIORS** (dir. Lee Tamahori, 1994) This grim film marks the promising debut of first-time director Tamahori. Jake (Temuera Morrison) is an angry man who drinks and beats his wife (Rena Owen) as a way of dealing with his somewhat disappointing existence in the poor section of Auckland, New Zealand. Meanwhile, their children try to find happiness in this atmosphere of poverty and despair.

14 **ONE FLEW OVER THE CUCKOO'S NEST** (dir. Milos Forman, 1975) In this adaptation of the book by Ken Kesey, Jack Nicholson plays Randall Patrick McMurphy, a clever but aimless migrant worker in the sixties who decides to get himself committed to a mental hospital as a way of getting free room and board for a while. Soon he's locked in grim battle with the system, in the form of Nurse Ratched (Louise Fletcher) and leading his fellow loonies in comic, and ultimately tragic, insurrection.

15 **ON THE WATERFRONT** (dir. Elia Kazan, 1954) Marlon Brando's Terry Malloy coulda been a contender back in his boxing days, but instead works for a pack of two-bit thugs on the Mafia-controlled loading docks of New York. He runs into trouble when he tries to fight for fair working conditions, while falling in love with a prim schoolteacher (Eva Marie Saint) whose brother fell victim to the Mob's reign of terror.

16 **ORDINARY PEOPLE** (dir. Robert Redford, 1980) Conrad Jarrett (Timothy Hutton) tries to get over the death of his brother and his

own recent suicide attempt in this portrait of middle-class despair. Mary Tyler Moore gives a stunning performance as Conrad's emotionally crippled mother, and Donald Sutherland stars as his concerned dad. A quiet, beautiful, nuanced film, even now.

17 **A PERFECT WORLD** (dir. Clint Eastwood, 1993) Forget *Dances with Wolves* (blech, hurl): Catch Kevin Costner's strong performance here as escaped convict Butch Haynes who kidnaps a young Jehovah's Witness boy (T. J. Lowther) as protection from the law, but soon finds himself attached to the boy and tries to give him some of the freedom and happiness that he thinks he lacks.

18 **PLACES IN THE HEART** (dir. Robert Benton, 1984) After her husband dies, Edna (Sally Field), a Texan wife in 1935 Waxahachie, has to support herself and her two children. With the help of a down-and-out field hand named Moses (Danny Glover), she plants cotton on forty acres of her land. Great performances all around, as Moses, Edna, her kids, her sister and brother-in-law (the terrific Lindsay Crouse and Ed Harris), and her blind boarder (John Malkovich) deal with storms, bigotry, infidelity, and toiling in the fields.

19 **PONETTE** (dir. Jacques Doillon, 1996) Teeny, five-year-old Victoire Thivisol won Best Actress at the Venice Film Festival for her portrayal of the poised, somber little Ponette, whose mother's death has left her questioning the nature of life, faith, and God. The intelligent, understated script provides some great scenes and dialogue that deal with a serious subject through the eyes of a child, without being at all cloying or condescending.

20 **REDS** (dir. Warren Beatty, 1981) Produced by, written by, directed by, and starring Beatty, this epic film follows the true story of John Reed, an intellectual Communist in the first decades of the twentieth century and the only American buried in the Kremlin. Diane Keaton gives a great performance as his journalist wife, Louise Bryant, and Jack Nicholson stars as the brilliant alcoholic playwright Eugene O'Neill.

21 **SCHINDLER'S LIST** (dir. Steven Spielberg, 1993) Boasting brilliant performances from such standout actors as Liam Neeson, Ralph Fiennes, Ben Kingsley, and Embeth Davidtz, this gorgeous, grim, black-and-white Holocaust film stands as one of the greatest ever made on the subject. Neeson stars as Oskar Schindler, a slick entrepreneur with ambiguous motives for protecting his Jewish factory workers from the Nazis.

22 **SHADOWLANDS** (dir. Richard Attenborough, 1993) Based on the life of C. S. Lewis, the gentle, retiring author of the Chronicles of Narnia, this touching film stars Anthony Hopkins as Lewis, whose sweet love affair with a lady (Debra Winger) of quite a different background and temperament changes both of them forever.

23 **SOPHIE'S CHOICE** (dir. Alan Pakula, 1982) Like *Schindler's List*, this movie centers around the Holocaust; also like *Schindler's List*, this movie is so devastating that most normal people wouldn't want to watch it more than once. Meryl Streep stars as Sophie, a Polish Holocaust survivor who lives in Brooklyn with her mentally troubled but fiercely charming boyfriend, Nathan (Kevin Kline).

24 **THE SOUND OF MUSIC** (dir. Robert Wise, 1965) Although set during World War II, this musical is much lighter than others of its ilk; it follows the story of irrepressible ex-nun Maria (Julie Andrews), the governess of the Von Trapp children, who are kept on a short leash by their authoritarian father (Christopher Plummer). Before long, the mischievous Maria is making the children cute outfits out of curtains, and they're all singing their way out of the grip of the Nazis.

25 **TENDER MERCIES** (dir. Bruce Beresford, 1983) A quietly moving tale of a down-and-out alcoholic country singer (Robert Duvall) who's trying to start a new life. When he meets a reserved widow (Tess Harper) and her young son, he finds a bit of stability and redemption. But the past can't be ignored, and Max's ex-wife (Betty Buckley) and rebellious daughter (Ellen Barkin) soon come back into the picture. This flick snagged a Best Actor Oscar for Duvall, and Horton Foote won an Oscar for his screenplay.

7 COMING OF AGE MOVIES:
Braces and Beyond

lthough coming-of-age movies tend to be about young people, a good movie from this genre speaks to people of all ages. See, "coming of age" inherently means awkward, grumpy, mopey, zitty, displaced feelings we can all relate to. It also more often than not means braces, training bras, first kisses, lunchroom humiliation, cars, kegs, living with your parents, crushes, bad jobs, and cool tunes—other things we can all relate to.

Sure, we're probably all partial to the coming-of-age movies we saw when we were at that age; for us, it would be **E.T.** when we were kids and the John Hughes movies when we were teens. But a great coming-of-age movie transcends that personal reaction; although **Diner** is about a bunch of twentysomething guys in the fifties, it became a favorite of Andrea's when she was in high school. And Clare watched **The Graduate** (made in the late Sixties), about a confused, sullen recent college grad, about a dozen times when she was in high school. Then there are movies like **Rebel Without a Cause**—that's just a classic, filled with young-man angst; it'll never be dated.

Since we Girls came of age during the heyday of John Hughes (before he became Mr. **Home Alone**), Molly Ringwald, Anthony Michael Hall, and the rest of the Brat Pack were our on-screen alter egos. These eighties coming-of-age flicks are heavy on familiar themes: family, romance, friendship, and social issues (with a lot of wrong-side-of-the-tracks stuff). The main kid always comes to some sort of turning point, a lesson is learned, and things almost always turn out okay. While we discussed some of these flicks in our Romance chapter—first love is often a rite of passage in itself, and makes a nice romance to boot—we've reserved plenty of flicks for discussion within the worthy genre of teen films.

Two absolute classics of this niche are John Hughes's **Sixteen Candles** and Cameron Crowe's **Say Anything. Sixteen Candles** is dead-on: it's sad, because Molly Ringwald is being ignored and humiliated by her family; it's funny, because Anthony Michael Hall is the leader of a pack of loser-geeks; it's ridiculous, because Molly's family has an exchange student named Long Duck Dong; and it's romantic, because everyone hooks up with the cute, way-too-popular person they've been crushing on in the end. Something about this movie just pushes Sibyl's buttons; she cries every time she sees it.

Say Anything stars another teen-movie regular, John Cusack. Cusack is much like the Ringwald character from **Sixteen Candles.** He is a nice guy, hangs out with the loser crowd in high school, and really wants a date with the class valedictorian,

WATCH THESE BEFORE YOU ATTEND YOUR HIGH SCHOOL REUNION!

Clueless
16 Candles
Grosse Point Blanke
Scream
Heathers
Dead Poets Society
Diner
Fast Times At Ridgemont High
Dazed and Confused
Ferris Bueller's Day Off

played by Ione Skye. Oh yes, there's love, biting humor (courtesy of Cusack's best friend, played by Lili Taylor), kick-boxing, bad advice from guy friends, brother-sister conflict, father-daughter conflict, and learning how to drive a stick shift. In one pivotal scene, Cusack attempts to woo back Skye by blasting the Peter Gabriel song "In Your Eyes" outside of her house. Good, hip music is another key component to any truly memorable teen flick. Just think: What would **The Breakfast Club** be without that opening Simple Minds song? What would **Pretty In Pink** be without the Psychedelic Furs? And **Valley Girl** without Modern English's "I'll Stop the World and Melt with You"? Nothing, we tell you! Nothing!

Sometimes, though, the mainstream movies don't do justice to the real angst-ridden experience that is growing up. Lise prefers indie coming-of-age flicks like **Gas, Food, Lodging**. (She also prefers indies when she's talking about love, as evidenced by her choices of **Ju Dou** and **Beautiful Thing**—two teen love films—in our Romance chapter.) These indies are more likely to deal with the reality of youth, alienation, family problems, and sexuality with the gloves off. These are not flicks with girls in pink cars (**Pretty in Pink**) or poor little rich boys (**Less Than Zero**). Rather, they're movies like **Europa, Europa** (listed in our Off the Beaten Path chapter), a beautifully told story about a Jewish boy hiding his identity from the Nazis. It's heart-wrenching, but it speaks to anyone who's felt self-conscious as a young person.

My Bodyguard and **Breaking Away** are two classics of a slightly earlier era. These movies are more pensive, darker, a little less cotton-candy than the Hughes stuff. These kids are grappling more with family problems and figuring out what to do with their lives than they are worrying about getting a prom date. Both movies are beautiful, kind of poetic, and well worth checking out.

Of course, there couldn't be any coming-of-age flicks if it weren't for the original teen angst/family feud/wrong-side-of-the-tracks tragic romance: Shakespeare's **Romeo and Juliet**. Any version of this story is worth watching, though the Franco Zeffirelli version has got to be the best traditional telling. While Baz Luhrman's MTV-style interpretation, starring Claire Danes and Leonardo DiCaprio, is another must-see. For the musically inclined, nothing beats the tragic gang warfare of the Jets and the Sharks in **West Side Story**—it's got teens, tunes, and Natalie Wood. (You can check it out further in Sibyl's Moving Pictures section.)

Fashion, music, and lingo are integral aspects of any coming-of-age movie. The classic tunes spun by deejay Wolfman Jack make **American Graffiti** feel completely retro. Director Amy Heckerling is responsible for **Fast Times at Ridgemont High** and **Clueless**. Let's see, would anyone be saying "totally awesome" or "as if" if Heckerling hadn't delivered these wild, California-style comedies?

Many coming-of-age flicks are about losing your virginity. These bad boys range from the cheesy (Jennifer Grey and Patrick Swayze doing the horizontal lambada in **Dirty Dancing**) to the sexy (Tom Cruise and Rebecca DeMornay on a train in **Risky Business**) to the terrible (admit it, you've seen **Losin' It**). Prepare to cringe, giggle, and hold your hands over your eyes while watching these kids fumble around; it's not pretty. Andrea uncovered a few movies that actually handle this subject well, such as the very creepy **Fear** and the dated but sweet **Little Darlings**.

Thank goodness some of these first-romance stories are really about love, not just getting in some chick's pants. A recent addition to the teen-flick canon, **Mad Love**, is actually a pretty good love story starring the always adorable Drew Barrymore (all the Girls here have huge crushes on her; she's just soooo cute) as a nutso girl who runs off with her sweet high school boyfriend (the reliably bland Chris O'Donnell). There's lots of good Seattle grunge music, cute outfits, tons of crying, and of course parental and class conflict.

You've probably gotten the picture already that many coming-of-age flicks manage to cram in all the required angst, romance, and jokes while fully functioning within some other movie genre; the aforementioned Off the Beaten Path, Romance, and Moving Pictures crossovers are good examples. But another great example of this two-for-the-price-of-one trick is the **Scream** series. **Scream** and **Scream 2** are clearly horror flicks, no doubt about it, but they're teen movies, too. They've got the heroine, plucky and pretty Neve Campbell. She's got family problems (involving a serial murderer eeek!), boy problems (seems her boyfriend may be a serial murderer), friend problems (the friends keep getting killed), cool clothes, and great hair.

The **Wizard of Oz** and even **Star Wars** also do double-duty. OZ is definitely a coming-of-age story, with Dorothy learning about courage, love, smarts, and family; her journey through the Emerald City is remarkably like high school. Yet **Oz** is also a crazy fantasy flick, and a musical, too. **Star Wars** is obviously a sci-fi, outer-space classic (listed in our Action chapter), but Luke's development into a Jedi warrior, his quest for his father, and his budding romance with Princess Leia provide plenty of lessons. (One of them clearly being, don't fall for your sister. Eww.)

Well, we've learned to wear trendy clothes and get along with our families and friends. We've learned that the coolest boy or girl in school will fall in love with us, and we've learned it's okay to burst out into song any old time, skip class, time travel, order pizza delivered to school, and kick some serial-killer ass. It's all part of being a young person, at least in the movies.

THE BRAT PACK, OR, WHAT A BUNCH OF BRATS!

By Clare

Every generation has its Rat Pack. For our parents (and for the grandparents of some), it was the Rat Pack: Frank Sinatra, Dean Martin, Sammy Davis, Jr., et al, people whose lives looked glamorous and rich and unattainable, on whom they pinned their every hope and dream. As teens in the eighties, we Generation X-ers had the Brat Pack. We identified with this group of actors; we loved them, we hated them, we watched them grow up, prosper and multiply, rise and fall. Then, one by one, they dropped out of sight entirely, like victims of a mysterious plague, only to reemerge in the strangest places, like on nineties' television sitcoms and in bad B-movies.

The eighties brought us this group of people whose on- and off-screen lives we found endlessly fascinating. Do the teen films of the nineties bring us the same? In various forms, sure. But nothing so cohesive and enduring as those teen actors of yesteryear. (Excuse me while I wax nostalgic.

I ADMIT IT! TEEN CRUSH

LISE: Andrew McCarthy and, yes, I am embarrassed.

SIBYL: Emilio Estevez all the way!!

ANDREA: Oh, the shame! I adored the entire cast of *The Outsiders* (even C. Thomas Howell and Ralph Macchio) But my heart belonged to Rob Lowe, with his faded jeans and too cool attitude. I even saw *Class* for him. Twice.

CLARE: Timothy Hutton. Cried through *Taps* about fifty times when I was thirteen.

Sniff.) Here they are, in all their glory: the teen idols of my youth, and a glimpse of the newest repositories of teen angst, nineties style.

Molly Ringwald has to be first on the list. Although Paul Mazursky's **Tempest** should really be considered her breakthrough role, **Sixteen Candles** was the flick that sealed her fate as the surly, lip-biting, eye-rolling, misunderstood teen that we all knew and loved. She continued on this hurly-burly bent with **The Breakfast Club**, then **Pretty in Pink**, then in lesser-known flicks like **The Pick-up Artist** and **For Keeps**. It was all downhill from there; Molly dropped out for two years, went to Paris, then came back (literally, if not figuratively) in TV movies like **The Stand**. Finally, she got her own TV show, "Townies." Has it been canceled? Has it been watched? Does anyone care? Alas, poor Molly, we knew you well.

Now, an even more interesting dropout has to be Ally Sheedy. Cast as the freakiest weirdo ever spotted in a milquetoast John Hughes film, Sheedy played the outcast Allison in **The Breakfast Club**. Despite her makeover, Ally didn't seem to be able to hold her place in the spotlight. Sure, she got to play a boring, pearls-and-suit-wearing lawyer in **St. Elmo's Fire**, but I really think that **Maid to Order** was the beginning of the end. She's been working steadily, you'll be happy to know, in such challenging roles as "New York ticket agent" in **Home Alone 2**, but she has yet to recapture her former luster. But wait! Is there a comeback on the horizon? Sibyl loved her performance in art-house flick **High Art**. I say, if she can stay away from movies in which she stars opposite a robot, she just might make it out alive.

Playing the yuppie to Ally's lawyer in **St. Elmo's** and the tough to Molly's princess in **The Breakfast Club**, Judd Nelson was the first sexy "teen" actor I'd ever been exposed to (he was actually twenty-six by the time he appeared in **Breakfast**—yikes!). What a bad boy! Naughty, hostile, nostrils a-flaring, hands-a-flexing (in his fingerless leather gloves), Nelson was the guy your mom told you to stay away from. He was soon supplanted, however; first by Rob Lowe (**St. Elmo's Fire**, **About Last Night**. . .), whose antics with a video camera and some minors proved that he was the real bad boy on the block; then by Robert Downey, Jr., who stole our hearts as the dangerous, sadly charming druggie in **Less Than Zero** (once again, life imitated art: Downey's been in and out of rehab and jail for the past several years). Now, a little older, a little puffier, but with that same peerless schnozz, Nelson has reappeared in "Suddenly Susan" as Brooke Shields's paramour-editor, Jack.

Talk of puffy has-beens leads me naturally to Anthony Michael Hall. Back in the eighties, his self-conscious brace-face stammering was something we mistook for "character acting." He was our Zero Mostel, our Billy Crystal, our Gene Wilder. His dorky brain in **Sixteen Candles** and his brainy dork in **The Breakfast Club** proved his range. When, five years after **The Breakfast Club**, Hall reappeared in **Edward Scissorhands** as a spoiled ass-hole jock (now there's range!), he was barely recognizable—more a balloon of his former self than a shadow. His role in **Six Degrees of Separation** dug him out of the muck somewhat, although he only came up for a brief gasp of air before diving back in with movies like **A Gnome Named Norm** and **A Bucket of Blood**.

Sometimes I'm hard-pressed to decide who among the eighties Brat Pack is the most talentless, but I come back time and again to the simpering Andrew McCarthy. Cast as the love interest in **Pretty in Pink** ("What about prom, Blaine?!") and as one of the friends in **St. Elmo's Fire**, McCarthy showed just how far you can get on middling talent and a pair of baby blues. His less-than-riveting performance in **Less Than Zero** (he even made hot standing-up sex with Jami Gertz look boring) involved a lot of facial contortions and eye-bugging, but no contortion in the world can save the guy from himself. Sadly enough, it seems that even stinkers like **Mannequin** and **Weekend at Bernies** couldn't best him. I therefore predict that he will be our generation's Charleton Heston: Someone we are doomed to see popping up occasionally for the rest of our miserable lives.

Interestingly, Emilio "Does Punching the Air Count as Dancing?" Estevez seems to have fared pretty well over the years. Perhaps because he is the son of Martin Sheen and the brother of Charlie, perhaps because he and Charlie discovered National Lampoon—**Young Guns**, **Loaded Weapon**—or perhaps because THE MIGHTY DUCKS came and saved his ass, this diminutive star has managed to keep his head above water. Just barely. He gave us some fine, angst-soaked acting in **Breakfast Club**, **St. Elmo's Fire**, and **The Outsiders**, then left us hanging. Andrea and I were actually psyched to see him in **Mission: Impossible**—but dismayed when he bought it in an elevator shaft a mere ten minutes in. We were rendered speechless with shock, our mouths hanging agape like carp. How dare they? *How dare they?!*

When you begin to unthread the long, long string of actors that continues unbroken from the core of the Brat Pack (which of course has its center in **The Breakfast Club**), it becomes impossible to stop the Six Degrees of Kevin Bacon madness. The actors just keep on comin': **St. Elmo's Fire** leads to Demi Moore and Rob Lowe, Rob Lowe leads to James Spader who leads to Jami Gertz who leads to Jason Patric who leads to Kiefer Sutherland who leads to Julia Roberts who leads to just about everybody, including Kevin Bacon himself. And I haven't even mentioned all the actors that **The Outsiders** brought us, among them Patrick Swayze, Matt Dillon, and Tom Cruise (who leads to Timothy Hutton who leads to Sean Penn). Argh! It's spinning out of control! What an incestuous bunch!

Today's teen actors (or, I should say, actors playing teens) are a less tight-knit group, and it's hard to pinpoint who exactly the nineties' Brat Pack will be, or where they will come from. The biggest emerging fad is the TV-to-film-crossover actor. We watched the entire cast of "Beverly Hills, 90210" sparkle with promise, only to fail miserably on the big screen, and now the entire cast of "Friends" is making the jump, with mixed results (Jennifer Aniston and Courtney Cox seeming to be faring better than their male costars). Then there are the new young hotties, starting with Claire Danes breaking out of "My So-Called Life" to become Juliet to Leonardo DiCaprio's Romeo. There's Sarah Michelle Gellar of "Buffy the Vampire Slayer," Neve Campbell and Jennifer Love Hewitt of "Party of Five," even Katie Holmes of "Dawson's Creek."

Where are the guys? Well, there's Leo. And there's . . . Scott Wolf. Sigh. Is it all falling apart? Probably not. I just don't know who the nineties Brat Pack is because (a) I am too ancient now, I don't care, and I'm not reading *Tiger Beat*; or (b) only time will tell. In other words, we won't know who they were until they're already over.

THE MOTLIER CREW . . .

By Lise

I love John Hughes films just as much as the next girl, but they aren't exactly a realistic representation of teenage life. Take me, for example. Every now and then, my Mom will dig out a photo of me in my teen years. In exactly none of these photos am I wearing a cute dress that I sewed myself, from a scarf, like Molly Ringwald in **Pretty in Pink**. In some photos I have a perm, the kind where it looks like a tumbleweed landed on my head; in others I am wearing tube socks pulled up to my knees. I had braces, I had purple-framed glasses, I had stirrup pants, I had a Forenza sweater. People, I had acid-washed jeans.

My personal bad fashion is really not the point, though. I want to tell you about my favorite teen films, in which characters often take the road less traveled. These films feature teens who are dealing with issues more serious than, say, a grandmother who grabs your newly developed booby and pronounces it "perky." They deal with issues like unplanned pregnancy, confusion about sexuality, and—okay, to be fair—how to score some freakin' beer crops up every now and again too.

I grew up in New Hampshire, where excitement meant driving to a field to sit on the ground and drink a couple of borrowed cans of beer; I am not unfamiliar with what some call the "master brew." (My younger sister and brother's friends have really upped the ante here by dragging a full-sized couch out into the woods. Such clever youth!) Maybe my rural upbringing is the reason why two of my absolute favorite teen films, **Gas, Food, Lodging** (dir. Allison Anders, 1992) and **Dazed and Confused** (dir. Richard Linklater, 1993), take place in the middle of nowhere.

The opening shot of **Gas, Food, Lodging** takes us down the highway in Laramie, New Mexico, where we see abandoned gas stations, a bone-dry motel pool, and the occasional tumbleweed. (Yes,

THE GROWN-UPS ARE SO COOL IN

LISE: Harry Dean Stanton is a cool parent to Molly Ringwald in *Pretty in Pink*, even though he's a little down on his luck.

SIBYL: *The Addams Family* (Raul Julia and Angelica Huston, supa-cool).

ANDREA: *Uncle Buck.* John Candy saves the day, again.

CLARE: The groovy, yoga-positioning, pot-smoking mom and dad are totally awesome in *Valley Girl.*

just like the tumbleweed I wore on my head—how nice of you to remember!) This is where Shade (Fairuza Balk), our protagonist, lives in a trailer park with her single mother, Nora (Brooke Adams), and her troublesome older sister, Trudi (Ione Skye).

While Trudi is out sleeping with every guy who puts in a request (in a sad scene, she confesses to having been gang-raped, saying "After that, I never said no again; why bother, they're just gonna do it anyway"), Shade comes to the realization that she too needs to find a man—not for herself, but for her mother. Shade says, in a sweet voice-over that gently leads us through the story, "Then we could do all the dumb normal stuff regular families do." But Shade's quest for a family is just part of the larger lesson that she learns, about being a strong woman, dealing with the hand that fate deals you, and staying true to yourself.

Allison Anders directs this story with such care. All of the details are right, from the David Bowie posters in Shade's room, to the alternative soundtrack featuring musicians like David Sylvian and Nick Cave. And the scene in which Shade dresses up like Olivia Newton-John to bust a move on a guy who she does not realize is gay, is hilarious and embarrassing.

Shade has her moments of confusion, but it's nothing compared to the traumas of the teenage girls in **All over Me** (dir. Alex Sichel, 1997). Ellen (Tara Subkoff) and Claude (Alison Folland) are best friends who live across the park from each other in Hell's Kitchen, a pretty tough New York neighborhood (let's put it this way: no one from a Woody Allen movie is hangin' out there). Their differences are made pretty clear in the first five minutes of the film, but it's also easy to believe that they are best friends, in that special, intense, and often abusive high school way. Sigh. It's all coming back to me. Pass me my silver shoes, would you?

Jeez, I thought I had it bad, but throw New York City into the mix, and Claude and Ellen have some serious obstacles to overcome. In one heartbreaking scene, we see teeny-weeny Ellen trying to walk normally in absurd high-heeled shoes that she wears with short-shorts. It reminded me of the day that I realized exactly how bad I looked in purple eye shadow—the kind of embarrassment that makes you hot, even when there's no one else around.

Ironically, Ellen and Claude's main obstacle doesn't really involve the drugs or crime in their neighborhood; their main obstacle is that age-old story, the fact that they are growing apart because Ellen has a new boyfriend, and she is leaving Claude behind—until she needs her, that is. Meanwhile, Claude is coming to terms with the fact that she is gay, which requires her to find a new support system. Yeah, **All over Me** can be heavy, but it's a simple and good story, which gives credit to both of the characters.

But, hey, you didn't think I was going to get all heavy and serious and then just up and leave you, did you? No way! Contrary to popular opinion, I am all about fun! My middle name ain't "I Really Do Like Lighthearted Movies, Because I Am Fun" for nothing! And a prime example of what I think is a fun and lighthearted flick falls into the teen category. I defy anyone to hold in giggles during a viewing of **Dazed and Confused** and, specifically, during Matthew McConaughey's scenes (yeah, he's the lecherous "I'm pushing thirty and still hanging out with high-schoolers" dude with the side-parted, wavy hair and skintight pants). If there's a more formidable display of feathered hair, bad cars, puka shells, baseball shirts, and classic rock, then I don't know about it. Throw in a few pot-induced conspiracy theories about the dollar bill, and a last-minute keg party in a field and—sniff—I get misty!

The truth is, if I am flipping through the channels and **The Breakfast Club** is on, then I am unavailable for the next couple of hours, period—the Ally Sheedy makeover scene is just too good for me to pass up. But if you're looking for some films that really give credit to all the royal crap that teens have to deal with, and that really convey a wider array of experiences (sadly, though, I must point out the dearth of good films about minority teens, with **Boyz N the Hood** being a noteworthy exception), put the John Hughes collection aside, and look for some directors who recently experienced some of said crap. Watch for Tamra Davis, the director of the semi-autobiographical 1998 film, **Slums of Beverly Hills**, and Lisa Krueger, the director of the seriously underrated **Manny and Lo**.

Let's face it: Unless you actually are Molly Ringwald, you probably didn't make it through the teen years without a few bumps and scrapes, and maybe even a wicked bad perm like mine. In fact, maybe I will write, direct, produce, and edit a film on teen angst, all about me and my hideous wardrobe. Clare? Andrea!? Sibyl?!? Will somebody puh-lease get my agent on the phone?

What's that? I don't have an agent? Rats.

LET'S TALK ABOUT SEX, BABY

By Andrea

My college boyfriend (let's call him Fred, to protect the innocent) once told me a story about his high school girlfriend. Seems that Fred dated this girl for eight months. During their entire time together, they made out exactly once, right at the beginning of their relationship. After that, they got into the charming pattern of going to parties, where Fred would spend his evening chasing her around, his finger down his throat, in an attempt to throw up on her. Yes, this is a true story. No joke.

Aside from the fact that this guy, um, Fred, obviously had some intimacy issues, I always thought this story was a good example of the nadir of teen behavior in the face of the megatrauma of emerging sexuality. Fred wasn't ready to be in a sexual relationship, but he definitely couldn't admit to that—not to himself, his friends, or his poor, long-suffering girlfriend who had no idea why her guy was so crazy.

WHAT I HATE MOST ABOUT *RISKY BUSINESS* IS

LISE: That scene with Tom Cruise dancing in his tighties. It's repulsive. And that song is awful.

SIBYL: Tom Cruise's hair. Tom Cruise's smugiliciousness.

ANDREA: Tom Cruise's annoying sweaters. Rebecca De Mornay's annoying pout. Every moment when that guy playing the annoying pimp is on-screen.

CLARE: That stupid line, "Sometimes you just gotta say, 'What the fuck?'" It became the credo for a generation of assholes.

And even when we're itty-bitty, we're already all confused and freaked out about what sex is, and what it's supposed to be, and what we're supposed to be doing. Lise was in elementary school when some older junior high guys were giving her a hard time, saying, "Hey, are you a virgin? You must be a virgin." Poor Lise got all confused and flustered. Not only was she not 100 percent sure what it was to be "a virgin," she wasn't sure what the right answer was. Was she supposed to be "a virgin?" Was that good? Bad? *Eek!*

As an adult, I look back on that era and just thank the heavens that I'm no longer going through all that angst and insecurity. However, I still like to watch films about teens, and now that I am at this nice, safe distance of adulthood, I can sympathize with all the awful stuff the kids are going through, yet be far, far away from the worst of it all. I remember the Will I or won't I? Should I or should-n't I? Am I ever going to or not, for the love of God??!!? But now I'm not right in the middle of it anymore, thankyouhigherpower.

There are different ways that teen films portray sex. Some are tongue-in-cheek, plenty are just stupid and gross, others try to treat sex and dating with some seriousness. The teen films I find most interesting are those that deal with the issues with at least a mod-icum of realism, whether adding a certain levity (**16 Candles**) or by exploring some of the scarier aspects (**Fear**, dir. James Foley, 1996.)

In the eighties, there seemed to be a whole slew of films that were about teenage boys trying desperately to lose their virginity. Why? No idea. The whole trend was kind of weird. Tom Cruise pops up in a true bowser called **Losin' It** (dir. Curtis Hanson—who actu-ally managed to claw himself out of this shitpile of his own making and direct the amazing **L.A. Confidential**—1982). The entire film centers on a group of buddies who head off to Tijuana to try to, yep, you got it, unload that monkey called virginity off their backs. Along the way they meet Shelley Long from "Cheers." If I haven't been clear enough, I'm saying it loud and proud: This flick is heinous. Still, it is part of an oeuvre.

A year later, Cruise showed up in another "please God don't let me die a virgin" film entitled **Risky Business** (dir. Paul Brickman, 1983). This flick really cemented his career. Who can for-get that snappy dance he did in his skivvies, sporting Ray-Bans? (Product placement? You be the judge.) Me and the other Girls seem to be the only people who didn't like this film, by the way. It launched every schlub and his brother in to the world of lip-syncing in public. The whole movie seems dated and annoying, with center-part-sporting Cruise playing a little snot-nose trying to get into an Ivy League school and romance a prostitute (Rebecca DeMornay) at the same time. Sometimes you just gotta say "overrated."

You might think that films with young girls being sexually active were a lot more serious and thoughtful than those with boys in the lead. Boys were in films like **Losin' It**, or **Porky's**, set in the 1950s about a bunch of guys in Florida who schlep around some brothel trying to get laid.

Girls, on the other hand, wound up having to actually deal with the repercussions of their sexuality. In **Baby It's You** (dir. John Sayles, 1982), Rosanna Arquette and Vincent Spano star as two kids from totally different backgrounds who fall for each other; it's a film I remember finding upsetting as a young girl, since the two leads obviously care about each other, yet grow apart as they mature.

Just as Sayles's heroine didn't have such an easy time of it, neither did Jennifer Jason Leigh in **Fast Times At Ridgemont High** (dir. Amy Heckerling, 1982). Leigh's character loses her virginity, and the experience sucks. Then she has sex with someone else, and gets pregnant. Plus the guy who got her pregnant didn't even have the guts to pick her up after the abortion! Lame, lame, lame! At the end, she realizes she has a great friend and she finds a super nice guy who treats her well, so that was cool, but she had some serious bumps along the way.

However, if you dig a little deeper, you'll see that there are plenty of teen flicks with male leads where the protagonists have a wide range of human emotions, and the topic of sexuality is treated with respect. Basically, this confirms my theory that a well-made film can carry any of us along, whether we share the same gender/race/orientation as the protagonist or not. I felt for and identified with poor John Cusack in **Say Anything**, especially in the scene where he missed Ione Skye so much that he stood in the rain outside her house, and I still remember weeping at the end of **The Last American Virgin**, because the sweet hero was just so heartbroken. Ack.

One of my personal fave teen films of the nineties has got to be **Fear** (dir. James Foley, 1996), because it really shows that teenage girls are dealt with so awkwardly by the adults in their lives. Either they get babied like they're still teeny weeny little girls, or, because their bodies are fully developed, they get treated as sex objects. Neither approach is too helpful for their emotional development. Sadly, this film delves into pulp towards the end, so this theme is dropped while Marky Mark overacts and trashes everything in his path.

Contrary to what you might expect, the tacky and dated **Little Darlings** (dir. Ronald F. Maxwell, 1980) is one of the more realistic portrayals of teenage girls I've seen in a Hollywood flick. Set at a summer camp, it stars Kristy McNichol and Tatum O'Neal as two polar opposites who somehow get roped into competing to see which of them will lose their virginity first. Their bunkmates are totally catty, cliquey, and peer-pressurey. All realistic. They also talk about sex a ton, feigning bravado, even though most of them don't know a thing about sex or boys. Ouch, this film is totally brutal, (though at least not all the men in it are dogs—that's such a cheap and easy way out of gender issues.)

Overall, I'm with Lise: I think it's cool to keep it real. Sometimes a more meaty flick can offer a perspective that perhaps is missing from those Corey Haim/Corey Feldman classics. Regardless of where your teen movie desires take you, for sure teens deserve films that treat them with the same respect that the rest of us are given. There's enough mythology and misinformation out there that when a film tries to do the topic justice, I just want to stand up and cheer! No more soft lighting! No more candles! No more asking your friend Bev to come spend the night with you at a guy's place so you won't have to deal with the consequences of being alone with him and having to tell him you don't want to fool around with him!

Um, not that I ever did that.

INNOCENCE LOST

By Sibyl

The lights go down. The music plays. The opening credits roll. Over shots of Midwestern suburban Anywhere, the voice-over narration begins: "I was seven years old when I crashed through the patio door, but I didn't get hurt." Or maybe, "The year was 1988. My mother bought me a miniskirt. I threw away my retainer at the school cafeteria."

All right, so maybe my childhood isn't movie material. But memories of childhood, the joy and more often the agony, are the focal points of some of the best movies out there. From art-house classics like Ingmar Bergman's **Fanny and Alexander** (1983) to pop-culture favorites like Steven Spielberg's **E.T.** (1982), the childhood years provide great material.

Rite-of-passage movies—and I'm not talking about sexual rite of passage, that's Andrea's turf—usually center on one event that marks the passage from childish innocence to a tougher, more adult perception of the world. Because we're talking about movies here (not my everyday boring life), these events tend to be dramatic, jarring, even violent.

Though all movies about children have a certain inherent sweetness, the good ones temper that quality with a harsh dose of reality that makes the young characters seem real. **To Kill a Mockingbird** (dir. Robert Mulligan, 1962) is thoroughly sentimental; both the novel and the film are considered rite-of-passage classics. Yet there's something about **Mockingbird**—the creepy score, the stark black-and-white film, the lessons about racism—that makes the story surprisingly adult and complex. Scout is a six-year-old tomboy growing up with her brother Jem in the South. Scout idolizes her widower father, Atticus (Gregory Peck), and loves her brother, too. Her life is pretty idyllic, but during the course of the film she must mature, and it's not easy.

Scout learns about bigotry when her father defends an innocent black man against false charges of raping a white woman. She also learns to overcome her notions about the neighborhood freak, Boo Radley (Robert Duvall). Scout and Jem's fear of the unknown drives the film; they make a habit of running rather than walking past Boo Radley's house, sometimes while screaming, but they are also curious about this so-called weirdo. Their curiosity is so fresh and naive that when Radley finally does appear, saving Jem from a knife-wielding drunkard, the children accept him openly. They quickly overcome the biases of the adults around them to understand the simple truth about Boo Radley: That he helped them, that he is lonely, and that he seems nice. That's enough for a child.

There is nothing further away from **Mockingbird**'s old-world Americana than **Welcome to the Dollhouse** (dir. Todd Solondz, 1995). **Dollhouse** is one of the harshest visions of childhood I've

WOW, THIS IS DATED

LISE: *The Legend of Billie Jean.* Does anyone remember this flick?

SIBYL: *Less Than Zero.* Jami Gertz as a model? And all those ruffly eighties styles!

ANDREA: *Top Gun.* Egad, how could I ever have thought this was a "quality" picture? I'm pretty sure we hit the zenith of overpec'd overactors and a soundtrack straight out of the K-Tel library in this rah-rah fighter-pilot dog of a film.

CLARE: *Splendor in the Grass.* Loved it in high school, cried and cried, then woke up and realized that it's about a guy and girl who literally *go mad* because of sexual frustration. So hysterical!

ever seen. Director Solondz is unflinching in his exposure of prepubescent misery and cruelty. For Dawn Wiener (Heather Matarazzo), junior high school resembles Dante's circles of Hell. She has no friends, her clothes suck, her little sister is perfect, her parents aren't very nice. This film is relentlessly grim, propelled by the bizarre contrast between Dawn's perpetual scowl and her happy, pink, flowery, ruffled clothes.

Dollhouse pushes the "childhood is hell" thing a little too far at points; Dawn's life is horrible at every turn. Still, there is a lot of truth in the film. Dawn is willful, disagreeable, contrary, even sour. The film is refreshing in its assault on the typical images of blissful suburban upbringings. Dawn's pure hatred for her sister (in a darkly funny scene, she bungles an attempt to kill her while she sleeps) resonates with anyone who's ever witnessed siblings fighting. Yes, **Dollhouse** is a creepy black comedy, but it's also an honest depiction of kids with the gloves off.

Set in the Louisiana Bayou in the early sixties, **Eve's Bayou** (dir. Kasi Lemmons, 1997) centers on young Eve's (Jurnee Smollett) discovery that her father, the town doctor (Samuel L. Jackson), is a serial adulterer. This knowledge causes her to distance herself from her mother (Lynn Whitfield) and to fight with her brother and sister. Eventually she seeks help from a witch doctor (Diahann Carroll, in eerie white-face makeup) to cast a spell on her father. Eve does not heed the advice of her aunt (Debbie Morgan), a practitioner of good magic, who tells her that the powers of evil are not to be taken lightly.

There's a fascinating exploration of a child's thought process in **Bayou**. Eve's sister tells her that their father molested her, but Eve also learns her father's side of the story from a letter he wrote. And, as the unseen adult narrator, we sense that she's still unsure of what happened. Perception and reality are never as jumbled as when you're a kid. Emotions are heightened, there's a lot of drama, and if you're ten years old like Eve, how do you know who or what to believe? **Bayou** leaves this puzzle unresolved.

There is an essential truth in every great film about kids (and I'm not talking about the Macaulay Culkin oeuvre or **Curly Sue** here)—the characters are fresh and their emotions are raw. Why else would all the greats make movies about childhood? There's a sadness in all of these films, a point in which we see a child getting her first taste of the cruelty of the adult world, feeling emotional, as opposed to physical, pain for the first time, and attempting to make sense of it. Still, these films also offer some sense of hope, too: the hope that a child's pain will create a stronger, more sensitive adult.

25 Coming of Age Films to Rent!

1 **ALL OVER ME** (dir. Alex Sichel, 1997) Set in New York's Hell's Kitchen, this film explores the ups and downs of a super tight friendship between a wild party girl and her shy, pensive friend who's coming to grips with being a lesbian. Great exploration of the power and pressure of friendship. Allison Folland (*To Die for*) as the quiet, chunky Claude is amazing.

2 **BEYOND SILENCE** (dir. Caroline Link, 1996) Up for Best Foreign Language Film at the 1998 Academy Awards, this incredible—and incredibly moving—German- and sign-language film follows the coming-of-age of Lara (Tatjana Trieb and Sylvie Testud), a young girl whose deaf parents are highly dependent on her. As she grows older, the usual parent/child rifts occur, exacerbated by the fact that Lara becomes a talented clarinet player, and her parents cannot share her love of music.

3 **BOYZ N THE HOOD** (dir. John Singleton, 1991) This wrenching flick was made by then—twenty-three-year-old Singleton. Wow, its vision of life in South Central L.A. is grim. Laurence Fishburne and Angela Bassett are parents trying to keep their kid out of the alluring gang life and away from the constant gunfire riddling their neighborhood. Definitely a tearjerker.

4 **THE BREAKFAST CLUB** (dir. John Hughes, 1985) This Hughes meditation on the agony of teen cliques (dork, princess, jock, freak, stoner) seems more preachy as it ages. Still, Ally Sheedy's whacked-out loner and Anthony Michael Hall's zealous goody-goodie make the draggy talk-fest sections endurable. Worth it just for the tunes and dancing scenes.

5 **BREAKING AWAY** (dir. Peter Yates, 1979) Ah, the young Dennis Quaid. He's part of a motley crew called "cutters" (kids who didn't go straight to the University of Indiana after high school). Bored with swimming in the local quarry, they take on the local rich assholes in a bike race, led by the kid who's transformed himself from Midwesterner to opera-singing, Italian-speaking, leg-shaving bike pro. It's grimy, very seventies, and totally great.

6 **DAZED AND CONFUSED** (dir. Richard Linklater, 1993) Oh, the glorious seventies. It's the last day of school in 1976. Set in suburban Texas, this instant classic features lots of bicentennial garb, tube tops, bell bottoms, and tons of classic rock. This flick represents every type: nerds, jocks, stoner-jocks, freak-stoners, junior high kids, and lecherous grads still hanging onto the high school scene. Like high school itself, *Dazed* is often hilarious and sometimes brutal. Amazingly realistic keg-party scene, plus Matthew McConaughey's best performance ever.

7 **DINER** (dir. Barry Levinson, 1982) Perhaps Seinfeld was inspired by this buddy movie set in fifties Baltimore. These guys (including Kevin Bacon, Paul Reiser, and Mickey Rourke) hang out in their local diner, eating off of each other's plates and grumbling about their jobs, girls, and who snarfed someone else's French fries. A funny yet sad meditation on friendship at that inevitable time when everyone starts going in different directions.

8 **FAME** (dir. Alan Parker, 1980) Probably best remembered for its musical scenes (the title song, "Hot Lunch," and "I Sing the Body Electric"), this flick is also a rather dark exploration of kids desperate to make it big facing the harsh realities of show biz, set against a really gritty-looking New York. Surprisingly sad and touching.

9 **FAST TIMES AT RIDGEMONT HIGH** (dir. Amy Heckerling, 1982) A thousand careers were launched in this totally California high-school flick. Look for Sean Penn as the classic surfer dude Jeff Spicoli, and Jennifer Jason Leigh as an inexperienced girl looking for love (and sex) in all the wrong places, using Phoebe Cates's absurd best-friend advice as a guide.

10 **FERRIS BUELLER'S DAY OFF** (dir. John Hughes, 1986)
Bueller? Bueller? A truly fun teen fantasy about getting one over on
everyone: school, parents, siblings. Matthew Broderick is perfect as
the smug, wily, thrill-seeking Ferris, bagging school and romping
with his best friend and girlfriend while eluding the classic teen-
movie bad guys: the principal, the cops, and his parents.

11 **FLIRTING** (dir. John Duigan, 1990) An intelligent, funny, and surprisingly powerful film about two kids (Thandie Newton and Noah
Taylor) at an Australian boarding school in 1965 who, though saddled with the usual teen awkwardness, manage to make crushing
and flirting and dating look almost graceful. The dark cloud of the
Idi Amin years in the girl's native Uganda hangs over the young couple as they struggle with school bullies, Sartre, racism, and young
love.

12 **GAS, FOOD, LODGING** (dir. Allison Anders, 1992) An original
and honest-feeling film starring Fairuza Balk as Shade, a teen who
lives in a teeny trailer in a New Mexico town where her mother is a
waitress and her sister, well, gets around. As tumbleweeds blow
across the street, Shade makes her first sexual advance on a guy
who is gay, and all three of the women have to come to terms with
their separate and communal lives.

13 **THE GRADUATE** (dir. Mike Nichols, 1967) A weird movie, but a
classic. Dustin Hoffman's befuddled college grad is confronted with
lame career choices (plastics), a sweet girl, her seductress mother
(the notorious Mrs. Robinson, the perfectly sly Anne Bancroft), and
his own panic and self-loathing. It's really pretty grim and sort of
surreal, but a better-looking, better-sounding (Simon and
Garfunkel) coming-of-age movie hasn't been made since.

14 **HEATHERS** (dir. Michael Lehmann, 1989) Friends are great, but in
the high school years, we all thought about dumping some of our
pals. Some of us did. Well, in *Heathers*, Winona Ryder begins to
knock off her color-coordinated princess friends with the encour-
agement of a Jack Nicholson-channeling Christian Slater. This is
some really dark humor, but it works wickedly well.

15 **THE LOST BOYS** (dir. Joel Shumacher, 1987) Long, feathered, hair. Dangling hoop earrings. Eyeliner. And that's just how the male cast dresses in this fun vampire thriller. Even though the fashion is dated, this eighties' flick stands the test of time surprisingly well. Not only do the two Coreys appear in fine form, but Kiefer "Sneer Like a Madman" Sutherland vamps it up as head of the blood-suckers, and Jason Patric has a starring role as a moody teen fighting his urge to join the dark side. Great fun.

16 **MULAN** (dirs. Tony Bancroft, Barry Cook, 1998) Disney gets progressive with this tale of a Chinese girl who joins the army to protect her ailing father. Mulan cross-dresses, kicks some samurai butt, and hooks up with a hunky young soldier. The songs aren't memorable, but the art direction of ancient China is pretty mind-blowing, and Eddie Murphy is hysterical as Moo Shu, the lame but loyal dragon.

17 **MY LIFE AS A DOG** (dir. Lasse Hallstrom, 1985) There's something amazingly Zen about this Swedish coming-of-age story. Twelve-year-old Ingemer's life is pretty grim: his brother is mean, his mother is sick, and he's separated from his beloved dog and shipped off to live with his uncle in the country. Yet in charming voice-overs, he considers everything to be relative, as he always reminds himself that he could be the poor dog that was sent up into space without enough food.

18 **ROMEO AND JULIET** (dir. Franco Zeffirelli, 1968) We thought we'd recommend Zeffirelli's version, rather than Baz Luhrman's glitzy, flashy, modernized one with Claire Danes and Leonardo DiCaprio, just because we're surly old farts. Actually, this film is so much more beautiful; the dialogue is mercifully intact, not butchered by shouting and bad acting; and the two stars, Olivia Hussey and Leonard Whiting, are luminous. This film could actually make you want to study Shakespeare instead of studying the thousandth unauthorized biography of Leo.

19 **RUNNING ON EMPTY** (dir. Sidney Lumet, 1988) Liberal parents who inadvertently injured some people during an antiwar protest in their youth are on the run from the government and haul their kids all over the place. River Phoenix is the teenage son sick of changing his identity, particularly since he's fallen for Martha Plimpton. Two of our favorite actors, the late Phoenix and the always riveting Plimpton, really convey the joyful misery of teen romance.

20 **RUSHMORE** (dir. Wes Anderson, 1998) Rushmore is more than just a prep school to Max Fischer (Jason Schwartzman)—it's his sole reason for being, until he finds a mentor in a depressed, drunken benefactor (Bill Murray, at his wry, weirdo best) and falls for a beautiful teacher (Olivia Williams). Max is both heroic and pathetic, passionate and ridiculous; if you didn't know someone like him in high school, it's because you were someone like him in high school.

21 **SIXTEEN CANDLES** (dir. John Hughes, 1984) The quintessential Brat Pack-era teen flick. Molly Ringwald is at her sulky, pouty, why-me best in this still-funny comedy about irksome dorks (Anthony Michael Hall), crazy relatives, a foreign-exchange student, a prom-queen princess, and the unattainable high-school hunk. One of the few teen flicks to devote equal time to the horrors of family and social life.

22 **STAND AND DELIVER** (dir. Ramon Menendez, 1987) This flick falls firmly in the "inspirational" category. Edward James Olmos teaches calculus to Hispanic kids at a burnt-out Los Angeles high school in the barrio. Lou Diamond Phillips is great as an aspiring gangsta who ends up jamming at math. It's sappy, but worthy.

23 **TO KILL A MOCKINGBIRD** (dir. Robert Mulligan, 1962) Based on the book by Harper Lee, this classic film follows the story of a gentle, ethical small-town lawyer, Atticus Finch (Gregory Peck), who defends a black man against a rape charge leveled by a white woman in the Depression-era South. Told from the perspective of six-year-old Scout, this film shows children learning about the injustice of prejudice. Look for Robert Duvall's film debut in a cameo near the end!

24 **VALLEY GIRL** (dir. Martha Coolidge, 1983) True, this film is not, shall we say, cinematic genius, but Nicolas Cage's performance as a new-wave dude is amazing. The whole Romeo-and-Juliet thing is pretty standard fare, with the added bonus of nonstop valley girl talk and an untragic ending. Unbelievably dated lingo and all-around evilness from Julie's girlfriends weigh this flick down, but the romantic prom-scene finale is a classic, as is all of the awful, lacy-peasant-blouse fashion.

25 **THE WIZARD OF OZ** (dir. Victor Fleming, 1939) If you're going to learn lessons about courage, love, brains, loyalty, and family, they might as well be set to music with a psychedelic background of witches, munchkins, and terrifying flying monkeys. This movie is way too scary for kids, but as a coming-of-age piece, it's breathtaking. Judy Garland in her signature role is amazing. Warning: this movie causes nightmares in viewers of all ages.

8 EVENT MOVIES:
Big Budget Mega-Blockbusters

There are about eight guys in Hollywood making action films these days. Mimi Leder (**The Peacemaker**, **Deep Impact**) may have broken through recently, and Kathryn Bigelow (**Point Break**, **Strange Days**) may pop up every once in a while to remind us that women can produce slick, big-budget fare, but for the most part, it's a man's world out there, baby. And you'd better love it or leave it, because it's not going away.

We here at the Girls on Film say, okay. We'll love it. How could you call yourself a red-blooded American girl and just say no to the excessive budgets, the pointless explosions, the throwaway love interests, the pithy catch phrases, and the improbably happy endings evident in such movies? How can you refuse the lure of all those cops and robbers, tough military agents, evil drug lords, gunfights, spies, aliens, spaceships, monsters, time travel, supernatural phenomena, and natural disasters?

Most important, how can you deny yourself the pleasure of a nice, air-conditioned theater on a hot summer's day, and the joy of watching a flick that doesn't require one bit of thinking from your overheated mind?

Answer: You can't. So don't even try it!

Ever since David Lean poured every single dollar and then some into **Lawrence of Arabia**, and André De Toth blew money on the **3-D House of Wax**, men have been obsessed with epic films that chomp up the dollars (and a few choice victims, if you're Spielberg et al) with special effects and other toys of the trade. Call it a Peter Pan complex, call it Size Does Matter, call it what you will, but it's the truth.

The good thing about big-budget Hollywood action films is that they usually look pretty good, are nicely art-directed, and have high production values in general. The bad thing about them is that they're often sorely lacking in character development and believable plots. But if a big-budget film is a true keeper, it's got to deliver Everything.

One of the men who usually delivers on the Everything (but the Kitchen Sink) front is our resident "king of the world," James Cameron. Remember, **Titanic** was originally slated for summer release, along with all the other brainless powerhouses—until Cameron went WAY over bud-

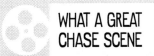

WHAT A GREAT CHASE SCENE

LISE: The end of *Speed*, where the rescue squad is chasing the bus on the tarmac. That movie was really fun to watch; the sequel stank. And sank—*hahaha!*

SIBYL: Han Solo's escape with Luke and the crew in his clunker of a space ship in *Star Wars*.

ANDREA: I loved that scene in *E.T.* when the kids all jump on their bikes to save the cute little alien, managing to outrun and outwit the Feds.

CLARE: The chase scene in *Seven* is amazing, when Brad Pitt ends up with his head pinned down by a boot, but his life is spared. All that rain!

get and took too long to wrap up his precious three-and-a-half-hour spectacle. You've got to admit that Cameron delivers on his characters, even if they are a bit stereotypical. That's what pushes his flicks to the top o' the heap. The King of the Bloated Budget, Cameron is known as an exacting control freak, demanding a lot of his actors and production people. The guy wants to do it right. And he has: flicks like **Aliens**, **The Abyss**, **The Terminator**, and **T2** all showed us that this guy isn't forgetting about giving us a strong plot around which he may drape his impressive special effects.

And the fact that two kick-ass chicks were the stars of three of Cameron's flicks doesn't hurt. Think of the rockin' Sigourney Weaver in **Aliens**: Man, she made that movie. And how about Linda Hamilton, who started off as a flaky tie-dyed chick in **The Terminator**, and then came back in **T2** with a rippling stomach and an arsenal of semiautomatic weapons? Awesome.

But the prototype of all female action characters had to have been Carrie Fisher's sarcastic, tough-talking Princess Leia in **Star Wars**. Now there was a spunky fighter! Saddled with that unfortunate hairdo and a full-length white gown, she still managed to kick some serious butt. In fact, Andrea also thanks George Lucas, creator of the Star Wars trilogy, for one of her favorite movie experiences of all time: **Raiders of the Lost Ark**, with Harrison Ford, was produced by Lucas and directed by Steven Spielberg, one of the Super Eight men in Hollywood out there producing big-budget flicks. Andrea says that **Raiders** was just such a good time that it opened a new world to her; for the first time she realized that a movie can just transport you and really take you on a ride. Whee!

Spielberg is certainly the champion of the special effect, but he's also mentioned in our Moving Pictures chapter because he's so good at manipulating our emotions in general. What better combination to fill us with wonder and awe? **Close Encounters of the**

Third Kind was a hallmark film for most in our generation. In movies like **Close Encounters** and of course **E.T.**, Spielberg gives us these quirky, funny, touching, true characters to relate to while we watch the money burn. Even **Jurassic Park** showed us the wonder of two scientists (Laura Dern, Sam Neill) seeing real-live dinosaurs after a lifetime of studying their fossils. (Then, of course, the killing begins. Remember, Spielberg also gave us **Jaws**.)

Which brings us to monsters and other menacing creatures (i.e., aliens), which brings us to Dean Devlin and Roland Emmerich, who, among the New World Order of filmmakers, have single-handedly brought the action film to a soaring new level of pointlessness. What they did with the pretty fun **Independence Day** was totally undermined by the flop that was **Godzilla**. Geez, we said we didn't mind a mindless big-budget flick, but we didn't ask you to suck our brains out along with it!

Speaking of sucking our brains out, a new type of action film seems to be pumping the testosterone level higher and higher, while brutally squeezing out the gray matter of everyone involved. The mantra here seems to be, "hey, it's just an action film!" but we Girls are feeling a little left out and jaded by the whole Bruckheimer/Bay phenom. This producing/directing team brought us (lucky us!) **The Rock** and **Armageddon** (and Bruckheimer has produced a long string of action flicks, from **Top Gun** to **Con Air**). Not to say these flicks weren't fun in their own special, violent way, but hey, where'd all the ladies run off to? And is it really necessary to blow *everything* up? For twenty minutes?

Finally, there's the stylish violence of John Woo, leader of the Hong Kong action-movie cabal, who has scores of drooling Tarantino-wannabes (and Tarantino himself) worshipping his every gunfight. Now, **Broken Arrow**, starring John Travolta and Christian Slater, was just silly. But **Face/Off** (also with Travolta, and with new action film star, Nick Cage), showed us that the public not only could swallow an alarming amount of violence, but loved it. Paid to see it. Came back for more.

We're a little scared of how far this violent trend is gonna go. When even Spielberg blurs the line between scary, R-rated action and fun, PG-rated antics (**Jurassic Park** and **The Lost World** are watched the world over by very young children), we all might be in trouble. And teenage boys especially seem attracted to the gunplay in movies like **Con Air** and **Face/Off**. Honestly, the rash of adolescent gunmen mowing down their classmates in the spring of 1998 gave us pause. Are we showing kids too much violence? Making it look too cool?

All we can say is, remember that action flicks are usually rated R with good reason. We can check our brains at the door, sure, but some of these flicks require that you check the ole ticker, too.

With that caveat in mind, let the action begin.

ADRENALINE JUNKIE!

By Sibyl

Recently I went to my local video store (it's an independently owned place; they've got a great selection, always have copies of new releases, and are damn nice—all qualities that set them apart from the big chains). I milled around, glanced at the musicals, glanced at the foreign films, then picked up **Say Anything**, a romantic comedy with John Cusack. Can't go wrong with that choice. Then I made a dash for the new release area, snagged a copy of the movie I'd been eye-balling all along, and darted discreetly to the counter (as discreetly as a grown woman with pigtails and oversized pink flip-flops can dart).

The video-store dudes and dudettes at Video Blitz are groovy. They've seen all the flicks and they're not judgmental about what you rent.

"**Say Anything**, that's a classic," said the video dudette.

Picking up the other box, she said, "**Face/Off**? Hmm? Okay."

ANECDOTES FOR BIG SUMMER BLOCKBUSTERS

Babe: Pig in the City
Beyond Silence
Dream with the Fishes
Groundhog Day
The Last Seduction
He Got Game
What's Eating Gilbert Grape
Pulp Fiction
The Opposite of Sex
A Simple Plan

I signed on the line and shuffled out, my contraband flick stashed discreetly in my huge yellow tote bag.

See, I was lured into this whole sordid, illicit world of action flicks by an older man. The scene: St. Louis. Summer, 1991. A do-gooder by day, I was working several part-time jobs and trying to save the world. A pleasure-seeker by night, I was cooling my jets, renting movies, and wishing I was twenty-one. So it only stands to reason that I would strike up some sort of friendship with the angry young video-store guy at my indie-owned rental joint. The guy was cute, an on-again off-again grad student (which sounded pretty glam to me, being a piddling soon-to-be senior in college myself). We would chit-chat about flicks, his dreams of moving to L.A. and writing screenplays, my grand scheme to learn French by watching lots of foreign films and paying close attention to the subtitles.

One day, he asked me if I wanted to go see a movie with him. Up to this point it had been strictly in-store banter. I said sure, why not? Really, what else did I have to do? He was all psyched because **Terminator 2: Judgment Day** (dir. James Cameron, 1991) was coming out. It was the big movie of the summer. We'd see it opening night on the biggest screen in St. Louis (at The Esquire, of course, the movie theater of my childhood). I kind of blushed, looking down. You see, although I fancied myself something of a movie buff, I had never really gotten into action flicks, and, well, at age twenty, I still hadn't seen the action flick by which all others are measured. I had not seen **The Terminator** (dir. James Cameron, 1984).

I had to admit it to him: I was an action-movie virgin. Shock, pandemonium, and taunting ensued. He insisted there was no excuse for my naiveté, my inexperience. I was a rube. Oh, the horror, the shame. But then, like any older man worth his salt, he taught me, in his sleazy yet kindly way, the ancient rites and secrets of the action flick. He bestowed upon me his personal copy of **Terminator** and sent me home to watch it. With directions. Big screen, high volume, not during the day. I emerged hours later, bellowing "SAH-RAAAH KOHN-UH!!" (That's "Sarah Connor" for those of you who don't speak Schwarzenegger.)

A few days later, we saw **T2**. Whoa. **Terminator** and **T2**, back to back. That's a lot of action for a rookie. I was hooked. That innocent summer dalliance with a guy whose name I have already forgotten drew me into a whole new world. A world populated by teenage boys in baseball hats, boys so jacked up on soda and Soundgarden that they don't know their own names; boys who rock in their seats, just waiting for the movie to start so they can ride that crazy adrenaline high. These punks aren't concerned with plot, character development, or the auteur theory—though the names Cameron, Bigelow, and Woo certainly mean something to them. They just want it loud, fast, and explosive; they want fire, bombs, guns, planes, cars, fights, and maybe some aliens. And guess what? That's what I want, too!

Ever since that fateful summer, I've been an action-movie fan. Sure, I'm still far from an expert, and I'm not exactly an action-movie omnivore (I don't like outer-space stuff like **Alien**), but I am easy. I like the **Die Hard** series, **Speed** was good, I loved **Independence Day** (so many cheesy stories! A little humor! Great explosions!). I even kind of liked **The Rock** (but don't tell). The experience of seeing these movies in the theater is key—all that screaming and yelling, fearing that maybe the kids will get too excited, have forgotten to take their Ritalin, will start a riot. Exhilarating.

So I watched **Face/Off** (dir. John Woo, 1997) last week, having missed it on the big screen. And, okay, sure, the story is totally unbelievable (a necessary element of any action movie—who believed that Nicolas Cage could grow all that con hair?), and the speed-boat chase at the end is totally boring and lame. Still, that movie did me right! Love the campiness of Cage and Travolta. Love the glam art direction. Love the heavily choreographed action scenes. I was pumped after seeing that flick. Ready to guzzle Big Gulps, skateboard recklessly, and play Nintendo until I was dizzy.

But instead, I just sipped a cup of tea, did some yoga, and read the New York Times. I did wonder fleetingly whatever happened to that St. Louis video-store guy. Perhaps he's living in L.A. now. Perhaps he's writing screenplays. Or perhaps he's still in St. Louis, working at that video store, luring innocent young ladies into his tawdry underworld, getting them all jacked up on action adrenaline.

SO THEY SAY IT'S A MAN'S WORLD

By Lise

Have you checked out the action section at your local video store? Anything you noticed? How about the faces of Jackie Chan, Arnold Schwarzenegger, Nicolas Cage, Wesley Snipes, and John Travolta staring at you from the video box covers? See where I'm going here? Testosto-rama! It's like the whole genre is aimed at men, in the same way that it often seems that all romance movies are aimed at women (that could be because, well, they are). Now, don't get me wrong, I like both men and romance films (depending on the particular man and the particular romance movie, of course), but what's wrong with this picture?

James Brown once said "It's a man's world," and I was beginning to believe that it was, at the very least, "a man's aisle" at the video store. That is, until I remembered women characters like Princess Leia, Foxy Brown, Bonnie Parker, and Barbarella—women who kicked some serious butt. And that was just the tip of the iceberg, ladies. It seems that, throughout the history of action movies, women have always played a strong role, and not just of the sidekick variety. So you still think it's a man's world? Well, how about trying to explain that to . . .

LINDA HAMILTON AS SARAH CONNOR In 1984's **The Terminator,** James Cameron introduced us to a nice waitress named Sarah Connor. Sarah drove a motor scooter, wore an incredibly ugly eighties' shirt with snaps all over it, sported feathered hair, and got stood up on a Friday night. She was nice. Silly guitar music played when she rode her scooter. Doesn't sound so tough, you say? Well, after a battle with a terminator, sent from the future to kill her as-yet-unconceived son, we see a very different woman, one who drives a

Renegade, wears a bandanna around her head, and isn't going to roll out the welcome mat for any more visitors for a while.

In **T2**, this becomes crystal clear when Sarah is first shown doing pull-ups in her room in the mental hospital. She is, as they say, cut. Phrases like "Miles, hand me the detonator" roll off her tongue. She handles weapons with the same ease and skill with which June Cleaver maneuvered her vacuum cleaner. And she's doing it all to protect her son. Whereas the terminator (Arnold Schwarzenegger) sent to help John Connor just does what he is programmed to do, Sarah Connor actually gets her strength from being a mother.

GEENA DAVIS AS SAMANTHA CAINE Sarah Connor isn't the only woman who's going to extremes to protect her kid. In Renny Harlin's 1996 film **The Long Kiss Goodnight**, we meet Samantha Caine, an amnesia victim who has rebuilt her life as a single mom and schoolteacher and is having a great relationship with a caring man. That is, until she . . . well, she finds out that she used to be a government assassin. Like Sarah Connor, she also goes through a transformation as she begins to remember her former life, changing into skintight clothing and the inevitable uniform of a tough woman: the tank top, preferably ribbed. No bones about it, Samantha is the woman in charge in this movie; if you're looking for the sidekick here,

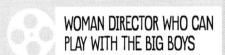

WOMAN DIRECTOR WHO CAN PLAY WITH THE BIG BOYS

LISE: Agnieska Holland, the director of *The Secret Garden* and *Washington Square*.

SIBYL: Amy Heckerling (*Fast Times at Ridgemont High*, *Clueless*) She's funny and has a way with bright California eye-candy.

ANDREA: Two words: *Point Break*. Directed by my fave femme, Katherine Bigelow.

CLARE: Jane Campion (*The Piano*, *Portrait of a Lady*). All that drama, tears, swelling music, and gorgeous, lush photography!

it's Samuel L. Jackson as Hennessy, a private investigator Sam hired to help her discover her preamnesia life. In Samantha, we have a woman who pulls some ridiculous stunts (except in the world of action movies, where they are par for the course) to save her daughter. **The Long Kiss Goodnight** is a surprisingly entertaining movie (save for one really gross and hateful torture scene). And I found it interesting that, at the end, Sam becomes kind of a combination of her old and new selves, a country Mom/trained assassin, and no one really seems to mind.

MULAN Sure, Mulan is an animated Disney character based on an ancient Chinese folk tale, but that doesn't mean she isn't as tough as the rest of these ladies. When Mulan's injured father is summoned to battle the Huns in the Chinese army, Mulan makes an exceptionally brave decision. She cuts her hair, dons her father's battle gear, swipes his sword, and goes to battle in his place, disguised as a man. Sure, she has a puny dragon named Mu Shu (voice of Eddie Murphy) and a purportedly lucky cricket with her, but the real skill and bravery is all Mulan, as she makes it through basic training and ultimately rescues the Emperor. Ming-Na Wen is great as the voice of Mulan, who is headstrong, different, and fiercely loyal to her family.

The animation in **Mulan** is beautiful and the battle scenes are action-packed. But the really cool thing here is that Disney has created a strong female lead, a girl who is not helpless, who is not willing to let her father fight another war, and who is not waiting to be rescued by a man.

SIGOURNEY WEAVER AS RIPLEY Can you believe that **Alien** (dir. Ridley Scott) was made in 1979? It's always fun to return to some older sci-fi films, made back in the day when Atari was cutting-edge technology and even action movies took their time and told a story.

The beginning of **Alien**, directed by Ridley Scott, is so slow that it reminded me of Stanley Kubrick's **2001: A Space Odyssey**—and I like that. Now, let's just temporarily forget about the continuation of this series (**Aliens, Alien Resurrection**), and concentrate on the original. If you have not seen this movie for a long time, or if you have a bad memory, or if you thought **Star Wars** was the first outer-space movie, I highly recommend renting **Alien**, pronto! I slept with the lights on last night, because this is some scary, spooky stuff.

As Ripley, one of seven crew members on board a cargo ship in space, Sigourney Weaver is youthful and fresh-faced, yet also appealingly no-nonsense. She's a career girl who wants to get the job done and who wants everything done by the book. When an alien gets stuck on the ship, Weaver's ability to show fear is what makes the simple saga so terrifying. Ripley kills Ash (Ian Holm), a crew member who turns out to be a robot; she detonates the ship when everyone else is dead; and she then battles with the alien single-handedly when it turns out that the slimy, toothy, wholly unsavory beast is on the escape ship with her.

QUEEN LATIFAH AS CLEO In 1997, F. Gary Gray directed **Set It Off**, a deserving movie that got overlooked. Queen Latifah is the star here, but you can take your pick of the four women in the movie, because every single one of them has been screwed over enough by what we have come to call "the system," that they believe robbing a bank is the only way to get even, to be free. Queen Latifah, Jada Pinkett, Vivica A. Fox, and Kimberly Elise play Cleo, Stony, Frankie, and Tisean, girlfriends in present-day Los Angeles who just want their piece of the pie. I think of **Set It Off** as a thinking woman's action movie; although I obviously don't believe it's okay to rob banks and kill people, it makes for an engaging story of right and wrong. These women work all night for Luther's Janitorial, just to make barely enough money for a baby-sitter, or to send a younger brother to college, or just to get out of the neighborhood. And, although their plans go wildly wrong, they've got each others' backs until the end.

Queen Latifah's performance as Cleo is gutsy—she really makes us wonder whether Cleo is the smartest, stupidest, bravest, or most loyal of the bunch. The ending is reminiscent of **Thelma and Louise**, but way more realistic.

Maybe the lack of women directors (Kathryn Bigelow being one of the few) is one of the reasons I never really cozied up to the megabudget action genre, unlike my self proclaimed "adrenaline junkie" friend Sibyl. As a drama aficionado, I need credible characters and motives in my films (no, I don't mean like two men switching faces, sorry Sib). I like to know what makes people do the things they do, and why they make the choices they make. I found all these qualities in the women characters above. These are no Spice Girl, faux-girl-power ladies; they are the real thing. And the five I chose were just the beginning of a long, long list. I'm thinking maybe Sibyl and I can have some video dates now, because damned if I didn't have a good time watching these movies, despite myself.

WHAT DO I WANT? EYE CANDY! WHEN DO I WANT IT? NOW!

By Clare

Okay, I'm no film aficionado. (There. I said it. Okay?) I don't really know the ins and outs of filmmaking itself; like most people, I just look at the screen for two hours and let a movie soak in. And that's what's so great about big-budget action flicks—they're trying as hard as they can to bombard you with colorful images, beautiful people, and maybe a little blood and gore (but spectacularly filmed and glamorized, of course). When a big-budget film doesn't work, it's pretty sad (think **Last Action Hero, Godzilla**); there's nothing more pathetic than filmmakers with a ton of cash at their disposal who still can't make a movie work.

But in the best action films, a director can afford (quite literally) to totally immerse you in a different world, replete with elaborate sets, gorgeous costumes, high-tech effects, amazing camera work, beautiful art direction, even great music. In short, they often have what the experts call high production values. I may not be an expert myself, but I know what looks good, and this stuff reels me in every time.

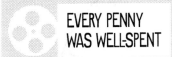

EVERY PENNY WAS WELL-SPENT

LISE: *Star Wars.* I have never loved another action or sci-fi movie as much.

SIBYL: *T2*—super-cool morphing.

ANDREA: *Blade Runner.* Ridley Scott's sci-fi western is so phenomenal-looking that each viewing of it brings new pleasures.

CLARE: Luc Besson's *The Professional* (actually, all his movies). He uses such great music and has such visual flair.

Science-fiction films can immerse you the most fully, since the director is, in effect, creating a total universe of their own imagining; they can really go nuts on sets and costumes and cinematic tricks. But a good old regular action film kind of creates a parallel universe, too—while I'm watching, I can actually buy into Tony Scott's male-dominated world of fighter jets and guns and ammo, or dream that I'm a glamorous woman in a Ridley Scott film, or just get caught up in the campy glory of a movie like Luc Besson's **The Fifth Element**.

Wow, when I start thinking of all the great-looking action films out there, I practically foam at the mouth. How do I pick my favorites? Where do I begin?

I guess I should begin at the beginning. The beginning for me, at least. It all started with **Star Wars**. From the double moons on planet Tatooine to the freaky aliens in that bar scene (all speaking different languages), to the battle scenes (created with models, wow), to the menacing Storm Troopers and of course Darth Vader, George Lucas really pulled out the stops here. My little nine-year-old mind was blown. In taking me into this completely alien world, Lucas didn't leave out one detail (apparently he even required cast and crew to familiarize themselves with an elaborate manual explaining all the "back story" for every single character and planet). Thought by Lucas's contemporaries to be a costly embarrassment at the time of its release, **Star Wars** has since been emulated and alluded to in many a film.

One of those films has to be Luc Besson's **The Fifth Element**. This flick is one bright, colorful, cheesy, rockin' good time. Now, I wouldn't go seeing this movie for any Deep Meaning, and I have to say that it doesn't bear up under scrutiny the way, say, **Star Wars** does, but for the two hours I was watching it, I was totally sucked in. Besson spent a reported $90 million on this puppy, and you can see where it all went: half to Jean-Paul Gaultier, who designed the costumes (yes, I'm kidding), half to Bruce Willis (kidding again), and the last bit handed to the production designer (Dan Weil), the director of photography (Thierry Arbogast), the art director (Ira Gilford), and the special-effects production house. (Too bad Besson, who also wrote the screenplay, couldn't invest a little more in a good script doctor. Ahem.)

What makes this film is the color. Wow. Milla Jovovich, as Leeloo the Supreme Being come to save the Earth (no, I'm not kidding this time), has bright orange hair. Which just happens to match

Bruce Willis's bright orange muscle shirt. Which just happens to match the bright orange lava-type stuff emanating from the dark fireball/planet/total destruction thingie that's headed for Earth. The sets have bright orange-and-red accents. Much of the light is purple and blue. There's a totally blue opera-singing woman who belts out a tune in front of a gorgeous space-view. Even Milla's blue eyes look art-directed (so pretty with her milky skin and fiery hair!). Besson's aliens are sort of dumb-looking **Star Wars** knock-offs, and Ian Holms's religious character wears an Obi-Wan-influenced getup (which makes for some of the only brown in the film), but no one has done as much with color than Besson in **The Fifth Element**. And Jean-Paul Gaultier should have gotten not only an Academy Award, but a freakin' Nobel Prize for those insane costumes.

Besson also directed two of my other fave action movies, **La femme Nikita** (1990) and **The Professional** (1994), both of which feature common Besson elements: fantastic, pulsating, Middle-Eastern-sounding music (both these and **The Fifth Element** were scored by Eric Serra), spectacular gunfire scenes, a beautiful girl (Anne Parillaud in **Nikita**, a newly discovered Natalie Portman in **The Professional**), and the character of Leon (Jean Reno), the Cleaner. Besson really lets his ladies kick some butt, let me tell ya. Nikita is a gun-toting, government-trained assassin, Mathilda (Portman) is a precocious troublemaker who can pack heat with the best of 'em, and of course, Leeloo (now Besson's wife, by the way) gets that awesome kick-boxing scene in **The Fifth Element**, juxtaposed nicely with shots of the blue lady singing. Amazing.

For a little more substance, one only has to turn to director Ridley Scott, who seems to fancy himself to be a little more arthaus than his fellow action/sci-fi filmmakers. Responsible for such fare as the original **Alien**, **Blade Runner**, **Thelma and Louise**, and **Someone to Watch over Me** (one of my personal guilty-pleasure favorites, with Mimi Rogers, Tom Berenger, and a feisty

Lorraine Braccho), Ridley can create a moody, dark, richly atmospheric film better than most.

As Lise mentioned earlier about Scott's **Alien**, **Blade Runner** (1982) not only holds up after sixteen years, but seems to have gotten even better with age. I was watching James Cameron's **The Abyss** the other day, and was shocked to see how dated it looked (the "underwater alien city" looks like Vegas; the aliens themselves look like something out of **Ghostbusters**). Not so with **Blade Runner**. I think that visually, **Gattaca** (dir. Andrew Niccol, 1997) learned a lot from this film, creating these immense cement cityscapes with glowing sepia tones and using a lot of smoky, back-lit shots within dark but highly detailed interiors. While **Gattaca** did a lot more with color (whole scenes were shot in cool blues, electric pinks, and glowing greens), **Blade Runner** gave me a fuller sense of the whole environment, with lots of overview shots and varying locations. When Harrison Ford jets past huge ads for Coca Cola, travels up hundreds of floors to his messy apartment, or visits a steamy noodle shop on the crowded street, you can feel how huge and cold Los Angeles, circa 2025, has become.

Ridley Scott's **Thelma and Louise** (1991), written by Callie Khouri, shows that he can create a beautiful mood even when he leaves the lights on. Mostly filmed in the daytime, in the red canyons and on the dusty roads of Utah and Colorado, **Thelma and Louise** is sometimes self-consciously but impressively shot. Heat shimmers off the road; sunlight glints off the convertible that the two title characters tool around in for the whole movie; Thelma (Geena Davis) looks into a rearview mirror and sees a full skyline of red mountains and startling blue skies. There's even a beautiful but senseless nighttime shot in which the convertible looks like it's lit from under the dash (whaa? Pretty, though!). As in all of his films, Ridley gets some great music together, for a haunting score and a soundtrack that leads you and our heroines inexorably to the powerful Grand Canyon denouement.

For some even slicker and infinitely more macho work, check out the movies of Ridley's brother Tony. Director of flicks like **Top Gun**, **Days of Thunder**, and **The Last Boy Scout**, Tony was once the favorite auteur of the late Don Simpson/Jerry Bruckheimer producing team before Michael Bay (**The Rock**, **Armageddon**) and Simon West (**Con Air**) came into the picture. Think glowing, indirect lighting, lots of silhouettes, shiny metal, and cheesy but memorable soundtracks over great scores.

I loved **Crimson Tide** (1995), starring Denzel Washington and Gene Hackman as two officers on a military sub who, in the midst of a radio-communications breakdown during the Cold War, clash about whether or not they've been ordered to fire a nuclear weapon. Lots of burnishing red bulbs and green control-panel lights bounce off the sweaty faces of the nervous crew, who encounter a life-threatening fire, mutiny, betrayal, and a cute li'l Jack Russell terrier, all in a few tense hours.

I think you could play a version of "Where's Waldo?" with Tony Scott's movies in which you pick out the sunset in every film—the movie just ain't over till you've gotten a nice, big, blazing one. **Crimson Tide**'s is pretty amazing; Denzel and Gene watch it from the deck of the submarine as they start crashing into the depths of the ocean. But I have to say this one's outdone by our huge, fat, orange sun at the end of **True Romance** (1993), Tony's best movie by far.

Displaying a similar smoky-rooms-and-back-lighting technique as Ridley's **Blade Runner**, **True Romance** is a great-looking movie. What makes it Tony Scott's best film, however, is the fact that it was penned by Quentin Tarantino, so it's not only incredibly violent, but it's also sweet and funny, if you can believe that.

True Romance starts in cold Detroit, where lonely Clarence (Christian Slater) meets saucy Alabama (Patricia Arquette) at a Kung Fu triple-feature. After some steamy sex (blue background, silhouettes of lips and tongues and bellies), Alabama crawls out of

Clarence's apartment window in front of a huge billboard (nice shot), where she cries because she's fallen in love—and he doesn't know she's a call girl. Soon, though, the young couple's gotten married, become embroiled in a huge cocaine scam, and run off to Los Angeles to escape the authorities and make their fortune.

Between Patricia Arquette's turquoise and red flouncy outfits; all the blue light and bright-red, syrupy blood; and a repulsive yellow scene with the repulsive yellow Gary Oldman as Alabama's erstwhile pimp (who is—get this—supposed to be black), this movie is saturated with dramatic lighting and rich hues. A final showdown in a hotel room finds machine-gun fire conveniently ripping open some sofa stuffing and filling the entire room with wispy, downy feathers, as though a chicken had just exploded. It's actually quite lovely.

So there's an incomplete account of my favorite eye-candy on the market today. Fluffy, sweet, and right on the money on a hot summer day, these flicks provide a little ambient escape to a world where all the men are buff, all the women are tough, and everyone knows how to fire a weapon.

HAVE A SPARE HUNDRED MIL? I'LL TELL YOU HOW TO SPEND IT

By Andrea

As we've been discussing in this chapter, the Hollywood action film is a slick, big-budget vehicle. Since you have to spend *mucho dinero* to make these suckers, studios produce them via committee. Basically, they think that if they're gonna drop over a hundred million smackeroos, they'd better be pretty confident they're going to see returns. And how.

It's tough to make a movie like this, since the room for error is nil. Jobs are going to be lost, entire studio departments will be entirely reshuffled, all due to just one big tanker.

A way to guarantee profits (or so these execs hope) is to repeat a successful formula over and over. This becomes fairly obvious for those of us in the audience who see a bunch of action films in a row. We begin to notice certain stock characters or plot lines popping up, hither and yon. This is not necessarily a bad thing, for every film has its place, and there's something to be said for this type of formulaic picture. Not only is it satisfying to check out a flick that doesn't require a huge amount of thinking, but on

ALL-TIME MOST ANNOYING ONE-LINER

LISE: *The Player*, a tortured artist's opus is turned into an action film by the studios; in the bastardized version, Bruce Willis saves Julia Roberts from the gas chamber, and she says, "What took you so long?" Ouch. Sob.

SIBYL: Princess Leia to Han Solo: "I'd rather kiss a Wookie." (Or her brother Luke. Eek! Holy intergalactic Greek tragedy!)

ANDREA: I'm going with Arnold Schwarzenegger telling Sharon Stone to "consider that a divorce" after he shoots her in *Total Recall.*

CLARE: Hey, Andrea, mine's an Ahnold line, too! When he shoots a runaway croc in *Eraser* (whatev) and says: "You're luggage."

another level, seeing certain "types" again and again definitely fulfills us in the same way that fairy tales did when we were children.

I had a bit of an epiphany about the action film formula after I saw **Volcano** (dir. Mick Jackson, 1997). I finally felt like I understood the potent mixture that makes for a successful action story, and because I'm so nice, I'm passing on my wisdom to you. Someday you might stumble into a cool 75 million, so you'll want to save this little "cheat sheet" in order to make your movie. Sometimes you have to mix and match a bit (e.g., the heroine doubles as the sidekick) but use this as your starting point, and I guarantee you'll have yourself one fine action film.

FIRST, THERE'S THE HERO: The Hero is brave and habitually reckless with his own life. Oftentimes, he has a teenage daughter who mouths off to him even though everyone else is intimidated by him and the five o'clock shadow that he seems to have even at ten in the morning. The hero also tends to be a renegade fella, not all stuffy or by-the-book. He's no big-city slicker, more at home on a farm than in an office on Wall Street. You've seen him before: He'd rather "do" than "discuss." A workaholic who drinks beer (not Schnapps or white wine, for chrissakes!), you can usually spot the hero pretty quickly. He is wearing faded Levi's. He is sexy. He is all man.

The penultimate hero is Bruce Willis in **Die Hard**, who redefined the action hero for an entire generation. I have seen this movie a ton of times and still love it. It is good.

THERE'S THE HEROINE: As Lise mentioned, women in action films can kick as much ass as any fella. Cool! Whether she's taking on the lead role, or working in tandem with the hero, there are certain things about the heroine you can be sure of.

The Heroine is beautiful, saucy, and doesn't wear much makeup. Supersmart, the heroine usually has her Ph.D. in something impressive (e.g., nuclear physics). Anne Heche's character in **Volcano**, Dr. Amy Barnes, is a seismologist. Zoinks! I am also partial to Laura Dern in **Jurassic Park**, who not only looks like Laura Dern but also happens to be brilliant and devoted to her job.

The heroine usually sets sparks off the hero, especially when they first meet, before they are united by their desire to thwart the mayhem or murderer wreaking havoc on their small town/large city/mid-size boat. Remember Marion (Karen Allen) in my personal fave **Raiders of the Lost Ark**? She was tough, ready to fight, spirited, sassy, smart, and attractive. And she sure could sure piss off Indiana Jones—until, that is, they wound up swapping spit on a ship at the film's end.

YOU MAY GET A TEENAGE DAUGHTER: Not a constant, but the Teenage Daughter pops up often enough that she should be considered a key ingredient. She's a wise-ass who gives her parents a hard time and usually winds up getting herself into serious trouble and has to be saved by her courageous father. She's obnoxious, but underneath all that bluster, she's a sweet little girl who realizes at the film's end how much she loves her dad.

Some classic performances of a daughter: There's Rianne (Traci Wolfe), Danny Glover's teenage daughter in **Lethal Weapon**; Jamie (Dominique Swain), John Travolta's kid in **Face/Off**; Dana (Eliza Dushku), Arnold Schwarzenneger's daughter in **True Lies**; and Kelly (Vanessa Lee Chester), Jeff Goldblum's child in **The Lost World**.

YOU'VE GOTTA HAVE SIDEKICK! Sidekicks have been around as long as heroes have. The sidekick is loyal. It's also important to note that the sidekick is scrappy and usually shorter than the hero. The sidekick exists to make sure everyone knows how cool the hero is. Sometimes the sidekick will provide much-needed comic relief, and, in a film with few female characters, the sidekick will provide emotional bonding. Often, the love between a hero and a sidekick is as strong as any (though these films to take great pains to point out that, sweet mother, our boys are not gay!). My personal fave hero/sidekick relationship is in **Butch Cassidy and the Sundance Kid** (dir. George Roy Hill, 1969). The two bicker like an old married couple, (a truly great script by William Goldman), put each other down constantly, and of course, love each other dearly. It's very sweet, and with Paul Newman and Robert Redford as the leads, it's not too tough on the eyes, either.

For many years, people of color were relegated purely to the sidekick role in mainstream Hollywood films (think Tonto to the Long Ranger). This has begun to change, albeit slowly. There's **Passenger 57** and **The Drop Zone**, two truly fun Wesley Snipes action flicks, and the tag-team of Will Smith and Martin Lawrence in Michael Bay's **Bad Boys**.

While Chow Yun Fat begins his ascension in Hollywood films, (such as in **The Replacement Killers**), I suggest you check out his work in such John Woo-directed films as **Hard-Boiled** (1992) and **The Killer** (1990), since Chow Yun Fat is tough, stylish, smart, and bold. In short, a real hero.

THE BAD GUY IS BADDDDD: A sick, twisted Bad Guy is of key importance to an action film. Without him, you got nothing! Nothing! A bad guy can make or break a movie. **Die Hard** has a great bad guy in Alan Rickman's Hans Gruber, with his oily charm and weird accent. **Lethal Weapon** has Gary Busey's Mr. Joshua (love that guy!). And of course, there's Darth Vader, who has become an icon from the **Star Wars** trilogy.

These guys are memorable, since they're evil to the core and have no compunction about killing people. Just as the hero is willing to risk life and limb to do good, the bad guy is willing to go all the way to obtain his goal, which is usually getting a load of money, or, even more frightening, just spreading evil for evil's sake, like Darth. Once in a while, embitterment and revenge drive the bad guy, like Dennis Hopper's freaky Howard Payne in **Speed**. The only time you can have a bad guy who's just kind of pesky, or a wee bit obnoxious, is when you have:

THE CALAMITY: Often, evil leaves the form of the human body and takes on the appearance of tornadoes (**Twister**), crazed animals/beasts (**The Birds, Anaconda**) lava (**Volcano**; **Dante's Peak**), celestial bodies (**Deep Impact, Armageddon**), and dinosaurs (**Jurassic Park**). This stuff is brought to you by some of the most impressive special effects teams in the world, and is way more believable than the hokey goop they used to fob off on audiences a generation or two ago. Calamity works because we're neurotic little suckers and believe anything cloaked in scientific jargon ("My God, planet Goodujeuglsg is heading on a collision course with Earth! The only thing that will stop would be to fire tons of Pepperidge Farm cookies at its center!").

Calamity works, too, because it sets up a David and Goliath situation. Since the hero is obviously not as powerful as the snake/goop/toxic ooze, he's going to have to outsmart it and beat it at its own game.

I think I managed to touch on most of the finer points of big-budget filmmaking here. This is pretty much all you need to start you off on making your very own action film. Good luck, and don't forget to thank me in your acceptance speech at the Academy Awards.

25 Action Films to Rent!

1 `2001: A SPACE ODYSSEY` (dir. Stanley Kubrick, 1968) "I'm sorry, John, I can't do that." This epic space movie starts with the apes and ends with humankind's greatest achievement: a computer named Hal who can think for himself. Problem is, Hal's agenda may not be what his fellow space passengers had in mind . . .

2 `ALIEN` (dir. Ridley Scott, 1979) Heralding Sigourney Weaver's rise as an action hero named Ripley, this incredibly suspenseful and moody film also takes us into space, where a crew on an exploratory mission finds a strange creature that attaches itself to one of their peer's faces. Needless to say, things go downhill from there.

3 `ALIENS` (dir. James Cameron, 1986) The alien is back and so is Ripley, in James Cameron's worthy sequel to the highly popular *Alien*. After hanging out in a suspended state of sleep for some years, Ripley finds herself once again face-to-face with the gooey, toothy creature of her nightmares. Poor Ripley just can't get a break.

4 `BARBARELLA` (dir. Roger Vadim, 1968) This super-kitschy flick from the sixties stars the scantily clad Fonda as the title character, who jets around in a fur-lined spaceship and gives sexual favors in return for fuel and other necessities. Not exactly a feminist statement (or is it?!?), but fun all the same.

5 `BLADE RUNNER` (dir. Ridley Scott, 1982) Get the director's cut without the intrusive voice-over, and then get lost in Ridley Scott's perfectly shot and art-directed, smoky, futuristic world. Harrison Ford stars as a type of contract killer hired to "terminate" rebellious androids (Rutger Hauer and Darryl Hannah); an ever-kooky, hair-sculpted Sean Young plays the love interest.

6 `BRAZIL` (dir. Terry Gilliam, 1985) Terry Gilliam's brilliant and elaborately constructed dystopia of a huge, gray, faceless bureaucracy finds Sam Lowry (Jonathan Pryce, pre–Infiniti commercial fame) working at the Ministry of Information, where everything gets documented, stamped, passed off, jumbled, fumbled, and destroyed. Meanwhile, he fantasizes that he is a hero bent on saving a beautiful damsel in distress (Kim Greist).

7 **CLOSE ENCOUNTERS OF THE THIRD KIND** (dir. Steven Spielberg, 1977) Five mysterious musical notes, unexplained facial burns, mountains made out of mashed potatoes—strange occurrences and themes repeat themselves all over the world in Spielberg's funny, eerie, wondrous movie about a UFO phenomenon that touches the life of regular guy Richard Dreyfuss.

8 **CRIMSON TIDE** (dir. Tony Scott, 1995) Gene Hackman and Denzel Washington star as two Naval officers in a nuclear sub; a cut-off transmission from the government finds them in conflict as to whether or not they've been instructed to fire a nuclear weapon. Tense, sweaty, and pumped full of testosterone, this is a satisfying suspense movie.

9 **DIE HARD** (dir. John McTiernan, 1988) This great flick definitely set the bar a bit higher for action movies that came after. McTiernan successfully incorporated the best of the genre: funny one-liners, a strong hero (Bruce Willis), and a tightly paced, compelling story.

10 **THE EMPIRE STRIKES BACK** (dir. George Lucas, 1980) If you don't know who Luke's father really is, you haven't lived! This second part in the Star Wars trilogy is, according to we Girls, the very best of the three. Slicker and darker than its predecessor, this film includes Luke deep in training with Yoda (who looks remarkably like E.T.). Filled with battles, love, and startling revelations.

11 **LA FEMME NIKITA** (dir. Luc Besson, 1990) Another butt-kicking female lead blows us away in this story of a juvenile delinquent (the gorgeous Annie Parillaud) who has to die for her crimes or become a government-trained assassin. Guess which option she chooses?

Avoid the crummy American remake (*Point of No Return*, with the lipless Bridget Fonda)—stick to this great French-language film.

12 **THE FRENCH CONNECTION** (dir. William Friedkin, 1971) Before giving us a little girl possessed by the Devil (*The Exorcist*), director Friedkin brought this gritty drama about two tough New York City cops trying to intercept a huge heroin shipment coming from France. "Popeye" Doyle (Gene Hackman), a piggish alcoholic but a dedicated police officer, finds his nemesis in the smooth Alain Charnier (Fernando Rey) and tracks him relentlessly, culminating in the most famous car chase ever filmed.

13 **FROM RUSSIA WITH LOVE** (dir. Terence Young, 1963) One of our faves in the Bond series. This time 007 battles a sinister Russia spy organization while still retaining his smooth, shaken-not-stirred stylings. Though some might argue that Bond is a bit dated (go ahead, you're preaching to the converted), we still say that once in a while, a little Bond can make you feel all smooth and cool.

14 **THE KILLER** (dir. John Woo, 1990) Director Woo is credited with bringing a new sensibility to action films here in the United States. To see for yourself, check out this film about a top-notch assassin who also happens to have a heart and a soul. Woo doesn't scrimp on style; he pulls in everything from Catholic iconography to doves flying throughout the movie, and his star, Chow Yun-Fat, plays the title character with all the class and elegance in the world.

15 **LETHAL WEAPON** (dir. Richard Donner, 1987) This truly original original in what has since become a tired franchise stars a young, feathery-haired Mel Gibson as a reckless cop and Danny Glover as his straight-man partner. The opening scene still makes us cry, as Gibson puts a gun in his mouth, despairing over the death of his beloved wife. Sob!

16 **POINT BREAK** (dir. Kathryn Bigelow, 1991) A young police officer (Keanu Reeves) and his weathered partner (Gary Busey) investigate a bank-robbery ring. In order to solve the crime, Reeves has to infiltrate a renegade band of surfers, led by Bodhi (Patrick Swayze).